Digging Up The Dead

Digging Up The Dead

The Life and Times of Astley Cooper,
an Extraordinary Surgeon

Druin Burch

Chatto & Windus
LONDON

Published by Chatto & Windus 2007

2 4 6 8 10 9 7 5 3

Copyright © Druin Burch 2007

First published in Great Britain in 2007 by
Chatto & Windus
Random House, 20 Vauxhall Bridge Road,
London SW1V 2SA

Random House Australia (Pty) Limited
20 Alfred Street, Milsons Point, Sydney,
New South Wales 2061, Australia

Random House New Zealand Limited
18 Poland Road, Glenfield,
Auckland 10, New Zealand

Random House (Pty) Limited
Isle of Houghton, Corner of Boundary Road & Carse O'Gowrie,
Houghton, 2198, South Africa

Random House Publishers India Private Limited
301 World Trade Tower, Hotel Intercontinental Grand Complex,
Barakhamba Lane, New Delhi 110 001, India

The Random House Group Limited Reg. No. 954009
www.randomhouse.co.uk

A CIP catalogue record for this book is available from the British Library

ISBN 9780701179854

Typeset by Palimpsest Book Production Limited,
Grangemouth, Stirlingshire

Printed and bound in Great Britain by
Mackays of Chatham plc

For Marion, who suggested she'd
been no help at all

Contents

List of Illustrations

The author and publishers are grateful to the following institutions for permission to reproduce illustrations: London Topographical Society 2, National Portrait Gallery 5, 6, 7, 19, 20; Reproduced by kind permission of the President and Council of the Royal College of Surgeons of England 1, 4, 14, 15, 21, 22, 32, 33.

x

Acknowledgements

Most books, particularly those requiring some research, thank the people that have helped and make a point of saying that any remaining faults and errors are purely the responsibility of the author. I have always viewed these announcements with a little suspicion, never having been quite sure whether they were completely sincere. One of the many pleasant results of writing this book has been to make me believe that they generally are, and I find it impossible to avoid repeating the sentiments that I have read so many times before. A great number of people really did go far out of their way to help me write this book. I am thankful to Bill Edwards, Keeper of the Gordon Museum at Guy's, to Simon Chaplain and Tina Craig at the Royal College of Surgeons, and to the many library staff who were friendly and welcoming to me. Those at the Radcliffe Science Library in Oxford were, as always, superb. John Barnard was kind enough to meet with me and share some of his expertise on Keats's years at the Borough Hospitals. Grizelda George and Tim Peto both went out of their way to help me combine writing this book with practising medicine. I apologise for causing them trouble, but rather hope to trouble them further in the future. Ann Wheeler of Charterhouse in Godalming and Bill Edwards of the Gordon Museum were generous with their time and provided highly informative answers to fairly obscure questions. The Royal Society of Literature's Jerwood Award helped fund some of the time I spent away from the wards.

I would like to thank Peter Buckman, my agent, for all of his help. We met when he dislocated his arm and arrived at my Emergency Department in some pain. The conversation that he began while I twisted his arm back into place was the first step towards this book. Had Peter been anything other than gracious and composed under pressure it would never have been written, and his help over the last two years is greatly appreciated. Roger Barbee, of the National Cathedral School in Washington DC, has provided helpful comments on an earlier draft. My real debt to him, however, is deeper, and his encouragement and helpful criticism go back over more years than I now care to remember. Richard Holmes first came to my aid when I was preparing for my medical finals; his biography of Coleridge was more real to me that summer than the seemingly dull collection of facts and traditions I was busy memorising and learning to repeat. Studying under him at the University of East Anglia was an absolute joy, and an educational one into the bargain.

Alison Samuel and Jenny Uglow have edited this book. Their skill, knowledge and effort have made a deep impression, and both the book and I have benefited as a result. Arjun Amar helpfully reminded me how easy it is for a biographer to misinterpret motives, even in the field of ornithology, by pointing out that the curious behaviour of the long-tailed tit at the close of the book was probably its method of feeding. The faults and errors that remain are purely mine, and I hope to be forgiven for them.

Prologue

When I was four or five years old my mother took me to see a dead man.

He was sitting about ten houses away, along the road from where we lived. My mother lifted me up to see into the front of his car. It was one of those small white transit vans. There were only the two seats in the front, the back part crowded with boxes of tools. Something happened when the man stopped for lunch, and he died.

Childhood memories are difficult things. Do I really remember seeing the dead man? Perhaps my mother told me the story so many times that I came to remember how I imagined it to be. It seems odd now that he should have been sitting dead in his car so peaceful and so undisturbed. How did people know he had died? Why weren't there police and para-medics there, trying to get him breathing again? How did my mother know – and how did she have time – to take her small son along in order to try and show him that dead people were not terrifying, and that corpses could be peaceful?

The experience did not stop me being frightened of death and corpses and skeletons, particularly at night, throughout my childhood. Yet it was not the original source of my fears, either, since those had grown up with me. Perhaps it had been noticing those terrors that prompted my mother to walk me up the street that early afternoon in London in the 1970s.

As I grew a little older I became fascinated by dinosaurs. There seemed nothing terrifying about fossils, or about huge carnivorous monsters with teeth bigger than my small body. Things that were so far away did not disturb me. What disturbed me, what made me shiver and look over my shoulder when it grew dark, was the thought of what lay close at hand. Skeletons were much more frightening than fossils. There is nothing very familiar in the vertebrae of a stegosaurus, or in the three horns on the head of a triceratops. But skulls are closer to home. You can feel them when you put your head in your hands. You can see their shape beneath the skin of your mother's face. There is very little that is troubling about death in the abstract, but walking past a quiet graveyard at night is to find death closer than is comfortable.

It took too much time and trouble to move aside all the earth and clay piled on top of a coffin. To snatch a body, a resurrectionist had to be quick. The work was paid at piece-rates, except for the bodies of children and fetuses. They were priced by the inch. You had to make haste to make money, even given the astonishing sums a good snatcher might earn in the late eighteenth century. And the work was dangerous: body-snatchers were not popular.

Men worked in darkness and in haste. The semi-literate diaries that some took pains to leave suggest they also worked drunk, lubricating their fears and stoking their courage. With strong arms they moved the soft earth, newly laid, but only from the head end of the coffin. The rest was left covered while they removed the body. The grave robbers forced a specially shaped crowbar between the head end of the lid and the casket. With muscular force and the weight of earth pressing down on the lower part of the lid, the wood snapped widthways where it passed over the corpse's chest. The hungry men dragged the body out, stripped it naked, bundled the shroud and clothing back into the coffin, and then pushed back the earth over the grave.

The technique varied to suit demand. When there was a local glut of deaths, several coffins might be placed one on top of another in a single grave. Then the prize would be richer, but a snatcher had to remove all the overlying soil in order to lift out the higher coffins and extract all the bodies. Sometimes the poor were buried in pits without coffins. That made it easy to dig up several at a time, but more likely some of them would be so decayed you would have to put them back again.

The more surface soil the thief had to move, the more care he had to take to tidy up afterwards. Graveyards were renewable resources, but only if the local parishioners believed no harvests were taking place:

> *The extent to which this precaution was carried, and the manner of accomplishing it, formed the chief point of distinction between what was termed a good or slovenly workman . . . A bit of stick, an oyster shell, a stone, or a planted flower, were marks which were recognised at once, and noted by the practised body-snatchers.*

A wooden spade was useful since it made less noise when it hit stone; earth with gravel in it had to be flung carefully away in order to deaden the sound.

You put the body into a sack, then, if you had one, onto a carriage. If you didn't, you wrapped the corpse tightly in cloth to disguise its shape and carried it over your shoulder to its destination. That was a hospital or a school of surgery, but often such buildings were inaccessible or closed in the middle of the night, and grave-robbing was not a daylight occupation. Sometimes the goods needed to rest overnight, perhaps in a pub or at a private home, perhaps tucked out of the way by the roadside. Surgeons were helpful here, making sure their homes could accept discreet deliveries at unusual hours and even offering temporary accommodation to heavy sacks destined for different destinations the next morning.

Sometimes the deliveries covered longer distances. The rural poor who had never left their parish in life might become better travelled after death. Trade wasn't limited by county or national boundaries, only by the pace at which bodies rotted. When the poet John Keats studied to be a surgeon he lived in the part of south London still known as the Borough, sharing the house of a tallow chandler, a candle-maker, with another surgical student. The student's name was George Cooper, although he was no relation to the subject of this book. John Flint South told of how when Cooper moved across the river to Brentford they arranged for a body to follow. Packed in a hamper it came by boat across the Thames.

> *It was a rather warm day, and, as the subject was known to be for skeleton making, it was probably not very fresh, and certainly rather odoriferous. The perfume was not long undiscovered. 'It is a very warm day,' observed one lady to the other. 'Yes, ma'am, it is very close,' was the reply; and this was immediately followed by – 'Captain, there is a very unpleasant smell*

from that basket.' 'Yes, ma'am, I dare say; I brought it from a tallow chan-
dler's in the Borough and very likely it is graves!' The basket went on its
way without further observation and was duly deposited by the boat's
captain at my friend's house, with the observation, 'Well, sir, I have brought
you a stiff 'un.'

The conjunction of the tallow chandler and the corpse is probably co-incidental, but that isn't certain. Surgeons often laboured over their cadavers when there was no sunlight to see by, or no window by which it might enter. They sometimes used candles made from the fat that was closest to hand.

Nothing is quite so strange as that which is half familiar. We know that bodies fail and die, that after death they change and decompose. We realise that much of what was familiar to us in a living person will still be present in the corpse. The overlap, the uncertain boundary, is what disturbs. As a medical student I had expected that going into a room full of half-dissected corpses would be nightmarish. It was, but that feeling quickly wore off. Soon I could reach into a large fluid-filled plastic bucket and pull out a flayed and bobbing shoulder without remembering how unsettling it had seemed a week before. But in other ways the experience was more intrusive, more insistent. It lingered. Memories came back during normal life, insinuating their way into the time I spent with the living. I may have left the dissecting room far behind, have scrubbed and show-ered and changed, but the recollections haunted me. They came back as I watched the living muscles moving in the bodies of friends and family. They came back – the intruding texture and smell of preserved human flesh – as I sat down to eat.

It wasn't surprising to find myself reluctant to pull dead flesh apart. You approach a face or a chest with a certain degree of reluctance, knowing the body will look a little less human as a result of your work. But I found the most difficult parts of dissection were unexpected ones, moments when something crept up and took me by surprise. You recognise that it will feel personal to dissect a head: it was far more haunting to be consumed without warning by the odd intimacy of dissecting a hand. I thought how familiar the contours of it must have been to the dead person, more than those of their own face. Then there was the slow surprise of touching someone

4

else's genitals, of carefully pulling them apart. Those who are cold and dead cannot protect their privacy.

Nothing makes somebody come alive so much as passion. For Astley Cooper, the great passion of his life was anatomising. Born into a large family in rural Norfolk he became the greatest surgeon of his day, his pre-eminence spanning the four decades between the start of the nineteenth century and the reign of Victoria. He was a strikingly tall and handsome man, imposingly physical and with a taste and talent for boldness. He soared to become the attendant of kings and prime ministers, chief among a surgical profession starred with scientific and social celebrities, a caste of tremendously innovative and adventurous men. But he never for a moment lost his interest in what first had captured his imagination. The bodies of the dead and of the living, animals strange and familiar, the subjects of his previous operations and experiments, the remains of those he had admired and loved – all served his consuming interest in the phys-ical stuff of life. The corpses he dissected were often putrid and as a result were frequently deadly to those who worked with them. The animals Astley vivisected were stolen at great expense and significant risk. What was it that interested him? What was it that pulled him, again and again, to take such risks and make such efforts in order to cut up the living and the dead? What made him so fabulously famous in his day and why is he so little known in ours?

I first came across Astley Cooper whilst reading about Keats, who himself trained and worked as a surgeon. For Keats, poetry and medicine were twinned. Apollo, the god of both, was frequently in his thoughts and letters and verse. Faced with a world full of pain and death, Keats felt compelled to address suffering, to relieve it or to make it bearable by finding meaning in it. Images of fever and illness, of the balms and cures and hopes and despairs that came with them, these things spilled freely between his hospital experiences and his poems. He never lost his feeling that the two activities – at least in the first decades of the 1800s – were related. The reality of pain, both of the body and the mind, had to be borne – 'because', as he told his friend Bailey, 'women have Cancers'. As a child he helped to nurse his mother through her own illness and early death from tuber-culosis.

The book that put me on the path to meeting John Keats and Astley

Cooper, who taught Keats when he trained as a surgeon, was off-putting. It had been on my shelf for a year or two before I got around to opening it. The front cover was garish: a coloured-in portrait of an affected and dreamy young man. It was a modern edition of Keats's letters.

My bed was along the back wall of the house, on the first floor. It was early autumn and there was sunshine everywhere. I read sitting on the bed, my elbow leaning out of the open sash window. There was a flowering privet underneath, and the scent of its flowers was particularly strong in the early evening. Each day I read the book after I got home from work. The days were long and light and felt as though they would never cease. In the mornings I made my way by a gloriously slow bus journey across the golden Cotswolds, to a town of warm and glowing yellow stones. There, in a beautiful three-storey Georgian house with a green wisteria across the front, was the doctor's surgery where I was working.

It was a General Practice of seven full-time partners. I was a medical student, attached to them for a few weeks. Each morning, the patients came to the surgery. They would hobble or limp or frisk their way into the consulting room: every class of person in every state of life, with the immediately noticeable presence of two groups that, back then, I was less used to seeing. There were the very young, the constant stream of babies and toddlers, with rashes, coughs and streaming noses, or flirtatious wide-eyed smiles and slobbering toothless gums. And in even greater abundance came the old. Moving slowly, thinking slowly, talking slowly. They came in couples or alone. They entered the consulting room full of independence and stoicism, or worried by fear and tormenting anxiety. Each appointment was ten minutes, and if it ran over, the next one had to be correspondingly shorter. It was exhausting.

One day I spent the morning with the senior partner of the practice. He was a relatively young man, full of vigour. He had lectured to my medical school some time previously, and I remembered him only as a tall figure standing in the shadows at the front of the theatre while we looked at his slides and made notes. In his practice – in Real Life, I want to say – he was transformed. Taken out of the darkness, he came alive.

That morning one patient, a man in his sixties, came in reporting that he had been bleeding from his anus. He was embarrassed and frightened. The energy with which the doctor dealt with it made it bearable for all of us. The intimate examination – a finger inserted up into the rectum and swept around to see what it could feel – the discussion of possibilities, of the bleeding blood vessels of piles or gut inflammation, of the growing menace of a cancer – the spirit of the consulting room made it all tolerable. It allowed the possibility of death to enter in without the existence of life becoming dimmed. It was the achievement of that particular doctor's character.

After lunch we went on home visits. There were decrepit houses, empty fridges and filthy rotting furnishings. There were places where every net frill was in place around the windows and the plastic cover had never been removed from the sofa. There was a young woman, heavily pregnant with her first child, in a home with scrubbed wooden floors and a kitchen crowded with books and herbs: a general sense of promise.

We visited an Italian couple whose elderly father had come over to stay with them. A fortnight before, he had still been at work, appearing in court as a barrister. Now he was demented and incontinent. The doctor examined him, and afterwards explained to us all that the old man was dying. He spent almost an hour on the phone, trying to arrange for care at home, so that the man could die with his family. He failed. Next he tried to get the old man into a hospice so that he could die with a moderate amount of peace and dignity. There was no room. Eventually he had him admitted to a general ward at the local hospital. It was the only place that would take him. The family were devastated, but they were also relieved. Someone had come into their home and taken away the uncertainty. They had known they were unable to cope without help.

The doctor was in despair, but I only realised that when we went outside into the sunshine and got into his car. The general hospital, he explained, was overcrowded and busy. The old man would die on a foul-smelling and noisy ward with little time for him. If it was a bad day he would pass away on a makeshift bed in the corridor of the emergency department. 'We need to cheer ourselves up,' the doctor said to me. So off we drove, across the Cotswolds again, past woods that were still green and gold, to a house where no one had called for a visit. 'He's a regular patient of mine,' the doctor explained. 'I pop in every month or so to see how he's doing.' All of which was true. But it was also true that the patient and his wife were delighted to see the doctor and clearly liked him. Even their dog was pleased. They brought out tea and a cake and gave us, despite the patient's wheelchair and his slowly degenerating disease, the sense that it was worth carrying on and that the sunshine outside was telling the truth.

That evening I took up the book of Keats's letters. A handful of tall yellow evening primroses grew across the garden from the flowering privet. I read until the sun faded away from them and then watched the swallows in the darkening sky. After that I went for a drink with my housemates. My first real tastes of Keats and Astley Cooper came at the same time as this early experience of what it meant to be a doctor. They remain vivid. A year or two later I heard that the doctor with whom I had spent that day died, himself eaten up by a cancer of the gut.

By the time I attended my first real autopsy I had been studying medicine for some years. The shock of the dead had worn off, and the dilapidation of old age was what most disturbed me. The hospital wards smelt to me of sickness and decay, the scents of institutional food and disinfectants mixing promiscuously with the stink of urine or faeces, incontinence and dementia. Hospital gowns and hospital curtains always gaped a little bit open, and what they revealed about human decay was sickening. For a long time physical disgust was the hardest part of becoming a hospital doctor. It persisted long after I learnt from experience what warm and friendly places hospital wards usually are.

So I was not worried about the autopsy. It had nothing to do with the wards that were so troubling me at the time. It had more in common with the science that previous research experience had made me familiar with. I had seen plenty of old people dying in their beds, and had often needed to look carefully to determine whether patients were old and sleeping or had actually died. I entered the post-mortem rooms cheerfully, curious as to what it might be like to be a pathologist. I had already discovered my own taste for what is called histology, for looking at patterns of human flesh that have been frozen and ever so thinly sliced, then stained with incandescent dyes. They make the most wonderful colours and shapes, and it is a marvellous feeling to look at those patterns and understand that they represent something; that this mosaic of bright pink and sky blue shows cells, that these coloured networks are the stuff of life. All one needs to enjoy life as a pathologist is to find corpses interesting too. I was ready to see one of these old people, to help cut them apart and have a look inside.

It was a coldly dislocating thing to find that the person laid out on the chilled metal slab (stainless steel with a gutter down the middle of it like a medieval street), was a young woman of my own age. She was lying naked and supine, her back slightly arched and a delicate tattoo of a butterfly displayed on her thigh. Nothing had been the matter with her body. She had suffered from despair, and jumped from a multi-storey car park. Some bones in her spine had shattered on landing, and the aorta – the great blood vessel emerging from the left side of the heart – had burst.

The pathologist opened her up and her smell was unexpected. She was not like the corpses preserved in formaldehyde; she was fresh. I thought that the smell as her abdomen and her chest were opened down the middle was distinctive. It was unmistakably the smell of Earl Grey tea.

The following week I went to visit some friends. They lived in the Cambridgeshire countryside, and since it was a warm summer day we walked over to a fruit farm nearby. We sat in the sunshine, surrounded by fields of ripe raspberries, and I was gripped by cold horror. In the midst of pastoral tranquillity I had the sudden olfactory hallucination of the young woman's insides, of the smell of hopelessness and of suicide: of Earl Grey tea.

Why was Astley Cooper such an important figure in Georgian London? From the early biographies, from the references to him in newspapers and journals of the day, I learnt that he was a man who had once had a fiery love for revolutionary democracy and who had relished a life of hard work. My own early experiences of wards and mortuaries had repelled me, even though I lived in a world of clean hospitals, antiseptics and effective anaesthesia. What could it have been about bodies and eighteenth-century surgery that had so gripped Cooper? I tried to think through how it fitted in with having an ardour for democracy and for days and nights of constant labour. He lived in one of the most fascinating periods of history – from 1768 until 1841 – and he spent much of it with the dead.

Even our own stories are untrustworthy, like mine of the dead man on my childhood street and the young woman's smell. I am no longer sure how my own memory may have altered them. Diaries and letters, newspaper reports and books are little more reliable. But they are often all we have, when it comes to figuring out our own lives and trying to understand those of others. What follows is an attempt to dig up the dead, to try to fix and stain and colour a world of two hundred years ago. It is an attempt to trace what is familiar in a vanished life, and to use that as a guide to explore what is endlessly strange – the experience of another person, living in another age. It is a form of dissection, of anatomising. It is a form of what is called an autopsy, which means 'to see for oneself'.

1

Endings and Beginnings

Sir Astley Cooper having been long at the head of the surgical profession in this country, his illness excited more anxiety, and his death produced a stronger sensation, both in and out of the medical world, than we ever before witnessed. We think it indisputable that no surgeon, in this or any other country, ever realised such a fortune, or acquired such widespread fame, as Sir Astley Cooper.

British & Foreign Medical Review, 1841

Astley died early in 1841. Fond and admiring obituaries were printed in the newspapers and the medical press. They commented with gusto upon Astley's successes and dwelt with particular appetite on his unmatched income. The *Quarterly Review* declared that he had made more money than any physician, surgeon or lawyer that had ever lived; *The Times* and many others agreed.

To the nephew that bore his own first name, Astley left the gifts that kings had given him: a hereditary title and a silver epergne from George IV, a silver breadbasket from William IV. To another nephew, Bransby, he left a greater treasure: his notes and diaries and journals. Astley's intention was that Bransby should use them to write his biography. It came out, in two orthodox Victorian volumes of life and letters, in 1843. But even before his nephew entombed him under hundreds of pages of hagiography, Astley had already been buried with a suitably Victorian degree of pomp. His body lay for a while at his house in the West End of the city. On 20 February, at six in the morning, it was taken by hearse to Guy's Hospital, the horses clattering southwards across London Bridge. The coffin bore the collar, badge and jewel of the Hanoverian Guelphic Order, along with the riband and cross of the French Légion d'honneur. From seven in the morning until three in the afternoon it lay, velvet-lined, in the hospital boardroom. Hundreds of visitors came to pay their respects and to file slowly past. A strikingly large number were women. At half past two the quadrangle outside filled with a swelling mass of people, among them many medical students, surgeons, apothecaries and physicians. When the bells of the city struck three o'clock the coffin was taken up and carried towards the chapel.

Away from London's bustle, the village church in Hemel Hempstead, where Astley owned a large estate, was hung in sympathetic black. *The Times* recorded Astley's medals and decorations in lavish detail, knowing its readers would wish to know the details of the great man's funeral. Astley was preceded into the chapel by the plume of black feathers projecting forwards from the coffin's head.

Samuel Cooper, Astley's father, had been a student of divinity at Magdalene College, Cambridge in the late 1750s. He went on to become a Fellow, but since all academics had to be celibate, the twenty-one-year-old Samuel Cooper then made himself unemployed by marrying. His career at Cambridge implied no particular academic gifts, any more than his leaving of it was a noble sacrifice. The sole two English universities of the day, Oxford and Cambridge, were backwaters when it came to learning. They existed as undemanding finishing schools for the aristocracy, and as spring-boards to successful Church careers for the less well-off. Samuel Cooper was only following the pattern of his class. His success – and it was some-thing of a family tradition – came from marrying well. Maria Susanna Bransby had a significant fortune, and her landowning father controlled a Church living which Samuel took up shortly after.

In 1768 Maria and Samuel were living in the handsome manor-house of Brooke Hall, about three miles from the Norfolk village of Shotesham. To the Reverend Samuel Cooper's tenure of the prosperous local benefice of Yelverton was added the living of Morley St Botolph, another gift from his father-in-law. Good connections and proper behaviour won him the approval of the corporation of Norwich, and they expanded his posses-sions with the curacies of Mundham and Seething. Samuel's marriage had been only the start of his worldly success.

Both Maria and Samuel were fond of writing, producing reassuringly conservative texts praising the virtues of England's established order. Samuel's were in the form of sermons while his wife wrote epistolary novels that gained her a much larger readership. *Letters Between Emilia and Harriet* came out in March 1762, a month after the arrival of the couple's first child, a son named Bransby (after his mother's maiden name). Maria then rapidly produced another two sons – Samuel Lovick in February of 1763 and William Houman in September of the following year – followed by two daughters, Charlotte Maria in September of 1765 and Marianne two years later. The rush of procreation was enough to pause her literary efforts but by 1768 she was gestating her two most successful creations: her son Astley and her next book. The book appeared in two volumes in 1769. *The Exemplary Mother* told the tale of a heroine who, through dogged virtue, saved her son from moral and worldly ruin. Successful enough to win a large national readership, it was painfully sentimental and piously sanctimonious. Maria's own letters to her friends and family were of a similar style.

Maria's sixth pregnancy was her most difficult, and she spent much of the time sick. When Astley arrived on 23 August, she was worn out. The baby was christened on 9 September and promptly sent away to live with a wet-nurse. It was a slightly odd decision, for all Astley's siblings were nursed at home. But it meant that Astley, as befitted a future Romantic, was suckled by Love, since his foster mother, Mrs Love, was a local farmer's wife. It isn't clear how long he stayed with the Loves and their children (they were his father's parishioners), but he maintained contact with them throughout his childhood, later referring to them as his adopted family. It was a significant relationship, and the early years Astley spent growing up on the Loves' large farm marked him permanently. Towards the end of his life, writing a treatise on the breast, Cooper advised against wet-nursing. 'All animals,' he wrote, 'even those of the most ferocious character, show affection for their young, – do not forsake them, but yield them their milk, – do not neglect, but nurse and watch over them; and shall woman, the loveliest of Nature's creatures, possessed of reason as well as instinct, refuse that nourishment to her offspring which no other animal withholds . . . ?' Maria Susanna Cooper, at the end of a difficult pregnancy, felt woman should do exactly that.

Brooke Hall, when Astley returned to live in it, was a busy place. It was large and impressive, an imposing brick-built Jacobean house, just the

13

thing for a successful young family. Norwich, then the second biggest city in England, was only seven miles distant. The village itself was pretty, with an open green in the centre where the schoolhouse stood among walnut trees. The grounds of Brooke Hall were bordered by an outer wall. A driveway ran through a large gatehouse, and Samuel Cooper took particular pleasure in making use of it, riding through on horseback or driving in his carriage. The grounds contained a large orchard and kitchen and flower gardens. An oak, upwards of a century and a half old, stood to one side of the drive, next to an encircling moat. It was a fine place to learn to swim and climb and ride, a place where a knowledge of natural history could be picked up while playing. There was a pigeon-house and a coach-house and stable-yards for the family's four-horse carriage, the smaller chaise and the handsome black horses essential to Samuel and Maria's professional and social lives. There was a pond for fish (and for swimming, when the children grew tired of the moat) with a boat moored at one side of it. No Enclosure Act had yet turned the surrounding farmland into large unbroken plots, and the village sat in a patchwork of commons and open spaces, cottages scattered amongst them. There were pheasants and woodcock in the woods and snipe in the undrained marshland of the nearby Fens – all fair game for Astley and his brothers. Growing up as a son of Brooke Hall was a privileged way to begin life.

The Reverend Cooper went to church, accompanied by his family, in a carriage pulled by four fine black horses. It was a show of vanity and wealth, there being no need to go to such lengths to travel to a church that was close to the house. And even if the Reverend's attendance at a more distant parish was required, the four horses remained a glorious indulgence. The *Quarterly Review*, in Samuel's obituary, commented pithily that such displays said more for the Reverend's living than they did for his life.

In the church where Samuel preached the family had a large pew close by the pulpit; on the other side, but in a similarly privileged position at the front, would sit the family servants. In the days before village churches had their own organs, the music was provided by the congregation. Astley and his brothers, when the time came for hymns, walked from their pew to a side door. A staircase took them to the gallery above where they and the rest of the choir sang.

The Coopers' contribution to the choir consisted of Astley and his three older brothers. Bransby was six years older than Astley, Samuel five and William four. And as if three older brothers weren't enough, Astley had to cope with the indignities suffered by any little boy in possession of two older sisters – Charlotte and Marianne.

Two younger sisters – Anna Maria and Margaret Bransby – were born in 1769 and 1770. Both died in infancy, as did a third girl born shortly after, Anna Maria Inyon. The disease that killed them was believed to be consumption, one of the many terms for tuberculosis – the 'Captain of the Men of Death', the 'White Plague' – a disease that was unsettling for many reasons, not least the uncertainty that came with it. Those who had been in contact with it lived under a threat, never knowing if they might develop the illness or not. Even those who definitely suffered from it lived under the shadow of doubt, for tuberculosis was by no means invariably fatal. There was always room for hope, even for painful and pointless hope. As a child Astley was also infected with tuberculosis, and the disease took hold in his lungs – 'phthisis' being the contemporary term. It was very much the family disease.

Despite the deaths and their shadow, Brooke Hall remained a home to six living children – seven from 1773, when Astley's youngest brother Beauchamp Newton arrived. (The Newton name was a nod to the Coopers' relations with the great mathematician and alchemist; there was also a link to Nelson, but in the 1770s it was not yet something to be treasured up in carefully chosen middle names.) The boys were brought up under the tuition of their father, a man who believed in the worth of an early education in conservative Christian values. As well as religion he taught his sons Latin and Greek. Astley progressed as far as being able to read Horace in Latin and the New Testament in Greek, but he had no interest in books. Whenever possible he escaped, preferring to stretch his legs rather than study his texts. From his mother he learnt English and history, while the local village schoolmaster came to teach the children reading, writing and mathematics. Astley made poor progress in them all. His favourite teacher was his dancing-master, a Frenchman who rode over from Norwich to give lessons. And when they were over, Astley plunged into whatever adventures he could find. He practised his riding without fear and without much respect for his mounts. Starting out on ponies he progressed as far as his size and skill allowed. Donkeys – pronounced 'dickeys' in the local slang of the time – were a particular childhood favourite. When he was large enough to manage a horse he taught himself to ride bareback without a bridle. He also made repeated efforts to ride cows. Growing bolder and more skilled, he caused havoc by scrambling up onto a bull and guiding it to drive a herd from the field.

When there was nothing to ride, there would at least be something to climb. Trees offered adventure in their branches and in their fruit: scrumping crops provided good experience in physical challenge, organised theft and the skills required in leading a gang through a successful raid.

Older brothers were occasionally to be feared, even as playmates. Bransby and Samuel, only a year apart, spent more time together than with the much younger Astley. Bransby was sedate but Samuel, although not as wild as Astley, would at least sometimes play with him. During one session Samuel managed to stab his younger brother. The two children were playing, and Samuel was holding in one outstretched hand a sharp knife. When Astley ran towards him, the blade happened to be at head height. It entered the lower part of Astley's cheek and travelled up and in, stopped by the lower part of his eye socket. The blood flowed briskly and a local surgeon was hurriedly sent for. Even when the bleeding had stopped, the wound caused serious concern: infections around the eye could be rapidly fatal or permanently disfiguring. The local surgeon visited for some weeks. Eventually the wound healed over, leaving only a small scar.

Brooke Hall was dominated by Astley's father. Samuel Cooper was an austere man, fond of his own opinions and the sound of his own voice preaching them. His wife, valuing her own strong sense of duty, followed his lead. Her grandson painted an evocative picture of their relationship:

> Perhaps she submitted rather too obsequiously to his will, either for his, or her own, happiness; for as my grandfather was naturally a little wayward, the pliancy of his wife's disposition encouraged a spirit of self-importance rather more than was quite consistent with that mutual deference to the wishes of each other, so necessary to conjugal happiness.

In the evenings, her children and her household at relative peace, Maria Cooper sat down to her writing. A brood of seven young children left her no space for a room of her own, but for all her 'pliancy' and conservative orthodoxy, Maria continued to write. Her books never had her name displayed prominently, but she grew confident enough to include it after their forewords. Women had a right to use a pen, she had her characters say, arguing that 'men . . . will scarcely be afraid of women, because they are capable of being agreeable companions, and useful friends'. She wrote

16

without a desk, her children spilling about her as she sat with a quill in one hand and paper in the other.

Of all her children Astley was the most active. He returned home covered with bruises on a regular basis: sometimes falling out of a tree, sometimes from tormenting a donkey into kicking him. The bruises made him neither bad-tempered nor secretive. Open, cheerful and brimming with physical courage, he was an attractive child. He was reckless both with his own safety and with the feelings of the animals, brothers and assorted friends that were around him, but his enjoyment of jokes and childish exploits made him popular, both with his peers and with his family – particularly the female half, fond of his spirit and his good humour. He had enough vigour and self-confidence to make him animated and independent, and enough openness to make others take as much pleasure in it as he did. The nearby common was open grazing land, a playground largely free of fences. Once, when Astley caught a horse there he turned it towards a resting cow, urging it on towards a leap. Seeing the horse and rider bearing down upon it, and unaware of its planned role as a surmountable obstacle, the cow rose up in alarm precisely as the child and his mount passed overhead. Astley returned home with a broken collar-bone and an undimmed spirit. There is no record of the fate of the horse or the cow.

If testing his adventurousness was one part of his childhood, another was trying out different identities, putting on stolen clothes and stolen voices. His brothers' wardrobes were raided, as were his father's mannerisms and speeches. Other people's property was also subject to Astley's childhood whims. He smashed the windows of a tailor he disliked and then, regretting his violence, returned to apologise and pay for the repairs. He altered the clock hands on the church while his father was inside, confusing both the villagers waiting outside and the Reverend alone within. From the top of the church tower he tore open pillows, sending a rain of feathers down onto the puzzled parishioners below, and another time he fell while clambering about the gallery, the drop onto the stone floor doing nothing to put him off heights. He enjoyed sprinting along the eaves of barns, falling sometimes but always luckily – on one occasion when the fall was steep enough to kill or seriously injure him, he landed softly in a large pile of hay.

Astley's experiments centred on seeing what he could become, what he could get away with, what role he could play. Aged about twelve he could still play a girl, and when he heard of a neighbour's reputation for making sexual advances to his maids he dressed himself up in the clothes of one of the family's servants and applied for the job. His mimicry won him both the post and the man's attentions, and when his new employer walked him halfway home after the interview the two paused at a stile whilst the master tried to kiss his young servant's lips. 'I have often heard you were fond of the maids,' declared the unabashed boy, throwing off his disguise, 'but I am Astley Cooper.'

Stories emphasising Astley's vitality and mischievousness come from different sources. His nephew Bransby, Samuel Lovick's son, collected them together from friends and family, and recalled Astley dwelling on others himself during his later life. Still more, written down by Astley in the years before his death, were presented to Bransby deliberately. They draw a consistent picture. It might not represent the truth of a young boy's child-hood, but it certainly shows how he and those close to him saw it in mature retrospect. Another story describes Astley hiding in his father's church, copying his voice and his words and puzzling the old man who commented afterwards that he 'had never noticed an echo in that place before'. In an odd Shakespearean episode Astley dressed as Satan, convincing the sexton's drunk wife to sell him her soul. She woke the next day, believing the memory to have been an intoxicated dream, to find to her horror that she was in the possession of some very real money.

Other anecdotes describe Astley experimenting with more helpful roles. Outside a local boarding school a boy snatched the hat from the head of a younger child and threw it into a nearby pond. Unmanned by the assault and the prospect of further punishment for losing his hat, the child stood and wept while his schoolmates mocked him. Astley, aged thirteen, was riding past on his way home from the village pub, where his dancing-master had held a lesson. Pleasure in his own striking appearance was evident in his dress. He wore a triple cocked hat, his dark hair emerging to fall in ringlets down his back, and a scarlet coat with black glazed collar. He stopped to find out why the young boy was crying. Hearing the story he dismounted, strode to the pond in his white silk stockings, and waded out into the water to fetch the boy's hat. When he came out he was soaked and muddy from the waist down.

In the 1843 biography, Bransby took care to insert one particular story among the handfuls of childhood anecdotes. It is familiar in form, for many biographies have a counterpart, and it shows the young Astley first having his head turned towards his future career. Bransby explains that when Astley's foster brother, John Love, was himself thirteen, he was run over by a cart. As he lay on his front in the dirt, the cart came to a halt with one of its wheels on top of his leg. When he was pulled free, blood was spurting in a strong bright red pulse from the back of his knee. The popliteal artery – the main vessel carrying blood to the lower leg – had been cut:

> *All was alarm and confusion, – when the young Astley, in the midst of the distressing scene, alone capable of deliberating, and perceiving the necessity of instantly preventing further loss of blood, had the presence of mind to encircle the limb with his pocket handkerchief above the wound . . . and stopped the bleeding. To these means his foster-brother owed a prolonga-tion of life until the arrival of the surgeon who had been sent for . . .*

One of the first operations I saw was an attempted bypass graft of a blocked popliteal artery. It had been blocked by fatty deposits brought on partly by age (the man was in his fifties) but chiefly by smoking. The operation went badly. While it was impossible to see the details of what the surgeon was doing – it was obscured by torrents of blood – I could read the progress of the operation on the surgeon's increasingly harrowed face. He sat on a stool with his patient's blood pouring over his lap and forming a congealing pool on the floor. An observant theatre nurse saw the effect the scene was having on me and advised me to step back and sit down in the corner for a moment. She gave me a small purple plastic dinosaur toy and told me to squeeze it until I felt less anxious. A lot of blood flows through the popliteal artery, and when the vessel is damaged more blood spurts out than one would think a man had in him.

Astley's own account of the episode remained vivid throughout his life, the emotions still strongly felt decades later. But the facts differed from those offered by his nephew biographer. As John Love lay bleeding in the Norfolk dirt, urgent calls for help were sent out to the local surgeons. One protested that he could not come because his attendance was needed by a patient dangerously ill with fever. Another said he had a labour to deal with, yet another protested a 'pressing case of inflammation of the bowels'. A torn popliteal artery was a thankless job for a surgeon, its only cure being an amputation of the leg at a level where the artery could be effec-tively tied closed. And there was little by way of a fee to hope for when the boy was not from a rich family. Throughout his life Cooper was scathing about the behaviour of these local surgeons. All were suddenly busy, and none could attend. Instead an old woman, held by some locals to have supernatural powers, was sent for. She sent back a message saying that by the time the messenger returned to John, the bleeding would have stopped. She was correct, for the boy had died.

The operation I saw continued to go badly wrong. The patient lost his leg at the knee as a result of the surgeon's inability to sort out the blood supply. A few days later, since the circulation to his stump was not very good, he was taken back to theatre to have a higher amputation, this time at mid-thigh where it stood a chance of healing. I lost track of him after that.

In 1781, through the patronage of the Dean of Norwich Cathedral, Samuel Cooper was awarded the perpetual curacy of Great Yarmouth. It was the reward for labour and most particularly for ambition, 'a large cure of souls, then amounting to 16,000 people, and supported by Easter-Dues, Fisherman's Doles or Gifts and voluntary contributions'. It was a rich and prestigious living, and upon securing it Samuel Cooper moved himself and his family over to the coastal town of Great Yarmouth itself. There they lived in the vicarage next to the church of St Nicholas. It still stands, and there is still some stained glass in an attic window with the youthful Samuel Lovick Cooper's name scratched into it.

Despite the step upwards in his family's fortunes, the move had a personal cost for Astley. He was coming up for fourteen and had formed an attachment with the daughter of a clergyman living near Brooke Hall. Great Yarmouth was almost thirty miles away, with no direct public transport.

After the move, Astley stole one of his father's horses and set off to ride back by himself to see his young lady. As an old man he was fond of dwelling on this story. He made it safely inland across Norfolk, and walked for a while with his sweetheart in her family's garden before attempting the journey home. The young woman played no visible part in his future life, but Astley had learnt something important, a lesson that made the memory of his trip stay vivid. Romance was heightened by adventure, and with risk went relish.

The church of St Nicholas at Great Yarmouth was larger and taller than the one by Brooke Hall. There was further to fall for anyone who took a fancy to clambering about in its rafters. But when the Coopers arrived there was building work being done, and when the workmen went home at the end of the day they left their ladders. It was too much of an invitation for Astley to resist, and he scuttled upwards. He slipped while walking along the joists, a bad mistake in what was the largest parish church in the country. It was said to be a seventy-foot drop to the chancel below. Astley caught his leg over a beam as he tumbled, and hung upside down for a while, horrified by the drop beneath, before managing to haul himself back upwards.

Resting awhile from heights, he took advantage of his new location near the coast and decided on a nautical adventure. Taking a small flat-bottomed boat designed to carry a man and his hunting dog across fenland shallows, he set out to sea. The River Yare was just about manageable, with a stone placed in the centre of the boat's floor to act as a keel and to give it depth and stability, but the craft still drew only a couple of inches of water, and when the ebb tide pulled Astley out to the rougher sea the swirling waters tipped the boat dangerously. The stone began to roll from the craft's centre, coming to rest between Astley's legs. Water came rapidly over the boat's side. Sinking quickly, he was fortunate to be able to reverse his course and make it back to the coast.

If the days were full of physical activity, they were also full of women. His older two sisters and his mother formed a circle of female company that Astley, admired and confident, moved in with poise and enjoyment. He grew up in a house full of mixed company, something that always gave him an easy pleasure. When his sisters wished to drive out, it was often Astley who took the whip on their behalf.

Yarmouth had its appeal, but Astley's strongest childhood memories were always those of his first home at Brooke Hall. As an old man he went back. The house had been torn down, the countryside transformed by the enclosures that had turned scattered cottages and commons into the larger, more productive – and less populated – farming estates. And Astley found that the years had diminished the views in other ways, too.

I walked down the village, along an enclosed road, dull and shadowed by plantations on either side, instead of those commons and open spaces [that were] ornamented here and there by clean cottages. The little mere was so much smaller than in my imaginations, that I could hardly believe my eyes: the great mere was half empty, and dwindled also to a paltry pond. On my right were the plantations of Mr Ketts, overshading the road, and for which numerous cottages had been sacrificed . . . I looked for the old Brooke Hall . . . for the road which led to it and its forecourt – its flower gardens and kitchen gardens – its stable-yard and coach-houses – and all were gone.

2

Apprenticeships

When Samuel Lovick Cooper scratched his name into the glass of the rectory window at Great Yarmouth, he was old enough to make it a slightly curious thing to do. It may have had something to do with the fragility of life, something apparent in a family that had already suffered three young deaths. Samuel was in his late teens, about to go up to his father's old college of Magdalene in Cambridge to study divinity himself. Bransby, the firstborn, was already at the university, reading law at Newton's Trinity College. William Houman's course had also been decided upon: weak in mind and body, his own family thought him unfit for any career. He was brought up under the extended protection of his mother. 'It seemed early to be determined that he should not be brought up to any profession, and he therefore had no other pursuit beyond that of his own amusement.' In this pursuit he may or may not have been successful. As they grew up together, Astley was frequently unkind to him.

Visions of wider society came through the regular visits of William Cooper, Astley's uncle and the senior surgeon of Guy's Hospital in London. Norwich was England's second city, but there was no doubt that London was the first. For a young man entering his teenage years, the stories of London society that William Cooper told conjured up a world of beck-oning promises.

The Coopers were prosperous and clearly willing to invest in the educa-tion of their children. Astley, however, had shown no pleasure in books.

With his vigour and his distaste for study, a career in the military seemed an attractive option. But family connections opened up other possibilities: not only was the Reverend Samuel Cooper's brother William a surgeon, their father had been one too.

The medical profession of the day was divided unequally into three. At the bottom of the hierarchy came the apothecaries. Officially their function was purely to dispense drugs and potions at the instructions of physicians. Given the scarcity and expense of these physicians, this official plan was never realistic. In 1704 the Royal College of Physicians successfully pursued an apothecary named Rose for having prescribed medicine to an ailing man. The House of Lords, offended at the self-interested behaviour of the college, overturned Rose's conviction on the grounds that the medical needs of patients were more important than the professional pretensions of doctors. It was the beginning of the formal erosion of the college's self-serving exclusivity. By 1803 the Manchester physician Thomas Percival commented that an apothecary was 'the physician of the poor in all cases, and of the rich when the distress or danger is not very great'.

Above the apothecaries, but not far above, were the surgeons. For an apothecary to bleed a patient was to encroach upon their exclusive territory. In 1540 Henry VIII had created the Company of Barber-Surgeons, men whose symbol was the red-and-white-striped pole representing blood and bandages. Only in 1745 had the surgeons split themselves off from their barber colleagues. Since then they had increasingly pursued their aspirations to be seen as something better than pullers of teeth and setters of bones. They moved to set themselves up as respectable professionals, aiming to acquire prestige and power and the ability to merit a more lucrative reward. The widespread establishment of large hospitals since the early eighteenth century had helped their cause, but surgeons remained second-class. William Cheselden (1688–1752) of St Thomas's was the first to achieve a social position significantly above that of a barber. It came to his aid in 1714 when the Company of Barber-Surgeons charged him with human dissection, an activity legally limited to themselves, the Royal College of Physicians and the universities.

Cheselden escaped punishment (and the legal restrictions on who was allowed to dissect were dissolved when the Surgeons & Barbers split in 1745), but even he had no ability to prescribe any medicines that were taken orally. That was the exclusive reserve of the final rank of the medical profession: the physicians. University-trained and proudly carrying the gold-topped canes that marked them out, these were the men able to command respect and rich fees. Formal surgical teaching in Edinburgh, the chief British city for medical teaching for much of the early eighteenth century, consisted of a few rather abstract lectures on anatomy delivered by physicians with little or no practical surgical training. The Company of Surgeons in London – located at the Old Bailey, the better to publicly dissect hanged criminals who made up their only licit source of corpses for study – still represented something that seemed to most people a craft or trade, nothing like the intellectually and socially respected physicians with their royal college.

To be a physician was to achieve something rich and rare; there were still only a couple of hundred in the whole country, and they could command heavy fees. But the exclusivity left a gap in the market, and while surgeons were trying to fill some of it the bulk of the work fell by default to the apothecaries: whatever their official role as functionaries, mere dispensers, they were the only source of medical advice available and affordable to the majority of the population.

Almost as soon as the family moved to Yarmouth, Astley started his training with Francis Turner, a local apothecary, a man who doubled as a surgeon for the excellent reason that there was no one else around who was any better qualified to do so. Apothecaries might become successful small businessmen, and if the training went well there was the potential for Astley to follow his brothers to university and a physicianship, or his uncle to a hospital and a career as a surgeon. And it went well enough, Astley proving himself friendly and adept without discovering any great calling to the apothecary's profession.

Standing behind his master one day, Astley was doing his best to make another of the apothecary's students laugh. He was successful enough with his face-pulling to collapse the other young man in laughter, and cause Francis Turner to spin round in an effort to discover the source of the mirth. Astley was caught with a bizarre grimace on his face, and quickly tried to explain away his contorted expression, exclaiming in pretended pain that a tooth was causing him agony. 'God bless me!' said Francis. 'Let me see.' He pulled Cooper's hand away from where it was pressed to his cheek and forced the young man's mouth open. Then, with the experience of speed and deceit which his profession had given him, he lunged without warning with a pair of powerful forceps, grabbing on to a molar. With a wrench he pulled the tooth away.

When he had recovered himself enough to think, Astley saw that the drawn tooth was decayed. There was nothing to be gained from complaining. He thanked the apothecary and declared the pain relieved. It was an early lesson in making the best of a painful situation. He was never sure afterwards whether Francis had been punishing him or making a genuine effort to relieve his apparent pain.

The period with the apothecary having gone well – at least in the eyes of the Reverend Samuel Cooper – Astley moved on. He was accepted on a trial basis as apprentice to Edward Rigby, a surgeon at the Norfolk and Norwich Hospital in the heart of the city. Before the age of fifteen Astley was living with him as his apprentice but without any binding indentures being signed. There was still enough doubt about Astley's career to make it desirable to leave the arrangements open. With the trial apprenticeship came attendance at the hospital, and with that came experience in the operating theatre. A single operation, the standard one of a man's being cut for the stone, was Astley's formative professional experience. He watched it being carried out by Dr Donnee, a colleague of Edward Rigby's, in the theatre of the Norfolk and Norwich Hospital. The operation seems to have taken place in the winter, as 1782 turned into 1783.

Astley was fourteen and a half. He watched as the patient walked into the operating theatre and climbed on to the table. It was raised up higher than a normal table, in order that the surgeon would not have to bend over awkwardly. The patient lay down on his back and let the surgeon's assistants position him. From the waist down he was naked. Following instructions he pulled his knees up to his chest and grabbed onto the outside of each foot with one hand. The assistants bound some cords tightly around his hands and ankles, holding him in that position, then slid a pillow or two underneath his head and his arched back to make him more stable and more comfortable. That done, further bindings were applied, this time passing under the man's knees and up over the back of his neck. His position was now fixed, his perineum – the stretch of flesh between his genitals and anus – exposed to unobstructed view.

An assistant took a slim curved silver tube in one hand and the man's penis in his other. He put the end of the tube to the opening at the end of the penis and slid it slowly inwards, down through the penis and into the bladder. A little urine bubbled out over the tube's exposed end, flowing over the assistant's hand and onto the table where the man lay. Now the surgeon, Dr Donnee, approached. His title proclaimed him to have a university training, to be one of the small number of physicians who had taken an interest in surgical practice, a man willing to get his hands dirty. He smeared animal fat over the index finger of his right hand, and then around the patient's anus. He pushed his finger through it and felt around in the rectum. It was empty, the result of enemas given before the operation. Clearing out the bulk of the faeces in the rectum made it smaller and less likely to get in the way of an errant scalpel as the operation progressed. Dr Donnee pushed his finger up against the front wall of the rectum, where it lay next to the back of the bladder, trying to feel the impression of the stone that he knew was in there.

When a large enough stone forms in the human bladder, it has no way of getting out. Sitting there it brushes against the inner wall of the bladder, causing pain and bleeding and often the intense desire to urinate without there being any urine to get rid of. The stone can block the urine flowing into the bladder from the kidneys, or stop its flowing out of the bladder down the urethra. Even a partial blockage of either type causes stagnation, and stagnant urine is a ripe bed for infection. If no urine at all can pass into the bladder then the kidney above is gradually destroyed by the back pressure. If none can pass out of the bladder then it swells, bursting once the pressure inside grows too high. A ruptured bladder meant a painful death. If a little bit of urine was able to squeeze by an obstruction then the bladder would swell like a balloon until the pressure was enough to force some of the liquid out. The pain and the bleeding and the infections could all kill, and if they became chronic could make people so miserable that there was no pleasure in being alive. People might be relieved finally to die.

The pain could be excruciating. It drove people to desperation. Anecdotes from the days when bladder stones were common – and operations expensive, painful and dangerous – illustrate the fact. One man put a long nail through his urethra – through the tube down his penis – and managed to get the end of it into his bladder stone. At that point he smashed repeatedly on the flat end of the nail with a blacksmith's hammer, frantic to break the stone up. Another man spent nine months inserting a home-made scraper by the same route, gradually clawing at the edges of the stone until it was in small enough fragments to urinate out. In his later lectures, Cooper described how his patients told him that the feeling of a bladder stone was 'as if boiling water or lead were passing through the urethra'. To try and avoid the agony of the stone blocking the opening of the urethra, sufferers would lie on their backs to urinate. Even then there was 'often, as the urine [was] discharging, a sudden stop to its flow . . . produced with violent pain'. They had no interest left over after such physical misery to care about how they wet themselves.

After Dr Donnee felt for the stone his assistant pulled the silver tube out of the patient's penis. He replaced it with a wooden staff, polished to smoothness and curved in the same way. It had a groove recessed into its convex side. The assistant held the staff as vertically as he could, pulling the patient's penis upright in doing so. The surgeon now made a cut beneath the man's scrotum, sliding his scalpel blade into the flesh diagonally from the centre of his body, parting the skin to about the length of a hand's breadth. With the same finger that he had put inside the man's rectum, the surgeon now pushed inside the wound, pulling the fibres of the exposed muscles apart. He took an instant to see where he was and then cut again, more deeply this time. He cut until he could feel where the head of the wooden staff lay in the patient's bladder. Locating it, he turned his blade upwards and cut through whatever was still between it and the staff's groove. It was there to serve as a guide for the scalpel, a safety mechanism to stop its slipping and making a fatal hole in the patient's rectum or intestine. (The original meaning of 'patient' was someone who was suffering, not someone waiting without protest.) Having reached the staff the surgeon knew that he had now cut all the way into the bladder. He took the scalpel out and pushed a blunt probe through the hole he had made, widening it, coring through the prostate gland that sat in its course. Through the larger hole he was then able to push a pair of forceps, his assistant pulling the staff out of the man's penis as soon as he had done so. What followed was a careful piece of fishing, as the surgeon attempted to grab the stone with his forceps. Once more he put a finger through the man's anus, trying to push the stone into the tool's jaws by pressing on it from within the rectum. It was a skilful job. If he pulled too forcefully he might tear away bits of bladder, rectum, urethra or genitals. If he pulled too timidly he lost the stone.

The operation impressed Astley. Witnessing it, he used to comment later, decided him upon a surgical career. Astley left no record of the details of Dr Donnee's particular technique, or of the success or failure of his operation on that day, but cutting for the stone was a stereotyped procedure, long established in a surgical tradition that had changed very little over the preceding century. What Astley did record was the impact on him of watching the operation. There was no doubting the importance of the surgery, no escaping from what an act of desperation it was – and no avoiding the vital role of the surgeon, the man at the centre of this dangerous piece of public theatre. Opium was commonly available, and could have done much to make the operation more bearable, but opium was also known to cause constipation, and full bowels were likely to get in the way of a knife. So opium was avoided. The patient's feelings were as naked as his thighs. And as he stepped up onto the operating table the patient was grimly aware – as was the surgeon – that the pain of the operation was not the greatest thing to fear. Both knew that while the majority of people survived, many did not. Bleeding was always a possibility, either at the time of the operation or afterwards, particularly if the wound became infected. Any local infection could spread, the perineum and the genitals becoming gangrenous and rotting away. Infection passing into the abdomen was another common cause of death, either through the bowels being punctured and faeces leaking out, or as a result of contamination from spilt urine or from the surgeon's fingers and instruments. None were sterile. Then the hole made in the bladder might not heal, leading to the acidic urine accumulating around the wound or ulcerating the genitals, slowly eating into them. And if there were stones higher up above the bladder, which the operating surgeon had no way of reaching, the whole procedure might turn out to have been pointless.

After the operation, but before the bindings were released, a man's scrotum and penis were strapped tightly upwards. That was to keep them out of the way of urine, for all patients found for themselves that urine leaked for a while through the hole that their surgeon had made. If they survived, and the wound healed, their problems were not over. Many men were left incontinent of urine. Faecal incontinence was also possible, as was impotence or infertility. And then there was always the chance, even if everything had gone well, that another stone would form anyway.

The pain of living with a bladder stone becomes palpable simply by appreciating how awful the operation was, and noting how many people risked it all the same. Samuel Pepys held a celebratory dinner each year, on the anniversary of his lithotomy, as the operation was formally known. It was partly out of pleasure at surviving the operation. But it was more from joy at being free of the stone.

It is not clear why bladder stones, which were once so common, are now so rare. Better health may be partly responsible, fewer infections and the use of antibiotics, as might changes in diet. Another possibility is that the medical potions of the day were actually toxic, altering the acidity and composition of the urine in such a way as to cause stones to form. The much higher frequency of bladder stones was partly responsible for the fact that a very much greater proportion of all operations was urogenital. It was also, however, the consequence of the contemporary surgical capabilities. Opening up the chest was impossible; operations in the abdomen were virtually doomed to failure since without sterile techniques the risks were overwhelming. If their patients were to stand any chance of surviving, surgeons had to limit themselves to the peripheries of the body.

After seeing Dr Donnee cut for the stone, Astley said, he decided to embark on a surgical training in London. To his family it seemed a sensible move for a young man with no taste for book learning and a clear stomach for blood. They knew it could lead to decent worldly success, for they had the example of Astley's surgeon uncle in London. And such a family link was part of the appeal, for Samuel and Maria Cooper knew that connections counted. Astley's father had been able to rely on his own father-in-law to find him a living. The careful preservation of names helped burnish family links. Astley's middle name – Paston – was that of a wealthy north Norfolk family. The recurring name Bransby harked back to a family of Norfolk landowners that had been rich for a century or more. Even the family crest – initially three torches – had been diplomatically changed. Given Maria Susanna's distant relationship to Isaac Newton, one of the torches had been replaced with the crossed thigh-bones of the Newton family. That suited a surgeon too.

3

London

In Maria Susanna Cooper's novel, *The Exemplary Mother*, the maternal heroine writes to her child as he leaves home:

> But, my dear son, remember, that you have yet been unassailed by temptations, and never been removed from the watchful eye of a tender parent . . . I tremble when I consider that you may be assaulted by all the destructive arguments of sophistry, exposed to the fallacious allurements of pleasure, and invited to plunge into the gulph of sensuality.

When his father locked him in his room for misbehaving, not long before his departure for London, Astley squeezed himself up the chimney and onto the roof. Walking near the house, Samuel saw his son perched overhead, calling out 'Sweep! Sweep!' at the top of his voice. His mother's warnings were not sensibly designed to dampen Astley's excitement about London and all it had to offer. He was not so timid as to tremble in fear at the thought of untried pleasures or experiences that his parents might disapprove of.

It was late August when Astley set off on the coach ride to the capital. The month was unseasonably cool, but that scarcely mattered compared to the heat of his youthful excitement. Confident of his own attractiveness and both physically and socially fearless, he was unlikely to be repulsed by the allurements of pleasure or the prospect of plunging into sensuality. He had just turned sixteen.

London in 1784, three years after the end of the war against the rebellious American colonists, was in a state of explosive growth. Fifty years earlier the population was around 750,000; by the end of the century it reached a million, and in the following thirty years that number doubled. But although the population was soaring, this was not because it was particularly fertile. People married late, had few children and died – on average – young. Growth came instead from inward migration. London had overtaken Paris as the largest city in the world, and it was a city dominated by men and women in the prime of their life and very likely to be immigrants to the city. When Astley arrived there were still more deaths than baptisms in London, just as there had been throughout the previous half-century of rapid growth.

Along with the massive increase in population had come a build-up of political and social tension. The Americans had won their independence, and discussions about the validity of their cause chimed with the growing politicisation of London's population. Commerce and the beginnings of industrialisation were spreading power to levels of society that had scarcely tasted it before. The year 1780 saw the anti-Catholic Gordon Riots, although later outpourings of public feeling in London were about politics more often than religion. George III, unhappy with the balance of power between himself and Parliament, felt the events of the American Revolution as a personal insult – both from the colonists and from members of his own Government who had disagreed with him over the issue. Following a series of political fights between Parliament and the king over who finally governed the country, William Pitt the Younger had been installed as Prime Minister. He arrived with the king's approval and a general election in March 1784 gave him the popular blessing as well – inasmuch as the strictly limited electorate could.

Astley had grown up in Norfolk surrounded by the conservative opinions and conservative friends of his 'Church and King' parents. That changed when he arrived in London, and the change was due to a peculiarity of his apprenticeship. Although his pupillage was with his uncle, William had either no room or no inclination to provide Astley with bed and board. So while his professional training was entrusted to William Cooper, senior surgeon at Guy's, Astley went to live with one of his uncle's surgical colleagues, Henry Cline.

Born in 1750, Cline had attended Merchant Taylors' School in London before his surgical apprenticeship began at St Thomas's Hospital when he was seventeen. He had been so unimpressed by the first lecture he attended that on leaving he declared 'he thought he should soon be able to do better than that'. A journey to Paris in 1774 did nothing to interrupt the flow of hard work with which he made good his boast. That was a momentous year for Cline, marking not only his trip abroad and his qualification as a fully trained surgeon, but also his attendance at the first course of lectures given by the famous surgeon John Hunter. Their learning struck him immediately, seeming 'so far superior to everything I had conceived or heard before, that there seemed no comparison between the great mind of the man who delivered them, and all the individuals, whether ancient or modern, who had gone before him'. Hunter's teaching was to be the foundation of Cline's professional approach and rapid success. A year later, having completed his apprenticeship and been appointed as lecturer at St Thomas's, Cline married. The wedding did not distract him from giving his scheduled lecture the same day.

By 1784 Cline's surgical master had died, and Cline had succeeded him as surgeon to St Thomas's. The hospital was across the road from Guy's, and together the two were known as the Borough Hospitals, named for their London neighbourhood. The two hospitals functioned as a unit, and when students trained they did so at both, shuttling between the two for their lectures, their dissections, their operations and their ward rounds. The Borough was a crowded, cramped place of narrow streets and winding alleys, edging inwards from the south bank of the River Thames opposite the City. There were three bridges over the Thames as it passed through London, and London Bridge crossed with convenient directness straight into the Borough. That made the hospitals close enough to the richer north side of London for its wealthier staff to live there. At the same time its situation in the south spared it from direct competition with other London hospitals and gave it a wide catchment area amongst the poorer part of the growing city.

Cline himself lived in 12 St Mary Axe, a grand detached residence with stables and outbuildings, in the heart of the City of London. Past Leadenhall Street to the south was the Thames, with Guy's and St Thomas's a short distance across London Bridge. To the west was Bishopsgate and beyond that the heart of the city – South Sea and India House, the Royal Exchange and the Bank of England.

The appointment at St Thomas's meant that in 1784 Henry Cline was beginning to enjoy success in his private as well as hospital practice. The two went very much together. Posts in the charity hospitals were generally unpaid, a surgeon profiting from them partly by the access they gave to the teaching, for which students paid well. What really brought the money in, though, was the reputation a hospital post brought with it. Alongside that came the lucrative private patients whose fees could make a surgeon comfortably middle class.

It seemed reasonable that the possession of a public office – an appointment in a charity hospital – should bring with it private wealth. Reputation and fame were a person's private property, as was his influence, and he might reasonably and justifiably seek to profit from them. Politics was seen by many as being no different. With a small electorate, and electoral seats often arranged to include as few voters as possible, landowners could choose their parliamentary representatives. Their 'ownership' of a constituency seemed to many no different from their ownership of farms or houses, or from a surgeon's possession of his reputation. All were a part of private property, which a good landlord had both the right and duty to cultivate.

Henry Cline was one of those who felt that such a conception was wrong, that parliamentary representation should not be the property of rich landlords, and that the payment of taxes brought with it a right to have a say in how they were spent, a right to a voice in the running of the country. The lawyer and radical campaigner Horne Tooke was one of the many like-minded friends who appeared regularly at Cline's house in St Mary Axe. 'I saw a good deal of Tooke at one stage,' said Samuel Taylor Coleridge. 'He left upon me the impression of his being a keen, iron man.' Coming up for fifty, and with a taste and ability in conversation that the *Encyclopaedia Britannica* later compared with Samuel Johnson's, Tooke had already spent half his life in political campaigns. In 1771, although his Society for Supporting the Bill of Rights (an attempt to increase the legal freedoms of British citizens) failed, he succeeded in establishing the right for parliamentary debates to be publicly printed. 'Horne Tooke's advice to the Friends of the People', said Coleridge, 'was profound: "If you wish to be powerful, pretend to be powerful."' In 1777 he was jailed for a year after siding with the American colonists and saying the British redcoats had effectively murdered their own people at Lexington and Concord. By 1784 his political life had acquired a temporary aura of peacefulness with the establishment of Pitt as Prime Minister. Tooke had campaigned viciously against Pitt's predecessor Lord North but had great hopes for the more democratically minded Pitt. He withdrew his own campaign for democratic reform, content to leave the matter in the hands of the like-minded new leader.

Given Cline's friendship with Horne Tooke and others, his living room rang with debates about the country's future. A description of William Hazlitt's (written in retrospect in 1825) pictures the effect of having Tooke in the house:

> Mr Horne Tooke was in private company, and among his friends, the finished gentleman of the last age. His manners were as fascinating as his conversation was spirited and delightful. He put one in mind of the burden of the song of 'The King's Old Courtier, and an old Courtier of the King's.' He was, however, of the opposite party. It was curious to hear our modern sciolist advancing opinions of the most radical kind without any mixture of radical heat or violence, in a tone of fashionable nonchalance, with elegance of gesture and attitude, and with the most perfect good-humour.

'Sciolist' was Hazlitt's pejorative, implying that Tooke was something of a dilettante whose interest in matters was always that of an amateur. None of this mattered to Astley, for whom the conversations of old men in the house where he happened to be a lodger were of no immediate appeal. The beginning of the academic season was early October. Arriving in London at the end of August, Astley had over a month in which to prepare himself. He showed no interest in doing so. He made friends easily, his boldness and his recklessness making him a natural leader. In London as in Norfolk he found plenty of friends. The groups became gangs and the adventures became more adult. A few years later, in 1800, the magistrate Patrick Colquhoun estimated that Georgian London contained fifty thousand occasional or professional prostitutes; about 10 per cent of the female population. Making use of their services was the norm.*

During his first few months in London Astley drank and ran wild, finding other like-minded youths to spend his time with. He made no serious preparation for the beginning of his surgical training, nor took any great interest in it when it started. Cline's house contained a handful of young

---

* Doing away with prostitution was impossible, Colquhoun argued, and so legislation and regulation to realistically try to improve the situation was the only proper human response. 'A prudent and discreet regulation of Prostitutes in this great Metropolis, would operate powerfully, not only in gradually diminishing their numbers, but also in securing public morals against the insults to which they are exposed ...'

medical men, boarding while they studied or worked. There were too many of them, and they were there for too brief a stretch of time, for the family to take either a disciplinary or an emotional interest in all of them, and while Maria Susanna Cooper may have wished to be an exemplary mother, her distant cares were not enough to keep her son from London's delights. For a long time Astley had found danger attractive. Now he also began to gravitate towards fraudulence. A story from these days relates how his uncle William came upon him by accident as he walked among the fashionable shops along the bustling pavement of Bond Street. Astley had dressed up in the uniform of an army officer, and was enjoying the gallant figure he cut. Caught out, he still showed some of the pluck expected of a promising young soldier. When his uncle stopped and challenged him in crowded Bond Street, Astley pretended not to know who he was. The fraud was obvious to William, but his nephew's strength of spirit unmanned him. William gave in and moved on, cowed by Astley's boldness. The young man continued his walk, safe at least in the confidence that his nerve matched his costume.

If William Cooper's parental control over his charge was weak on the public streets, it was no better at the Borough Hospitals. William was attached to the newer of the two, Guy's. It had been built during a period in which much private money was donated to the foundation of hospitals: in the early eighteenth century large charitable ('voluntary') hospitals sprang up around the country, with several in London. Westminster Hospital was the first of the capital's modern establishments, begun in 1719, but it was still operating from a converted residential house when the more ambitious purpose-built structure of Guy's began rising in 1721. It was a time of booming mercantile wealth. Thomas Guy was the son of a successful coal merchant, and had begun his life as a bookseller and publisher. The illegal import of high-quality Bibles from Holland brought him early success and he moved into printing them in London, this time legally, on behalf of Oxford University. By middle age Guy was a rich man, and in 1720 he invested his money in the South Sea Company. The value of the stock soared and Guy rapidly sold out. Between April and June of 1720 he got rid of stock that had cost him £54,000 to acquire. It brought him £234,428 in return. In late August of that year the South Sea Bubble burst and the value of the company's stock crashed. Guy had got out in time, and with his other available wealth he had around £300,000 to spend as he wished (considerably more than £20 million in today's terms). He put it towards a hospital, an 'Asylum for that stage of Languor and Disease to which the Charity of Others [has] not reached'. The words come from the inscription above the hospital crypt where Guy is buried. 'He provided a Retreat for hopeless Insanity, and rivalled the Endowments of Kings.' The reference to kings probably had in mind St Bartholomew's Hospital, the foundation of Henry VIII and in some disrepair by the eighteenth century. But the mention of a charity beyond others and a refuge for the hopeless meant something else. Hospitals were traditionally places where medical men attempted cures. Guy had been a governor of St Thomas's and had overseen many discharges – these might come when a man or woman was cured, but were just as likely to be an acknowledgement that as far as the hospital was concerned, the patient was incurable.

Thomas Guy's hospital was to be different. It was specifically intended to house those that the traditional hospitals like St Thomas's shut their doors on. That didn't quite mean that it was to be a general refuge for the needy, something like a cross between a hospice and a large almshouse. Instead the founding charter decreed,

> the Hospital was to receive and entertain therein four hundred poor persons or upwards, labouring under any distempers or disorders, thought capable of relief by physic or surgery, but who, by reason of the small hopes there may be of their cure, or the length of time which for that purpose may be required or thought necessary, are or may be adjudged or called incurable and as such not proper objects to be received into or continued in the present hospital of St Thomas's.

The foundation of Guy's explicitly intended to bring hope for the hopeless. With that came the ambition to extend the powers of medicine beyond those possessed by any other English hospital. Guy's would take in those whose cures were too unlikely, difficult or time-consuming. The intention to be an institution devoted to research and experimentation was there from the foundation. The eventual benefit was to be the patients', but for the medical staff there was the immediate attraction of being able to explore the limits of what was curable. Guy's provided the first opportunity in England for a modern teaching and research hospital. Oxford and Cambridge, with their collegiate structure and entrenched traditions, had hardly shifted their teaching since the days when the second-century medical dogma of Galen had been unchallenged. The modern innovations of the

Italian anatomists in the fifteenth and sixteenth centuries had not stirred them from their ancient slumber. The work of physiologists like the seventeenth-century William Harvey had largely passed them by. The universities of Glasgow and Edinburgh – modelled more on the style of such leading institutions as Padua, Leiden and the Sorbonne – had been more progressive, far outstripping anything that England had to offer. Guy's started off in the shadow of the great Scottish medical schools, and drew greatly on them for other, quite different reasons. 'That Guy's for long was dominated by Whigs and Dissent', said Cameron in his history of the hospital, 'resulted in the election to its staff of many men who, because of their religious principles, were denied admission to the universities of Oxford and Cambridge.'

Modern though they were, St Thomas's and Guy's were heated by open fires and lit by tallow candles, and their layout reflected the origins of England's hospitals in the medieval monasteries. By 1784, St Thomas's consisted of three quadrangles, each containing open cloisters, with the wards up on the first floors above the exposed colonnades. Guy's was built on a similar model, initially with two cloistered quads. It was an architectural design originally meant to cope with the heat of much warmer climates: a walkway shaded from the heat of the sun and unglazed to allow the free movement of air. In eighteenth-century England it was deemed attractive for other virtues. Richard Mead was an eminent physician, a governor at St Thomas's and a friend of Thomas Guy. 'Nothing approaches so near to the first original of contagion', he wrote,

> as air pent up, loaded with damps, and corrupted with the filthiness that proceeds from animal bodies. Our common prisons afford us an instance of this, in which very few escape, [with] what they call the gaol fever . . . all houses of confinement, should be kept as airy and clean [as possible] . . . as nastiness is a great source of infection, so cleanliness is the greatest preservative.

Guy's had not only fresh air but basins and towels for all patients and – still enough of a wonder for a visitor in the 1780s to comment admiringly upon them – flushing toilets. (The mechanism of the toilets protected them from any negligence on the part of their users when it came to disposing of bodily wastes. Flushing was activated automatically, the toilets 'always charged with water, being supplied afresh every time the patient leaves the closet. The door acts on the cistern by the common level, and the same operation discharges all that is left in the basin.') Every ward consisted of thirty beds, each covered with a wooden canopy and, when inspected in 1788, infested with bedbugs. In 1778 the front quad of Guy's was refaced in stone and given a classically inspired portico with pillars reaching upwards from the base of the first floor to the top of the third. The intention was to add a bit of grandeur, the previous brick façade having disappointed many. 'At your approach,' wrote one observer in 1761, 'which is a very narrow street, you first see the side of the square, which is very elegant, and a noble iron gate, with very handsome piers, but are much disappointed when you come nearer, to find the most contemptible front you can imagine.'

There are no records of Astley's initial impressions. The Portland stone façade with its five bays and three central Ionic columns above a 'pediment of Greek proportion' was ornamented in such a way as to proclaim the ancient origins and grand intentions of the hospital:

> In the pediment is a medallion with a female figure holding an infant and accompanied by a pelican and young; on each side is a reclining figure, one representing a male, one a female patient. Three bas-relief panels represent the practice of blood-letting: in the East is depicted a child with a leech, in the centre a child with a tourniquet and on the West a child with a lancet in one hand, a many-bladed scarificator in the other. In the niches are statues also by John Bacon representing Aesculapius and Hygeia.

Students, like everyone else, were meant to realise that the Borough Hospitals combined the authority of ancient nobility with a modern taste for development and innovation. Guy's even had a specifically built lecture theatre, something unknown in any other English hospital. Clinical training was beginning to move away from the private surgical schools of London and the Latin and Greek bookshelves of Oxford and Cambridge. The construction of the lecture theatre at Guy's also represented co-operation between the two Borough Hospitals, for while pupils were able to attend either, most of the teaching was concentrated at Guy's. Many students came to round off the education they had acquired at one of the country's many private surgical schools, or to walk the wards for a few months before setting themselves up as an apothecary or a surgeon. There were lectures on the principles and practice of the medical sciences, there were operations and ward rounds to be attended, admittance to all of them usually gained by the payment of a separate fee to the clinician involved. The privileged few among the students were apprenticed to one of the hospital staff, who took a personal responsibility for their education, training them up to be a deputy and often a successor.

To begin with, the architectural glory, the intellectual ferment and the concentration of human hope and suffering made little impression on Astley. Young, attractive and impatient for excitement, he found that other parts of London appealed to him far more than the Borough. He had grown up moving between different families: his conservative parents, his foster family the Loves, the Norwich apothecary and the surgeon with whom he began to train. Throughout his life he showed a gregarious desire to always be at the heart of a social group. Perhaps it had something to do with living in so many homes as a boy, perhaps it was strengthened by the immediate emotional rewards for a youth who recognised he excelled at both liking and being liked. Whatever the reason, Astley had an urge to belong. His attendance at Guy's and St Thomas's was poor.

Astley had no educational achievements and no financial possessions to preserve him if he slipped down the unforgiving class structure. To spend months in professional idling and teenage adventure was one thing in the security of his parents' Norfolk vicarage. On the streets of Georgian London it was quite another, but then what was a young man to do in 1784? The adoption of an officer's uniform was more than a device to impress the girls and evade recognition. For a boy with a stock of physical vigour and a taste for adventure the military was the obvious choice. The family links in surgery were at this point more attractive to Astley's family than to him. How was an adolescent to find in surgery what so obviously existed in the field of war? Where was the exciting risk, the allure of advancement and the reward of worldly and feminine acclaim? There was more appeal for Astley in passing himself off as a military man than in genuinely becoming a medical one. Watching Dr Donnee cut for the stone had won his consent to a surgical apprenticeship, but it became clear in London that it had not won over his heart. Dr Donnee's skill with his knife could not match the panache of an officer's sabre.

As the winter academic season of 1784 got under way, William Cooper tried to encourage his nephew. On Saturday evenings, in the operating theatre of Guy's, the Physical Society, including the most prestigious members of the Borough Hospitals, met during term times. 'Certain gentlemen', declares Wilks and Bettany's history of Guys, 'desirous of improvement in medicine and other sciences nearly allied to it, and convinced of the numerous and great advantages arising from a free communication of observations and opinions, have determined for that purpose to enter into an association, which they chuse to distinguish by the name of the Physical Society.' Effectively it was an informal university, feeling its way towards an emerging syllabus. '*Nullius in verba*' was the motto of the Royal Society, and it derived from Horace: '*Nullius addictus jurare in verba magister*' – 'I do not have to be bound to the judgements of my masters.' It was the motto for a club that desired intellectual freedom. The Physical Society had similar ambitions, and it was no accident that it had been founded at Guy's, a hospital set up with a mission to change the reach of medicine. The society was founded in 1771, before anything similar had been set up in the capital, and it met weekly during term times. Medicine and surgery were of particular interest, but so were a wider range of subjects. The borders of the medical sciences – partly because they were developing so rapidly, partly because they had porous connections to other fields of human thought – were open.

The Physical Society owned the only library of medical books available at the Borough Hospitals, and its weekly meetings served to focus the continuing education of its members. For the men who made up the society, that education was research – the best and the most modern in the country. Case reports, experimental therapies, the dissection of human and animal corpses, vivisection and untried surgical techniques, studies of electricity and of chemistry: all were potential subjects. Physicians, surgeons and apothecaries, many of them members of the Royal Society and many of them the leading figures of London's medical profession, gathered in the tiered amphitheatre surrounding the worn operating table. The meetings started at six in the evening, early enough that the London streets were still light at the beginning of the academic season. At five minutes past, a list of the society's members was read out, followed by the 'public business'. All those with an interest were welcome to attend, and many members of the public did. Medical research was intellectual common property, a field comprehensible enough and pregnant with enough wider implications to attract many of those with no professional link. That members of the public came to these meetings was a sign of the general intellectual appetite in the capital for trying to understand things that were still dark and hidden. They were all welcomed for the main item of the society's business, the 'medical news'. This news was little more than a haphazard collection of case reports, but the collecting together of individual cases was at the centre of the Physical Society's interests. From such reports the society tried to build up an advancing body of common knowledge. Minutes of the meetings give us a detailed picture. At his first meeting Astley listened as these serious, prestigious and often puzzled men talked. They discussed a child whose windpipe was inflamed – the child was bled and then put into a room full of warm steam – then the use of elixirs to try and aid a woman whose belly was swollen and tense with diseased fluid. Next came the report of a young girl with hugely swollen tonsils, and of her experimental treatment: her tonsils not tied tightly at their bases until they died and fell, nor cut sharply away, but gouged deeply at several places and then burnt weekly with acid until they wasted to nothing. It was 2 October, the first Saturday of the winter season, and nothing tied the cases together except their function as part of an effort to share experience and to learn.

For the 'private business' which followed the cases, starting at about half past eight and finishing an hour or two later, visitors were asked to leave the theatre. The members of the society then turned to their bureaucracy, to their system of fines and elections and to a discussion of what books they should buy for their library. At the end of that first evening, Astley was proposed by his uncle William for membership.

The atmosphere of the society was off-putting to a vibrant sixteen-year-old who had better things to do than spend his Saturday nights listening to older men. On his second visit, a fortnight later, Astley sat without relish through another evening of case reports. A member reported on an artificial leg ingeniously designed to move not only at the knee and ankle but at three constructed toes as well. Then came a story of a man with a headache who had turned yellow and suffered pains around his liver, before being restored to health through cupping.* Thirdly:

Mr Ogle stated the case of Cancer in a Jew, whose tongue was so totally destroyed as scarcely to be visible. In this state he lived for nearly a fortnight, till the coats of the sublingual artery being destroyed, a considerable haemorrhage came on, & soon put an end to his existence.

---

* In which air is heated inside a glass cup to create a vacuum. When the hot glass is applied to the skin the vacuum sucks up the underlying skin. Sometimes this was done just to the extent of leaving a circular red mark, sometimes carried on until the skin blistered. The intellectual principle was similar to that of bleeding and many other treatments: if it hurt, it must be doing some good.

Following that, came a report on a man who had accidentally stepped on a spring gun, showering metal pellets into his calves and thighs. Then there was a case of an ulcerating breast cancer. That led on to a general discussion of what members of the society had found useful for such conditions. Surgery was expensive, dangerous and not easily available, so it was common for women with breast cancers to visit doctors only when their overlying flesh had been completely eaten away by the cancer. There was no easy or obvious way to manage the ugly stinking infected mess that patients were left with. No one knew what the answer was, so the best they could do was to share their ignorance and their stifled desire to move forwards.

After the discussion of breast cancer the meeting moved on to talk about cancers of the lip, and what success members had had in treating them with dilute arsenic solutions. Then the meeting finished on hemiplegia: the paralysis of one half of the body most commonly seen after a stroke. At the end of this second meeting, as required by the constitution, Astley submitted his subject for the dissertation he would read to the society. He chose cancer.

The next week he presented it. With the benefit of a patchy home education and his brief attendance on Mr Turner, the Norfolk apothecary, Astley lectured to some of the world's leading medical scientists. There is no record of the content of his talk, and no reason to suspect it was of any quality. The fact that he avoided attending the society for most of the subsequent meetings that year suggests it wasn't. Even on the evening he spoke, Astley was fined 6d 'for leaving the room without permission of the president' – the small effort of sticking quietly to the society's pernickety rules proving too much for him.

For the remainder of his first winter season in London, Astley stayed away from the Physical Society. Even when Henry Cline and William Cooper were attending, the wayward nephew and apprentice was often elsewhere. He left the old men to their talk in the cold and gloomy operating theatre, amongst the stains and smells of the previous operations. In later years the society complained bitterly to the hospital about the conditions in which they held their debates. But they kept at it, weekend after weekend, buoyed by a sense of their importance and their potential for discovery.

Astley, however, had better things to do. The Coopers, along with many others in the eighteenth century, saw nepotism as being no more than an admirable sense of loyalty and family values. It says something for the deterioration of his relationship with Astley that William, a man greatly attached to such traditions, began to form an active dislike for his dis-obedient nephew. The disciplinarian uncle, stiff and childless, was no match for the fierce youth. Within months of Astley's arrival in London the apprenticeship began falling apart.

Henry Cline's manners were not so authoritarian as William Cooper's. Cline had children of his own, and less of a belief in the efficacy of unwavering strictness. The two senior surgeons were friends, but they were quite different people. There was nothing austere about Cline, and nothing conservative either. In fact his radicalism – something Astley had never before encountered – was his defining characteristic. 'In surgery,' said Astley later, Cline was 'cool, safe, judicious and cautious; in anatomy sufficiently informed for teaching and practice'. But Astley also commented that Cline liked 'other things better than the study or practice of his profession'. He did not mean that Cline was either shoddy or superficial when it came to his hospital work, only that he had a greater passion. It was democracy.

Cline's large house in St Mary Axe echoed to intense conversations. Many of the friends who dropped in were surgical, but many more were not: healing the body politic was as likely to be discussed as tending to the warmer flesh of living people. A stream of the most articulate and ardent reformists in the country moved through the house that Cline and Cooper shared. Men like John Horne Tooke and John Thelwall were the leading figures in England's growing movement for democratic reform. In Cline's house, Cooper found the opportunity to listen and to try out his own voice in argument. He began to feel the excitement of it.

Many medical students took their turn as residents in Cline's large house. Astley, a character attractive despite his occasional delinquency, began to move into the Cline family circle. His professional laziness gave him time in the house when Cline was not there, and he became friendly with Cline's mother, an intelligent and well-read woman with a sharp knowledge of current affairs. The sixteen-year-old boy and the grand-mother sat for hours together, talking and growing fond of each other. Astley spoke with a thick Norfolk twang, but his words were quick-witted and his figure was lively. His need to belong and his gift for doing so went hand in hand. There were three other young surgical students living with

Cline but only Astley began to turn his lodging into something more like a mutual adoption. Increasingly he spent the evenings sitting with Cline and his family. It was a new home, warm with fresh ways of thinking about the world. As the autumn months fell into winter, the evenings of discussion grew longer and Astley's interest brighter. The discussions of Cline's family and friends began to grip him. Democratic principles had a glamour born of novelty and the profounder appeal of the shared social idealism that underlay them.

Unavoidably mixed up with these new ideas was religious freedom. The two went together. Cline, Astley said, was 'in morals thoroughly honest; in religion a Deist'. This Dissenting belief held that while there was a God, the words of the Bible were never meant to be taken literally, and the superstructure of organised religion – heaven and hell, the Holy Trinity and the importance of church hierarchies – were the flawed creations of mankind. 'Mr Cline thought there was a cause superior to man,' wrote Astley, 'a prevailing law, influence, or deity, but believed that nothing was known of the future. The only clergyman with whom he was intimate was . . . [a] democrat.'

With alarm, Astley's parents began to notice these Deist views appearing in his letters home. 'Wherever you go, and whatever you do,' wrote his worried mother, '[remember] that the happiness of your parents depends on the principles and conduct of their children. Remember, also, I entreat, and may your conversation be influenced by the remembrance, that there are subjects which ought always to be considered as sacred, and on no account to be treated with levity.'

Outside his house Cline was a quiet man: within, he was animated and allowed easy expression to his wide knowledge and the sympathetic judgement that drove it. Astley warmed to Cline's generosity and gentleness and his brave spirit of honesty. By Christmas 1784, only three months after it had begun, Astley's apprenticeship with his uncle was formally dissolved. In its place was a new agreement. Astley transferred his indentures to Cline.

Cline was the better surgeon, but his new apprentice had seen little of his hospital work and the change did only a little to encourage him. 'I was articled as pupil to Mr Cline, and now I began to go into the dissecting room and to acquire knowledge, although in a desultory way.' As the winter set in, politics and Dissenting religion increasingly interested him but surgery continued to lack allure. By the end of the winter session he had been fined for his absence from the Physical Society's weekly meetings on fifteen different occasions: since his introduction he had scarcely turned up at all.

By the new year of 1785, Astley had little to show for his months in London. There was no professional mileage in having acquired a leaning towards Dissenting religion and democratic politics. And Cline, like William Cooper, was a man who believed that labour was an essential quality of manliness. Astley's laziness offended him. But while William Cooper found Astley's lack of application infuriating partly for the personal disrespect it displayed, Cline was not upset at the perceived slight to himself. By contrast, it seemed intolerable to him, in a world that urgently needed improvement, a world in which both society and disease pressed down their suffering with a heavy weight, that Astley should not make an effort to involve himself in the struggle. For a young man to have a mind and not to use it, to possess working limbs and a clear eye and to do nothing with them, was to waste the good luck and the privilege that he had been granted.

Cline, therefore, had no more sympathy for his charge's laziness than William Cooper had, but his values, and his experience of being a father, gave him patience, imagination and hope. Failing to see any response from Astley in the hospital or the dissecting room, Cline decided to take action. It was at home in St Mary Axe that the young man seemed happiest and most grown up, so it was there that Cline confronted him. Coming back after yet another day in the hospital dissecting room when Astley was absent, Cline brought home a human arm. He threw it down on the table in front of Astley and challenged him to dissect it then and there.

The scent of the dead could be many things. It could be putrid with rot or sweetened with the wine and spirits that were used as preservatives. There in the domestic setting of St Mary Axe it had enough of an edge of radicalism, of novelty and of promise, suddenly to take hold of the young man. Astley's adventurousness had always responded to dares, and here was a man he had learnt to admire confronting him in the most brazen of ways.

The skill and industry with which Astley dissected the arm astonished both the apprentice and the teacher. Astley was transformed. The fraudulent military uniform was gone, and in its place was the dress of a surgeon. For the first time in his life he found himself taking an interest in work.

*

The story of Cline giving his new protégé an arm (and presumably a piece of his mind at the same time) is almost too good to be true. In fact the entire narrative of Astley's youth keeps almost too well to a pattern. The future hero's qualities of energy and daring are present from his earliest days but are misapplied in lovable mischievousness and then almost thrown entirely away in adolescent disobedience. Then comes the epiphany. The wayward young man has a vision of his sins, a revelation of their consequences or of the shining appeal of virtue, and changes his ways. The story is similar whether it tells of a religious or an intellectual revolution. John Hunter's childhood – his dislike of labour, learning and study, so opposite to his adult appetite for them – is often presented in the same way. It was a characteristic biographical habit, whether talking about poets or clerics or Fellows of the Royal Society, to portray subjects as having experienced some kind of revelatory experience that set them on their adult path.

To an extent this should make us a little suspicious of such stories. Their details are untrustworthy when they fit so neatly into such a frequently repeated narrative pattern. But the sheer repetition of these kind of tales – wilful and unruly lives being saved by powerful realisations of purpose – should also alert us to their truthfulness. All childhoods are myths when they come to be remembered in adult life or written down for others. But the qualities of such myths tell us something important. The growth into adulthood is portrayed as being dependent upon falling in love with higher values than an individual has previously held – in Astley's case those of professional devotion, made possible and supported by his filial attachment to Henry Cline and his radical beliefs.

Coming up to his seventeenth birthday, Astley found a home and a way of living that allowed his character to develop and his career to progress. It was certainly the story he believed about his own youth, and that in later life he told to others. The emotional content of the story seemed to Astley to represent the truth about his growing up. In retrospect it seemed that something, and perhaps it was the arm, suddenly reached out and gripped him.

4

The Use of the Dead to the Living

The hospital academic season ran from October through until the warmer weather of May. That was partly in line with all academic seasons – long summer vacations for leisurely country retreats or time to help with the harvest, as means permitted – and partly for more pragmatic reasons. Bodies rotted more quickly in the heat.

Invigorated by his success with the arm, Astley began to pour his energies into his surgical training. That meant lectures and book work, which he began to attend to assiduously, but more than anything it meant anatomy. The setting for most of that effort was Henry Cline's dissecting room.

The composer Berlioz, unwillingly taking a course in dissection about three decades after Cooper started, described his first experience of such a place. Harold Schonberg quoted him:

> When I entered that fearful human charnel-house, littered with frag-
> ments of limbs, and saw the ghastly faces and cloven heads, the bloody
> cesspools in which we stood, with its reeking atmosphere, the swarms of
> sparrows fighting for scrapings and rats in the corners gnawing bleeding
> vertebrae, such a feeling of horror possessed me that I leapt out of the
> window, and fled home as though Death and all his hideous crew were
> at my heels. It was twenty-four hours before I recovered from the shock
> of this first impression, utterly refusing to hear the words anatomy,

*dissection or medicine, and firmly resolved to die rather than enter the
career that had been forced on me.*

The room where Cooper and Cline did most of their work was in St
Thomas's. There, laid out beneath two east-facing windows, were the
corpses. Their vapours rose upwards to a square lantern hanging from the
middle of the ceiling. The western wall of the room was covered with glass
cases displaying previous dissections, bobbing up and down in their liquid
baths if they were muscle, skin and fat, or held up and articulated by pins
and wires if they were bone. Other glass cases were scattered around the
walls and shelves wherever there was room for them. Under the windows
was a large sink for the students to wash their hands. They could also
wash the hands of their subject – or whatever part they were currently
investigating. It was the place for disposing of the more liquid bits of the
corpses, for washing the faeces and the last meals from within pieces of
bowel or stomach.

To the south side of the room stood a large fireplace with a copper pan.
Extracting the bones from a body could be done slowly, by careful dissection. It could also be done in more of a hurry, or the fiddly bits of the task
completed, by boiling. That added to the smell that lingered in the room
and worked its way into the living people who moved and breathed inside
it.

Smells came in abundance from the bodies laid out on the dissection
tables. Their strength and character depended upon the degree of decom-
position, and on what steps had been taken to preserve them. Every corpse
in the dissecting room had been illegally obtained. The majority had lain
in graves, or in readiness for burial, for days. It was not just the historical
convention of the long summer vacation that caused anatomical studies
to be concentrated in the winter months. (It is difficult to spell fetus with
an extra 'o' after hearing the explanation that it was originally inserted as
a confusion, the unborn dead being so often foetid when they were examined.) The stench was part of what had initially put Astley off his studies.
Now as he became devoted to the work he found the experience of its
smells changing. The scent of rotting flesh and the alcohol that much of
it was pickled in was as strong as ever. He grew used to the stains on his
shirt-sleeves, to the smell that lingered, that remained on his hands when
he woke in the mornings, and to the odd little pieces of fat and tissue
that he found later in the day on his boots or his stockings. But the

association changed, and rather than conjuring up horror or the experience of shabby boredom, now he had only to walk towards the dissection room for the smells to call up in his mind the experience of effort and exertion and satisfying labour.

The corpses were laid on tables, of which there were a dozen or so. To each table were a group of students, sometimes six, sometimes up to eight. So as a whole the room held seventy or eighty living people, the majority of twelve or so dead ones, and the partial and more carefully selected and preserved parts of many others. (Pickling in wine or spirits was common. Curing through heat or smoke, the way one does salami, was a rarer method but also used.)

The students and teachers were dirty. Some wore dissection gowns to try and absorb the sweats and smells and stains of their work, others kept to their own everyday clothes. When it came to immersing themselves to the elbow, day after day, in decomposing bodies, fastidious cleanliness was neither terrifically practical nor thought to be obligatory for safety. Anatomists were filthy, crammed together, and at risk. The risk came from the infectious organisms that bred so readily in putrid flesh. Death was not merely there in prospect, in the contorted corpses that they cut and pulled, boiled and macerated and injected. Death was also there in the jab of a needle, in the sharp stab of a flake of bone suddenly entering a palm. It hung in the air above the dissection slabs and followed the students home in the evenings.

In May 1778, only a few years before Astley began his dissections, the twenty-one-year-old Charles Darwin, eldest son of the Lichfield physician Erasmus Darwin, was in his second year of clinical medicine in Edinburgh. Dissecting the body of a child, his hand slipped and he cut his own finger. It was a trivial cut, but the flesh of the dead could infect. A few hours later, Charles began suffering from terrible headaches. The next day, delirious and haemorrhaging, his blood no longer able to clot, he died. In 1809 his name was given to a nephew, who later abandoned his own medical studies and made it famous.

Despite his declarations, Berlioz in the early nineteenth century returned to his dissections:

I consented to return to the hospital and face the dread scene once more. How strange! I now felt merely cold disgust at the sight of the same things that had before filled me with such horror. I had become as callous to the

50

revolting scene as a veteran soldier. It was all over. I even found some pleasure in rummaging in the gaping breast of an unfortunate corpse for the lungs, with which to feed the winged inhabitants of that charming place.

'Well done!' cried Robert, laughing. 'You are growing quite humane! Feeding the little birds!'

'And my bounty extends to all nature,' I answered, throwing a shoulder blade to a great rat that was staring at me with famished eyes.

Neither filth nor stench nor risk now deterred Astley. He would dissect until the strain of hunching over a stinking corpse made him physically sick. Then he would leave the dissecting room, vomit until he brought up blood, and return once more to his work. Astley's newfound immersion was as marked as his previous delinquency, and in their extremism both approaches marked a split with the more moderate Enlightenment world of his parents. 'Enthusiasm', the Bishop of Durham, Joseph Butler, exclaimed, 'is a very horrid thing.' There could be something almost unseemly, to the older generation, about passion.

Much of the business of the dissecting room is still unpleasant. Modern corpses are preserved in formalin, and the smell never quite left my hands at the end of the day. Latex gloves and frequent washing did nothing to help. And although we took care to dispose of the human parts properly, cutting someone up proved to be a messy occupation. I got half used to finding bits of fat and connective tissue later in the day, trodden onto the sole of my shoe or hitching a ride in a fold of my jeans. It made no emotional or practical sense to treat such unpleasant surprises with any sacred reverence. A half-preserved and half-rotten piece of fat trodden into the carpet cries out for no formal burial.

My anatomy teacher alarmed me one day when, without warning, she reached her bare hand deep inside the pelvis of a corpse and pulled out a uterus. 'Look at these!' she exclaimed. 'Aren't they simply beautiful?'

She was an elderly woman, the skin of her hands and face deeply wrinkled. She stood there in front of us, gently stroking the fimbriae that dangled limply from the end of the corpse's Fallopian tubes, the delicate fingers that catch the unfertilised egg when it is released from the ovary and help it on its way towards the womb. As I watched her, with her ungloved finger caressing the frond-like endings so that they repeatedly opened up for our gaze, the sincerity of her feeling was apparent. I was not ready to share in it, but it made me realise for the first time that dissection could be more than simply tolerated, that it potentially held an odd and unexpected loveliness.

It was very satisfying to find an aesthetic where I had previously seen only something to be disgusted with.

As his education began to get seriously under way, Astley was alarmed to recognise some of the symptoms and signs that a lecturer was describing. He recognised them too well from personal experience. The lecture was on hernias.

When Celsus described hernias, about ten years after the birth of Christ, he apologised for using slang. An unexpected lump, bump or protuberance was impossible to hide in the public baths of the day. When one was exposed it was commonly called a hernia, and this was the Greek word Celsus used and felt slightly shamefaced about, embarrassed at its vulgarity. The word stuck, and now sounds technical.

A hernia is a protrusion of a part of the body into a place where it was never intended to be. Through holes in the diaphragm, the twin-domed muscle that normally divides the chest from the abdomen, the stomach or loops of bowel can herniate upwards. A catastrophic rise in pressure inside the head can push the brain downwards, herniating out through the base of the skull. Far more commonly, bits of the gut herniate out of the abdomen. They do this in predictable ways. They follow the great blood vessels and nerves of the thigh, burrowing alongside them to emerge at the top of the leg. Or they track along the furrow that allowed the testicles (which originally form in the belly) to descend into the scrotum. Sometimes they just bulge right out through a gap in the muscles at the front of the abdomen, through a defect caused by trauma or surgery, or through the muscular weakness that can come from fat or from a fetus making the belly swell. Whenever you strain, the pressure in your abdomen rises, and the guts are squeezed. If the boundaries surrounding them are weakened, or the straining particularly great, a hernia forms.

Although still well known to those in late middle age, hernias have disappeared to a great extent from our cultural world. They are fixed so easily, the anaesthetics and the surgery are so reliable, that no one has much cause to suffer from them for long. Not that they necessarily even cause that much trouble. Small ones can just sit there, harmlessly.

On the day when Astley heard the lecture on hernias he returned home, terrified, and threw himself on his back on his bed, shoving his legs up against the raised bedposts. It was the position he believed least likely to make his hernia worse. But before rushing to his room, he left a message that Cline should come and see him immediately on his return home. It was desperately urgent.

'Mr Cline', said Cooper later, 'laughed and gave me a common truss.'

The laugh was typical of Cline's sure touch when it came to deflating his apprentice's tendency to lose his sense of proportion. But for the next three years the teenager wore the truss constantly, night and day. It was a device, strapped around the abdomen, for forcing the hernia back where it had come from by applying external pressure. At the end of those three years Astley examined himself, and found that the hernia had gone away. Relieved but still anxious, he put the truss back on for two further years. At the end of that time he felt bold enough to remove it, and the hernia never returned. What had worried him so much?

A piece of flesh in a place where it should not be, hernias can get themselves so tightly trapped that they cut off their own blood supply. The tissue in them dies. Without surgery, such an event not only kills, it does so in an excruciatingly painful way. The dead gut rots from within, becoming gangrenous, and the infection spreads internally. More commonly, though, hernias do not choke themselves to death but simply get bigger and bigger. They become increasingly unsightly. Teenage boys, then as now, do not like the thought of appearing physically deformed. And large hernias not only look disabling, they actually are, for anything that acts to increase the pressure in the abdomen will make them bigger. All lifting, all muscular activity, becomes something one seeks to avoid. The travel writer Eric Newby wrote of helping at Tuscan grape harvests in the years after the Second World War: there were two types of men attending, he explained, those who had hernias and could not actively help, and those who were helping and about to get a hernia. He was welcomed as being one of the latter, and enrolled to lift the heavy barrels of grapes and their fermenting juice.

To be physically limited by an unsightly bulge, and know that it was likely to get worse with time, was an unpleasant prospect for a youth who drew confidence from his good looks and vigour. Cline's reaction to Cooper was surgically appropriate – wearing a piece of strapping to try to shove the hernia back in place was precisely the correct contemporary treatment – but it was also fatherly, as much in the way he prescribed it as in the prescription itself. Cline was willing both to encourage Astley and to puncture his occasional paroxysms of melodrama. He could see both the promise in the boy and his need for reassurance. He helped him grow up, and Cooper loved him for it.

When Cooper was dissected, after his death, the remains of the healed hernia were found. It was on the right-hand side, and had projected downwards towards his testicle. That was the deformity which had so frightened him.

In the year 1543 Andreas Vesalius, freshly appointed to the position of dissector in Padua, published *De Humani Corporis Fabrica* ('On the Structure of the Human Body'). He had written it the year before, the same year Copernicus inverted the order of the heavens. For the first time in history a man had systematically looked at the insides of a human body and attempted to see what was there. For centuries anatomy had followed the Roman doctor Galen when he had summarised classical medicine in the second century AD. From that point on, until Vesalius, when men had looked at corpses they seemed unable to see for themselves. Leonardo da Vinci drew gorgeous pictures of dissections that were half-human, half-animal, and in part based upon Galen's imagination. To look and to see what was in front of one's face seemed the most difficult thing. It was not a polite business. 'The violation of the body would be the revelation of its truth,' wrote Vesalius. And there they were in his book, skeletons digging their own graves and bodies posed with superb grace against classical backdrops. The violation and the revelation were equally startling, the dead shown not in cold prostration but in the attitudes – and clad with all the spirited beauty – of the living. The body was not only a remnant, exposed by default when everything else had worn away, it was there in the heart of everything, of all joys and tragedies, for those who could summon up the determination to see it.

But where to get the bodies from? The swinish multitude – Burke's contemporary phrase for the unwashed masses – had a horror of being cut up after their deaths. The upper classes felt the same. This was part sentimentality and partly a mix of pagan and Christian superstition about the afterlife. Corpses were things to be cared for and to be frightened of: the ambivalent balance might shift unsteadily, but the one constant was that some sort of care must be taken. For all that many religious Dissenters doubted the odder and more literal stories of heaven and hell, most people were unwilling to take any chances. While one or two liberals might occasionally offer to undergo a post-mortem, there was no mass volunteering for dissection. The two terms referred to different procedures. A post-mortem was a limited exploration, usually aimed at identifying the cause of death. A dissection was more brutal. In a dissection the body was used freely by students or by surgeons, and its parts dealt with however they pleased. When Berlioz fed lungs to sparrows and shoulder blades to rats he was engaged in dissection.

The philosopher David Hume passed away in 1776. He died, as he had lived, an atheist, a man devoted to the rational understanding of life. Yet Hume had a watch set upon his grave, in order to prevent the theft of his body.

The legal status of a corpse was such that it could not be regarded as goods. It was not property, so it could not technically be owned, bought, sold or stolen. That was why the body-snatchers took such care to leave shrouds in their graves – it meant no theft had been committed. But the law defined what was criminal, not what was right and wrong nor what was practical. Hume was being consummately rational when he suspected his corpse would be attractive to some of those who stirred in the quiet of the Scottish nights. Surgeons were in demand, and to be able to attract and to serve patients they needed training. Learning anatomy could be done from the printed page, but that was not a sufficient education for those who would have to make their way – with bloodied fingers and with unsterilised steel – through the flesh of fully conscious patients. Anaesthetics were not to arrive until the middle of the nineteenth century. Until then, surgeons needed to be quick, delicate, and unmoved by pain. And they needed a good grounding in anatomy. A father who visited the London surgeon John Hunter was disturbed to find very few books around, and demanded to know how Hunter was planning to teach his son surgery. 'These are the books your son will learn under my direction,' Hunter replied, pointing at the dead. 'The others are fit for very little.'

Such human books, since they weren't legally available, had to be acquired in other ways. A great deal of surgical training went on in Edinburgh, and some of the precautions the inhabitants took as a result are still on display. Greyfriars in the centre of the city has several 'mort-safe' tombs, their iron cages reaching up from the earth where the coffins lie, sealing off the surface above from intruding spades and grubbing muddy fingers. The Scottish philosopher Hume was wealthy enough to hire a guard for his own corpse, but the Anglo-Irish writer Laurence Sterne was not so lucky. He died in 1768, the year of Astley's birth, and despite his literary successes he died in debt. Like all who died poor, he was buried cheaply. That made him cheap to dig up again.

With the explosion of urban populations the city churchyards filled up quickly, and there was not always room for the freshly dead. Sterne was buried in the overspill cemetery of St George's Hanover Square on London's Bayswater Road. The author of *Tristram Shandy* outperformed Christ by twenty-four hours, coming back from his grave on the second day. But unlike Christ, Sterne came back very much as he had left: stone dead. Two days after his burial he turned up on a dissecting table in Cambridge. He was recognised, and rather than being dissected he was reburied. Fame might not be a guarantee of wealth, but it had some privileges.

When Henry VIII united the companies of Barbers and Surgeons in 1540, he also gave them the right to the bodies of four hanged felons per year. Other than the rare opportunity to anatomise a willing volunteer or helpless dependant (William Harvey, the seventeenth-century anatomist, examined both his father's body and his sister's), the corpses of those four hanged felons a year were the only ones legally available. The situation was little different on the continent. Rembrandt's 1632 painting – *The Anatomy Lesson of Professor Nicolaes Tulp* – shows the dissection of a man called Aris Kindt, executed for robbery on 16 January and anatomised the same day, the only man to suffer such a fate in Amsterdam that year.

Charles II added a further two bodies a year to what was both a gift and a duty – for the surgeons were required to undertake their dissections in public, both pursuing their urge to learn and at the same time acting as agents of the state in inflicting post-mortem punishment and mutilation. In 1752 an Act of Parliament made the gift more generous and the duty more clear. Judges were able to decide for themselves on the fate of the bodies of those executed for murder. With an increasing number of trivial crimes against property attracting a death sentence, post-mortem humiliations were all that made the punishment for murder more off-putting than that for stealing a few shillings. You might be hanged either way, but for murder you might also be gibbeted, your corpse covered with disfiguring tar to prolong its putrefaction then hung up in an iron cage. The towns and countryside of England were littered with these creaking monuments. But with the same intention of inflicting a fate worse than death, judges could direct that a corpse should be dissected. It was, in the words of the 1752 Act, a 'further Terror and peculiar Mark of Infamy'. John Bell was typical. A tough young man, he stood upright for virtually the whole eight hours of his trial, refusing the offered seat. At the end he was found guilty of murdering a boy and stealing a shilling and sixpence from him. John heard his sentence of death without flinching. On the scaffold he was as brave. 'Lord have mercy upon us,' he was reported as saying, standing in front of the noose. 'All people before me take warning by me.' He was fourteen, and the only time he showed any vulnerability was when the judge told him that he was to be dissected after death. When he heard that, he cried.

In 1783 hangings were moved from Tyburn – now the site of London's Marble Arch – to the prison at Newgate by the Old Bailey. The move was a practical one. To stop the relatives who fought for the body, to stop the crowds accidentally obstructing the machinery of death, it was easier to move the whole business within the walls of a prison. But from the crowded noisy courtrooms to the streets outside, hanging stayed an open spectacle. Pamphleteers would rush to sell cheap sheets with accounts of unspeakable crimes, described in detail and preferably illustrated. Those about to die were on display, they were celebrities. Small groups, the wealthy and the well-connected, might be admitted to their cells the evening before, or be invited to breakfast with the prison governor and be included in the hidden preparations. Most people's view began, though, on the day of the killing. These were often early in the morning, and a working man or woman could brighten their routine by taking one in on their trip to work.

The new scaffold projected out from the west wall of Newgate Prison, where recent house demolition had cleared a space amongst the tangled streets. A porch attached to the stone prison walls contained two boxes, the best seats in the house – the two sheriffs took them. But there were plenty of other good spots to watch from: on the three empty sides of the stage galleries were built, for the reception of whoever was privileged enough to secure a place. The public were kept back by some strong railings five feet away, manned by constables to control the crowd. In the middle of the stage was a raised platform. The convict climbed onto it – it was only six inches high, but that was sufficient to make sure the view was good – and was attached to the noose overhead. Beneath was a trap-door. The executioner had only to pull a lever.

Keen Londoners had to pick their hangings, though, for there were a lot to choose from. In the 1770s London held about one a week; the next decade it increased by a half again. The walls of Newgate Prison – often termed the English Bastille – formed a backdrop for up to twenty dangling corpses at a time. Only a few thousand might turn out for an unexciting death. For someone whose crime or sentiment or celebrity had caused a sensation, tens of thousands were common. On rare occasions crowds of up to a hundred thousand people were claimed. They were the excep-tions, but in a city of only a million they were remarkable.

About thirty-five thousand people were condemned to death between 1770 and 1830 in England and Wales (Scotland was kinder). Most had their sentences commuted to prison or to transportation, although these were often fatal sentences themselves, for death rates were high aboard the boats and within the prison walls. About seven thousand actually went to the scaffold.

For the surgeons, it was not enough. Only a small proportion of those executed were murderers, and only some of those were given over for dissection – and then they were given only to institutions like the Company of Surgeons, possessed of long-standing privileges but taking little part in the daily training of medical men. No legal corpses were allocated to the actual surgical schools, to the institutions serving men willing to read and reread the moist book of the human body. The Company of Surgeons, the Royal College of Physicians and the universities of Oxford and Cambridge were keen to keep control of licensing, but scarcely stirred themselves to provide much practical training. 'Your theatre is without lectures, your library without books is converted into an office for your clerk and your committee room has become an eating parlour . . . I am sorry to observe that you have instituted lectures neither in surgery nor indeed in anatomy of any degree of importance,' announced John Gunning when he took over the Company of Surgeons in 1790 and set about changing things. It was too late for him to change the fact that surgical schooling had become a private business, in both senses of the word. Students paid to enrol on fee-paying courses run by their teachers, whether in charity hospitals or in privately owned schools. To attract their students these teachers needed hundreds of corpses a year. Since the crowded gallows of England did not supply them, they looked elsewhere. The people above were unwilling, so they sought out the people below. Around the hospitals and the training schools congregated groups of men who were willing to dig up the dead, or steal them from wherever they lay.

Astley's hernia had come on at an unusual age, particularly for someone who did not make his living by heavy manual labour. Until the lecture, Astley had been unaware of what the swelling near his testicle might signify. He never recorded when he first noticed it, so there is no way of knowing if a certain strain brought it about. While any physical effort could have caused it, there is the possibility that a particular one might have done so. The poorest surgical students were occasionally forced to help in these body-snatching expeditions, trading their labour for a share in the goods. There was no need for a relatively well-off student like Astley to do the same, but the excitement of it appealed to him. In the long winter London nights the Norfolk vicar's boy disappeared into the mists with the body-snatchers. In the graveyards and cemeteries of London he went to help dig up bodies that he would spend his days working on. It was heavy work.

January and February of 1785 were cold, with snow and strong winds and the temperature spending more time below freezing than above. But the days were getting noticeably longer. The feeling of general hopefulness and promise was increased for Astley by his new habits. Body-snatching and dissection were gruesome but riveting. In the mornings he walked from St Mary Axe, making his way across the river over the stonework of London Bridge. The houses that had once lined it had been demolished in 1757, but it still had the large waterwheels of the London Waterworks Company attached beneath, capable of being raised and lowered to suit the tide, drawing water from the Thames for the city around. Across the bridge were the teeming streets of the Borough, the wooden houses and crooked roads crowded close together near the stairs that led down to the river. St Thomas's was due south of the bridge, but the roads to get to it were crooked. Guy's lay immediately across from its sister hospital, on the southern side of St Thomas's Street, and each hospital was flanked by its own burial grounds, and its wards and theatres.

After a disagreement in 1760, it took eight years until the two hospitals finally got round to formally agreeing the way in which teaching should be shared. St Thomas's took the lectures on surgery. Henry Cline was in

charge, and the fee for admittance to his lectures was seven guineas –
with an extra five payable if a student wished to attend the dissecting
room as well. Guy's set up courses in the newer fields, for which demand
was initially slight but which still managed to charge ten guineas per course.
In the new hospital Dr Lowder lectured in midwifery for an hour from
half past seven in the morning. Then came a break before the next lecture
at ten o'clock. That alternated between Mr Babington on chemistry, and
Dr Saunders, also of Guy's, on medicine (or 'the Practice of Physic' as it
was contemporaneously described). Both men were eminent. William
Babington was an apothecary whose chemical knowledge and research
drove his ascent to the rank of a physician. He became a Fellow of the
Royal Society and founder and president of the Geological Society. His
death was marked by a bust at the Royal College and a statue in St Paul's.
Saunders had come to London after an early training in Scotland, arriving
with his reputation established by the chemical analysis he had supplied
for Sir George Baker's *The Devonshire Colic*. His independent publishing
success began with his 1780 *Elements of the Practice of Physic*. Two years
before Astley's arrival he published *Observations on the Superior Efficacy of
the Red Peruvian Bark in the Cure of Fevers*, a work that went into four
editions within its first year and was subsequently translated into Latin,
French and German. Astley had a mixed opinion of him. 'He was a most
entertaining lecturer, but [a] superficial person . . . He would give out that
he should lecture next day on Absorption and ask someone to get him
Cruikshank [a surgeon, and one-time assistant to John Hunter's older
brother William, who had written on the topic], that he might not come
down entirely ignorant.' Nevertheless, said Astley, Saunders had 'a considerable share of genius'. The Borough Hospitals held men whose researches
and publications were gathering high national and international opinions.

Anatomy classes in the St Thomas's operating theatre ran from one
o'clock until Cline wrapped up at three in the afternoon. At least one
surgeon visited each hospital each day, checking on ward patients or seeing
accidents that his dresser (effectively a junior doctor, the equivalent of an
American intern or a British house officer) wished help with. If the case
was urgent the dresser could summon the surgeon from home: both men
worked shifts of a week's length during which they were responsible for
newly injured patients. Operations were usually performed at midday on
either Monday or Friday. There were few of them, perhaps two or three
a week, and they were planned and advertised in advance so that the staff

and students of both hospitals could attend. Lists at Guy's tended to start an hour later than advertised, since by one o'clock the operations at St Thomas's would have finished and the combined Borough audience would be available. Routine admissions for planned operations took place generally on the Wednesday or Thursday preceding the date of the surgery. On Saturdays there were joint ward rounds, with physicians and surgeons collaborating in the care of patients, and the surgeons would attend at eleven in the morning three days a week (Monday, Wednesday and Friday at Guy's, Tuesday, Thursday and Saturday at St Thomas's). The ward rounds lasted a variable time, but in the order of an hour or two. Whichever hospital a student had originally registered with, he had the right to attend ward rounds and operations at either and to get what knowledge he could by watching and asking questions. Whether students would receive any teaching or any answers in return was at the whim of the staff member concerned – unless the student were an apprentice, in which case a personal training was part of the agreement.

Above all the other ways for a surgeon to study, though, there was dissection. As Astley began to learn his way around the human body, he found there was pleasure to be gained from being able to answer the questions of the students who worked alongside him. They needed his help, and he theirs, for the man appointed to teach them in the dissecting room was notoriously bad-tempered and unhelpful. Cline took charge of the lectures, but in the dead-house the students were under the care of John Haighton, a Fellow of the Royal Society and a man whose reputation as a leading scientist was not accompanied by a great love of teaching. He was 'a suspicious, irritable and argumentative man', said a historian of Guy's. As the Demonstrator, the man appointed to oversee the dissecting room and help the students within, he liked being on the winning side of an argument more than imparting any information. Haighton's interest was in physiology – he gave London's first lectures devoted to the subject – rather than in encouraging young surgical students. Scalpels and probes were the perfect tools for teasing apart flesh, but the structures the students peered at were as likely to be destroyed as outlined by their efforts. Even with an instructor keen to help them, it was a difficult job knowing how to proceed. It was made harder by being presided over by someone whose pleasure was to browbeat and demean.

Astley had two advantages. He had an habitual ease with people and he was able to seek Cline's advice in the evenings. Amongst his circle of friends, he began to take on informally the office that Haighton occupied but did not care to properly fill. Astley relished the success he found as a result, and it cemented him in his new role as a surgeon-in-training. Perhaps partly as a result, his attendance and application through the spring of 1785 were exemplary. When Henry Cline went to the wards now, he took Astley with him. The young man moved along the beds with his note-book in his pocket, ready to record what he saw. When patients did badly he saw them afterwards in the dead-house, tracing the connections between their deaths and their diseased corpses.

Soon enough the winter season was over; it was time to leave the hospi-tals. Astley vanished into a summer-long void, probably spending the summer at his parents' house in Yarmouth. Certainly no letters survive that suggest he stayed with the Clines.

A medical training at the end of the eighteenth century was not a limited apprenticeship in a specific trade. It was perhaps the most complete and modern course of education available, at a time when neither univer-sity had much scientific education to offer. From the lecture theatres of the London hospitals avenues of thought opened up, reaching into virtu-ally every field of contemporary natural and moral philosophy, ranging from chemistry to discussions of the nature of the self, or the relation of mind to body. The lecture theatres of Guy's and St Thomas's rang with the confidence and optimism of the Enlightenment, the galvanising belief that the problems of human suffering and disease could be understood and tackled with unprecedented success. Humans and their lives were improvable, as much as the animals and productivity of any farm. The drainage of fields and the irrigation of souls were equally achievable, and much that seemed presently incurable might seem very different when it was better understood. Heroism and the demand for individual influence over events, the need for knowledge and courage and action: those things were present in the military, in the Church and in politics. But there they were all weighed down by history, by the centuries of time and effort that had made such institutions rigid and hierarchical, wedded to orthodoxies and opposed to new ways of thinking. By contrast, in the field of medi-cine, individual ardour had as much room to breathe as it did in art, in poetry and in literature. And in medicine that ardour was no solitary thing, but took place within a community. Even the hours of potentially lonely human dissection were often done alongside others, or with a view to preparing specimens that would be shared and discussed. An apprenticeship at the Borough Hospitals had the flexibility of the arts, the technical knowledge of the sciences, the sense of purpose of the Church and the army. For Cooper, who had spent his childhood thriving as part of a community, on a sense of challenges and dangers, confident in his own physical and mental abilities to support him, it was perfect.

5

All Creatures Great and Small

Despite his almost total failure to attend any of the meetings of the Physical Society, Astley was elected to its committee for the following academic year, 1785–6. It was no sign of merit, only of good connections, of being the apprentice of Henry Cline and the nephew of William Cooper. William had been unable to shift Astley from teenage disobedience, but he was pleased that Cline had fared better. As his industrious dedication gathered widespread notice, Astley won back his uncle's regard.

The year 1785 started much as the previous one had finished, but this time Astley spent his Saturday evenings at the Physical Society. He was growing more sure of himself when it came to anatomy and surgery. The processes of disease and healing were becoming firm in his mind, as he studied his corpses and followed Cline attentively on the older man's ward rounds. As a result he could take an interest in the society's discussions. And he found himself, as he did so, rather good at them. There was something about his voice and manner that pleased people, that made it a pleasure for him to stand up and speak, and for all that his knowledge was a long way behind the other members of the society it was regularly ahead of his own contemporaries. The experienced doctors and surgeons responded to his youthful assurance and his sincerity. In the academic season of 1785 to 1786 he was absent from only one meeting. The death of his elder sister, Charlotte, aged twenty and engaged to a clergyman, did nothing to upset his schedule of work. She died, like her sisters before her, of tuberculosis.

Astley's parents wrote with the news, but also spoke approvingly and at length of their satisfaction in hearing of his newfound love of labour. Even their son's novel ideas in religion and politics could not unseat their happiness at his professional change of heart. But within his own crowded days all three lines of thought continued in parallel. In the evenings came spirited discussion around the fireside at St Mary Axe, and at weekends Astley accompanied Cline both on professional and on social visits. He was being steadily introduced to Cline's democratic friends, and forming links and friendships with them on his own account. He joined the Athletae, a primarily medical sporting club whose members (the physicians wearing the traditional wigs and carrying the gold canes of their profession) met in the evenings for exercise. The sports were those of the day – running, leaping and bowls – but also the more pugilistic ones that equipped men to walk the streets with as much confidence as they could. There was shooting and boxing and, along with them, something called singlestick – a form of fighting with a wooden staff: the canes that physicians carried were not always ornamental.

It was a violent world, and men had better be prepared for it. The point was brought home one evening when a man came breathlessly running onto the ward where Astley was working. Every other doctor in the hospital had left, or could not be found. The second-year student busy with his studies was the closest thing to a doctor that the frightened man could find. He had looked everywhere, he said between his gasps, and there was not another surgeon nearby. He begged Astley to follow him to a nearby Borough house where a woman lay bleeding and badly injured, her throat cut. Astley picked up a small supply of surgical tools and did as he was asked, hurrying out of the stone quadrangle of the hospital. The two men ran through the streets, reached the house and clambered hastily up the stairs. Astley was shown into one of the rooms. The woman was lying collapsed upon the floor next to her own bed. She had slit her own throat with a razor.

She was almost naked, covered only in a linen shift and in her own blood. It poured in a dark red slick down from her throat, staining the shapeless cloth beneath. Astley hauled her up into the nearby bed and tried to get a proper look at her throat. There were four gashes, one of them deep. Taking a suture, Astley stitched the edges of each wound closed. When he had finished she was able to speak, and he asked her what had happened. Why had she cut herself? Her reply was incomprehensible, except for one repeated word: 'stomach'.

Realising what she meant, Astley took hold of her sodden shift, the blood congealed into jelly in its folds, and lifted it up. Beneath it was the other cut that she had made. It ran from the base of her sternum down to the top of her pubic hair. From the gaping hole emerged her bowels, their loops and coils glistening wetly in the ill-lit room as they moved with each of her fast and shallow breaths. A faint steam rose from their moist surface.

The bowels themselves were inflated and full of air, noted the student surgeon, which meant they hadn't been punctured. With their smooth coverings they had simply moved aside as she had pushed the blade into her own flesh. It was a hopeful sign. Astley struggled to push the warm lengths of intestine back inside, the guts slipping too easily past his bloody fingers and once more out of the woman's body.

Footsteps sounded on the stairs outside the room. One of the hospital's fully qualified doctors now arrived, taking over and closing the wound in the woman's belly. Her guts were apparently all intact and inside, but the procedure was not enough, and the woman died nine hours later.

The experience held little physical horror for Astley, but the woman's suicidal despair unsettled him. Depression and the mental suffering of hopelessness never lost their ability to distress and occasionally unman him. He took what he could from the experience and went back to his work.

The summer of 1786 was spent in Yarmouth, where by now Astley felt confident enough of his new persona to display it at home. Not only did he seek out the apothecary to whom he had been briefly attached, he also began seeing patients on his own behalf. It was a bold move for a young man without qualifications and with only two seasons' student experience behind him, but it was not out of tune with the times. There was so little health care on offer in the English world, and its quality so often poor, that an earnest student could frequently do better than the local professional.

Now, when Astley sought out new friends he did it with a purpose, and they tended to fall into one of two camps, the medical or the political. Local debating societies were everywhere and provided rich ground for the latter. For the former it was a straightforward matter to build on connections: the social and professional worlds of the upper middle class were not so large. A Yarmouth physician introduced Cooper to a young Dissenter named Peter Holland, himself a surgical student. Astley was the junior by two years, but they quickly became friends, walking daily by the Yarmouth beaches as the summer went by. Holland was planning on continuing his studies in London, and Cooper wrote to Cline to ask if his new friend might come and join them in St Mary Axe. Cline sent back his agreement, trusting Astley's judgement on the new man. The arrangement was settled, and the two students agreed to share rooms. Holland had a wife, Mary, but she would stay at their home in Cheshire whilst he completed his studies.

As the September days grew shorter and the autumn mists began to rise off the Fens, the two young men set off for London. They stopped briefly at Brooke and then took a coach down through the Norfolk town of Diss, across the rural expanse of Essex, and into the capital. They arrived excited, ready for the start of the new academic year, and went together to the Borough Hospitals to buy their tickets for that season's lectures. Those on anatomy and surgery were to be given by Cline.

Holland had been a student for longer than Astley, with two years of provincial study under his belt before his arrival in London, but he found himself outclassed in the face of the muscles, tendons and nerves of the dissection room. Cooper and he worked together under the square lantern of the St Thomas's dead-house, jostling at the crowded tables for the elbow room they needed to properly anatomise their corpse. Cline was a popular lecturer and many of those who were drawn to the Borough to hear his lectures paid the extra five guineas for the accompanying dissections.

Although his popularity as an informal adviser was to Astley's taste, the crush was not. He discussed the problem with Holland and the two men agreed that from then onwards they should do their serious dissection at home. Cline had shown them it was possible to take material back with them, and a whole body was not so much greater a challenge than a single arm. That left the hospital dissecting room for socialising and for teaching, themselves both excellent ways to learn.

In Cline's house, the two men had a second-floor bedroom facing onto the street. There was an attic above them where the servants slept. Their own window looked out towards the street but was too high up for passers-by to see inside. The houses opposite, likewise, had no view of what went within the bedroom. This was fortunate, because it was there that the two students carried their corpse, laying it out on a table near the window.

Dissection was feared and loathed, and there was no organised police force at hand to put down a mob intent on violence. So it was with real fear that Cooper and Holland looked up from their dissection one day to see that they were being watched. The house on the other side of the street was having repairs done to its roof. But the men working on it sat unmoving amongst their slates, watching enthralled as the students anatomised their corpse. Cooper and Holland took one look at their audience and fled, rushing to the inner part of the house and carrying their cadaver with them. They hid, waiting apprehensively to see if the roofers would raise an outcry against them, the tension gradually subsiding into relief as the minutes passed silently and it became apparent they would not. From that point on they were too afraid to use their bedroom for dissections. The two men also shared a living room on a lower floor. Its windows did not face the street, and they took their bodies there from that day on.

Cline's house was a busy place. There were other students living there, some personally attached to Cline and others pursuing their studies with other masters or independently. Most of them struck Cooper as being fools; lazy men with no taste for work. It was a measure of how much and how quickly he had changed. Now it was the more serious character of Holland that he found attractive, and that had a profound effect on him. The daily walks the two had taken in Norfolk had changed into a sort of bachelor partnership of study. They worked, ate and slept in the same rooms. And they talked ferociously, about their studies and their world. Holland also got on well with Cline. 'He gave me a turn for study,' said Cooper of Holland. 'His conversation improved me, and the conversation between Mr Cline and him still more.'

The two men were on a sound footing in the hospital, and they pursued their studies with increasing devotion in their own time. In order to do so they bought admission to a series of evening lectures unconnected with the Borough Hospitals. They were those of John Hunter, who had been such an influence upon Henry Cline.

John Hunter was now in his early sixties. Born in 1728, he grew up hating the books his parents offered him but with a great interest in the Scottish landscape around him and the creatures that lived in it. When his father died John was thirteen years old. For a while he tried an apprenticeship as a cabinet-maker to his brother-in-law in Glasgow, but the attempt was not successful. Instead he went to London to help his older brother. William Hunter was a surgeon, and an increasingly successful one. Since the training of surgeons was beneath the interests of the universities, there was a demand for private schools. William had set one up, and it became John's job to help him. Rowlandson's famous etchings reputedly showed scenes from William's school. Of all of the Scottish medical men that poured south during the seventeenth and eighteenth centuries, the two Hunter brothers did most to change the world.

As William pursued life in the full glory of society, John preferred the company of corpses and the sort of men who could supply them. He tried orthodoxy with a surgical training at St Mary's in London but again the apprenticeship failed. Next he attempted training as a physician at Oxford – 'They wanted to make an old woman of me,' he declared, disgusted, after that effort also crumbled away. Somehow he stumbled his way into military service as a surgeon, and for the first time he came to grips with the living as well as the dead. The processes of healing fascinated him, and he came to understand that much surgical practice simply made things worse. 'To perform an operation, is to mutilate a patient we cannot cure,' he declared.

Hunter began to experiment. He explored physiology, anatomy and pathology through an insatiable appetite for the dead and the living, for the knowledge that human surgery and animal vivisection could provide. A Fellow of the Royal Society and a member, like Cline, of the Company of Surgeons, Hunter was at the peak of his career when Astley's apprenticeship began. He owned a large country estate at Earls Court outside of London, an ideal home for the large menagerie of animals he kept for his experiments. The dead came by the cartload to his door, and when he moved in 1785 to Leicester Fields – or Square, as it was rapidly becoming known – he bought not only a large and elegant townhouse but also the plot of land it backed onto. Opening on to dingy Castle Street, it provided him with a convenient rear entrance at which discreet deliveries could arrive. His exploration of the dead was comprehensive and meticulous. To explore pregnancy he acquired corpses in various stages; to investigate sexual function he procured a man who had died in the moment before ejaculation. When held in the mouth for a period, Hunter noted, there was a slightly spicy taste to the dead man's semen.

Hunter established himself as an excellent practical anatomist, devoting himself to cutting up the dead (and acquiring them) in a manner and on a scale which no one had ever contemplated. The space between the two sides of his town property was soon filled in with newly built rooms for lectures, experiments and for the museum of specimens he was building up. The carriage that took Hunter between his Leicester Square town-house and his country house was pulled by three Asian buffaloes. Each home contained a large copper pot for boiling down corpses. Comparative anatomy, physiology, experiments in transplantation and healing: his scope of interest was seventeenth-century in its breadth, and his scientific ability nineteenth-century in its sophistication. 'When I heard this Man,' said Cline after attending Hunter's lectures, 'I said to myself, This is all day-light. I felt that what I had previously been taught was comparatively nothing. I felt that I was now enabled to judge of what my experience and Observation had taught me; and thought I might, like Mr Hunter, venture to Think for myself.'

Despite his eccentric manners, his punishing lifestyle and his wayward looks, Hunter was a notable success. For a surgeon to become such a prominent scientist was still a novelty, as surprising as if he were a butcher's boy. His wife Anne, a noted beauty and society entertainer whose poetry Haydn set to music, took care to have Hunter's official portraits altered to make him look more respectable. He worked over his corpses while his wife dazzled in her drawing room, and the couple, with their wholly different interests, had a successful marriage. He paid for his astonishingly ambi-tious life with the money he took in from surgical practice and teaching – a sum that reached the phenomenal amount of £6,000 a year at its peak, the literal equivalent of about £400,000 today but with far greater buying power in a world where property and servants' wages were relatively cheap. Although Hunter spent some of his wealth on his homes, the bulk went to support his research. To attend lectures given by such a man was an exciting prospect for any ambitious student of surgery. For Cooper and Holland, who had heard Cline tell them about how magnificent Hunter's impact was, it was exhilarating. Early in October 1786 the two men walked to Leicester Square to listen for themselves to the man whose lectures they had heard so much about. The lecture series was to run on alternate evenings right through until April.

Mixed with the exhilaration was a certain nervousness. Although both young men trusted Cline, feeling the force and soundness of his judge-ment, they were aware of Hunter's reputation. For all of his genius – and often because of it – he was a bad lecturer. Astley's uncle William was one of many who spoke ill of Hunter, declaring that his lectures were entirely unintelligible. Far from opening a new era in his existence, said William Cooper, Hunter's words had simply put him to sleep. Such a derogatory estimate was widespread, as Astley later recalled. 'Although Mr Hunter and his opinions were so much esteemed after his death, yet I remember that the surgeons and physicians of his day thought him a most imaginative speculator, and anyone who believed in him a blockhead, and a black sheep in the profession.'

Like Coleridge, Hunter felt the need of opium before attempting to speak in public, and dosed himself with laudanum before each lecture began. But entirely unlike the poet's, Hunter's delivery was notoriously poor. Livelier members of the audience would grow restless, impatient for him to begin, whilst the less highly strung subsided into a doze. The classes were small as a result, usually less than thirty people, and many were put off from coming altogether. A skeleton was once wheeled into the room purely to allow Hunter to begin his talk with the traditional greeting of 'Gentlemen'. For those who were present and managed to stay awake there were the difficulties of Hunter's delivery. Uncertain, occasionally wandering, he was 'compelled to read his lectures and seldom raised his eyes from his manuscript'.

Cooper and Holland had to pay attention. First of all, Hunter told them, they were not to take any notes – or, if they did, they should burn them later. What he was telling them was no fixed body of facts to be handed down as doctrine but only the current state of his knowledge, changing as rapidly as he could improve upon it. It was an attitude characteristic of many of the leading thinkers of the day, and it reflected the sense of unexplored boundaries and discoveries waiting to be made. Even at the Physical Society and within Guy's and St Thomas's most of what was said was part of a long tradition, unchanged in large part since it had been laid down by ancient Greek and Roman authorities. After arriving at Cline's that autumn, Astley's mother had written to remind him that he had left his copy of Celsus – the Roman writer on medicine – in Yarmouth. Now Hunter was telling them that knowledge was too mercurial and rapidly advancing to be noted down even for a year or more. That posed some practical problems for students whose textbooks were often the home-made longhand rewrites of their lecture notes.

The title of Hunter's lecture series was 'The Principles of Surgery', but it contained startlingly little on operating. There wasn't even much anatomy. Instead Hunter tried to give his students a course on how the body worked, in health and in disease, and to view surgical interventions only in the context of this overall 'animal oeconomy'. 'I do not intend to give my lectures as a regular course,' he told the students, 'but rather to explain what appear to me to be the principles of the art, so thereby to fit my pupils to act as occasion may require.'

Hunter warned them that not only his ideas but even the words he used to explain them were new. And he began with a discussion not on any particular disease, or operation or anatomical structure, but on rocks. What made minerals different from living animals? What, for that matter, made dead animals different? What was it that made up the stuff of life? It was a puzzle he could not answer, but to which he demanded attention must be paid. What was a surgeon or physician to aim for if they could not even understand the basis of the difference between a creature being alive or dead, or an object animate or inanimate? As they walked home in the autumnal darkness of the City of London, Holland and Cooper were able to continue in a new way the discussions they had started on the Norfolk beaches. They were to hear this inspiring man teach them, in language that was hard to understand, with a delivery that was hard to follow, theories and approaches that were difficult to believe. 'Many of my ideas, and the arrangement of my subject,' apologised Hunter, 'are new, and consequently my terms [become] in part new.' A fresh language was needed for a man who found 'we have no language existing answerable to all my views of the animal economy'. Holland and Cooper, at least, were riveted. 'Mr Hunter was a man who thought for himself,' said Astley, 'but he was more; he was the most industrious man that ever lived.' Independent thought and hard labour had become two of the qualities he most deeply admired. Hunter demonstrated what they were worth not only in his lectures but in his worldly achievements. During the course of the lectures came the news that Hunter had been awarded the Royal Society's greatest honour, the Copley Medal. Now an annual award, Hunter's 1787 prize was the first time in two years it had been given, no work of a suitable standard having been judged to have been done in the previous year. Hunter's award was not for any single discovery, but for his three papers published that year in the society's *Philosophical Transactions* – 'On the Ovaria', 'On the Identity of the Dog, Wolf and Jackal Species', and 'Observations of the Structure and Oeconomy of Whales'.

Over the subsequent evenings Hunter took his audience on a tour of current knowledge in the life sciences. He started with the 'living principle', the superadded quality that gave life to physical bodies, 'which is not matter, but a property belonging to it' since 'what is simply mechanical, that is made of inert matter, must have, as it were, a soul to put and continue it in motion'. Hunter was a vitalist, a believer in the necessity of a soul to explain the difference between what was alive and what was not, the 'inert matter' of stones or corpses. 'In treating of any animal body I shall always consider its operations, or the causes of all its effects, as arising from the principle of life, and lay it down as a rule than no chemical or mechanical property can be the first cause of any of the effects' of life. 'The living principle . . . in itself is not in the least mechanical, neither does it arise from, nor is it in the least connected with, any mechanical principle.'* Following his framing of the contemporary debate on the definition of life, Hunter launched onto the functioning of the human body. He dealt with health, and how it was maintained, and with growth, and how it was patterned. These basics, he wrote in an article about the course, 'are to the surgeon what the first principles of mathematics are to the practical geometrician, without the knowledge of which a man can neither be a philosopher nor a Surgeon'.

To those who had the ears and stomach to listen to him, what Hunter said was revolutionary. If he occasionally found himself unable to explain to his audience his own notes, or grew caught up in his own confusion, that in itself was electrifying to young men hearing for the first time how much was still unknown, how much was still to be revealed. Cooper loved it. It was an education in the state of surgical sciences, and the best that the late eighteenth-century world had to offer, but more than that it was an instruction in method. Being taught to understand was a pleasure; learning how to experiment and discover for oneself was altogether greater. Science, Hunter taught, following the values and motto of the Royal Society, was not defined by the virtues, professions or educational backgrounds of those who pursued it. It did not carry weight on the basis of the personal authority or reputation of those who professed it. Science was method, it

---

* Part of Hunter's conviction came from his observation that living creatures produced substances that chemists could not: 'No chemist on earth can make out of the earth a piece of sugar, but a vegetable can do it.' Hence the definition of 'organic chemistry', meaning compounds that could only be created in the presence of the living principle. Not until 1828 did the German chemist Friedrich Wöhler synthesise the first organic molecule, urea, and prove this definition of 'organic' to be nonsensical.

was observation and experiment, and it paid no attention to authority or tradition. Hunter stood at the front of the lecture theatre that he had built out of his own ambition and his own funds and he lectured on the basis of his own experiments. He spoke of bone growth, of transplantation, comparative anatomy and embryology, of the treatment of gunshot wounds and the descent of the testicles. It was all from first-hand knowledge. Even so, Hunter's knowledge was less influential than the mental agenda that drove it. 'I think your solution is just,' Hunter wrote to his student Edward Jenner in August 1775. 'But why think? Why not try the experiment?'* That was precisely the attitude that linked the eighty-six hour-long lectures, each of them crowned with a question-and-answer session in which Hunter's baffling oratory was replaced with the wit and spontaneity of his conversation, and occasionally the reportage of his anecdotes. Laurence Sterne, Hunter told Cooper's group of students, had believed that a person only died when they had lost the will to live, and during his own last illness had jumped forcefully out of bed to prove that his will was still healthily intact. 'Death, which soon followed,' said Hunter, 'showed his mistake.'

Hunter's exhortations had an immediate impact upon his handsome Norfolk student. Hunter illustrated his talks with practical examples. When he spoke about aneurysms – abnormal dilations of blood vessels that could burst with fatal consequences – he handed around the preserved chest of a man whose aorta, swollen far beyond its natural size, was still contained within it. The ribs had expanded outwards to try to contain the massively bloated blood vessel. Another discussion was illustrated by a human tooth transplanted into the comb of a cockerel. The new blood vessels that had grown to nourish the tooth were clearly displayed. Hunter also showed a cockerel's testicle growing inside the belly of a hen, adhering to its guts (which, as a way of turning a hen into a cock, said Hunter, was 'such an improvement as that of Dean Swift when he proposed to obtain a breed of sheep without wool'). There was a portion of reindeer hide, a maggot burrowed within. The lessons of surgery were all around, and animal experimentation was even more important than operative practice when it came to ferreting them out.

---

*In later life Cooper repeated to others this injunction he had heard from Hunter. 'You must think for yourselves,' he wrote, 'only do not rest contented with thinking, make observations and experiments for without them your thinking will be of little use.'

So it was an unfortunate stray dog that saw the two young men walking together early in the New Year, and tentatively followed them home, hoping for friendliness and an escape from the cold streets. They called the animal Chance, and for a few days simply left him locked up in their room, worried that an angry owner might suddenly appear to claim him. When no one appeared, they decided to put into practice the kind of researches that Hunter described.

Aneurysms were a pressing surgical problem. Many were incurable. Dilations of the aorta or of the carotid arteries rising up into the head could not be fixed by surgeons. But aneurysms of smaller arteries, dilations of the femoral artery in the thigh, the popliteal behind the knee or the brachial down the arm: these at least were amenable to surgery, although the risks were great. The standard treatment for such aneurysms, or of traumatic wounds to those arteries, was amputation. Hunter was keen on a different technique.

In the spring of 1785, with permission from George III, Hunter had captured a stag from Richmond Park. He had cut into its neck and tied shut the carotid artery supplying blood to one side of its head. The stag's half-grown antlers became immediately cold on that side. But not only did the stag survive the operation, and appear healthy, but a week later the antlers were warm and growing once again.

Hunter had the animal brought to Leicester Square. He killed it and injected its great arteries with a brightly coloured resin. When it hardened he carefully cut away the overlying flesh, leaving a map of the blood supply to the creature's head. The carotid artery remained sewn shut, as he had left it, but countless delicate small leashes* of new blood vessels had formed alongside it, together capable of carrying enough nutrients to restore the animal to health.

It was a seminal experiment, and it helped to encourage Hunter in his belief that there was a better way to deal with aneurysms than despair or amputation. He advocated efforts to tie shut blood vessels at the point immediately upstream from where the dilatation began, relying on the body's ability to grow new arteries alongside those that had been surgi-

---

* A 'leash' of new blood vessels sounds a little fanciful, but is a standard piece of contemporary medical vocabulary. Most commonly it is applied to the new arteries and veins that grow on the retina in patients with diabetes, the body's attempt to compensate for damage that the disease has done. Seen through an ophthalmoscope these vessels do look like miniature leashes or whips, snaking their way over the back of the eye.

cally closed. Hunter spoke with passion about this odd technique, an approach that most surgeons thought was reckless, doomed to failure and therefore needlessly cruel. He also spoke with experience, for he was not only carrying out the procedure repeatedly on animals but also performing it on men and women. During the time in which Hunter first lectured to Cooper, he performed the first of a new type of operation for popliteal aneurysm. It proved successful.

In emulation of their hero, Cooper and Holland carried out a similar operation on Chance. It bore witness to their skill, their ambition, and their willingness to inflict pain. They tied the dog down and cut open one of its back legs. They teased out the femoral artery from its membranous sheath and neighbouring vessels, and sewed it shut where it began to run down the leg. It was precisely what Hunter was suggesting would be the operation to cure any aneurysm that might exist lower down the artery.

To their pleasure, the dog not only survived the operation but appeared to recover well. So Cooper and Holland, after a few weeks of looking after it and continuing to make their way three times a week to Leicester Square, did it again. This time they tied shut the artery supplying one of Chance's front legs. Once more the dog recovered.

Then they killed it. With as much care as they had performed the operation, they injected the blood vessels of the dog's legs with resin. The two procedures had been effective, and the major arteries had stayed closed. And there, in front of their eyes and beneath their fingers, were the networks of new blood vessels that had rapidly grown in their place, restoring the dog's health. It was precisely the alternative to taking notes that Hunter wished his students to choose.

Four hundred and fifty years before the birth of Christ, Alcmaeon of Croton investigated the function of the optic nerve in animals by slicing it apart. The writings of Hippocrates – which are those of several authors, grouped under the single name – came 150 years later. They describe a method for studying the process of swallowing by carefully cutting the throat of a pig, then giving it coloured water to drink. They also describe opening the same animal's chest in order to watch its heart beat.

Galen, the second-century AD physician whose writings were to be treated as gospel for the following fifteen hundred years, was a keen vivisectionist. He recommended using pigs or goats for experiments, complaining that he found it disturbing to see the expressions that experiments could produce on the faces of primates. It has been seriously argued that Galen was putting forward a purely aesthetic view, that he believed animals incapable of emotion and their apparent distress only upsetting because it superficially looked uncannily similar to the genuine distress that humans might feel. It is a difficult argument to believe.

The early Roman medical writer Celsus, whose book Astley had left at Yarmouth before returning to London that year, believed that some pioneering vivisectionists had avoided the use of other animals by carrying out their experiments on human criminals. He may have been right. In 1474 Louis XI of France gave his gracious permission for the vivisection of a condemned soldier. The man went on to have his abdomen opened up whilst fully alive. After that he was killed.

In the second half of the seventeenth century, Robert Hooke and Robert Boyle, those pioneering members of the newly established Royal Society, carried out many animal experiments. They were disturbed by at least some of them. In 1664 Hooke cut away the chest of a dog in order to investigate its breathing. Lungs have no muscle within them; they expand and contract as a result of the movement of the chest wall that contains them. When that wall is removed, no breathing can take place since the muscular means for achieving it has been taken away. To keep the dog alive during his experiment, Hooke pushed a hollow cane down its throat and into its windpipe. He pumped with bellows for an hour, watching the lungs expand and contract in response. The dog, unable to control either its lungs or its throat, could not even whimper. Hooke was praised for the experiment but he refused 'to make any further trials of this kind because of the torture of the creature; but certainly the enquiry would be very noble, if we could find any way so to stupefy the creature, as that it might not be sensible, which I fear there is hardly any opiate will perform'.*

The pain of vivisection was extreme, but it was carried out in a world where animals were killed not only for research but also purely for fun. The Borough, in Astley's day as in Shakespeare's, was a place of bear-

---

* He was wrong, and an overdose of opium would have provided just the effect he needed. Excessive opiates kill by switching off the body's urge to breathe; not only would a dog stupefied in such a manner have been spared any pain, but it would also not have made any respiratory efforts that might have interrupted the work of the bellows.

baiting and cock fights. In the 1780s Smithfields, on the site where Henry VIII had had judicial executions performed by boiling people alive, was the main live meat market. 'The shameful place, being all asmear with filth and fear and blood and foam, seemed to stick to me,' wrote Charles Dickens, who encountered it years later after many decades of improvements. Through the offal and excrement of their predecessors, animals were driven to Smithfields for sale and for slaughter. To keep them in order, and to make them look lively for buyers, sharp 'goads' were used – sometimes on the flesh of limbs and bodies, sometimes on their genitals or their eyes. Sheep were skinned while still half-alive and horses left to rot and die knee-deep in the carcasses of those that had gone before them. It was against this background that Astley broke the bones of rabbits to see how they healed, and performed experiment after experiment on the blood vessels of dogs and cats. It was a world in which brutality to animals was routine. All the same, some were against it.

One of the public debates relating to vivisection revolved around whether cruelty to animals taught men and women to be cruel to each other. William Hogarth engraved pictures of just such a process, in his 1751 series *Four Stages of Cruelty*. They show Tom Nero's fictional progression from his boyhood torture of animals for entertainment, through his mistreatment of horses as a grown man, to his murder of a woman carrying his child. The series culminates in the dissecting room where Tom is himself ripped to bits by the surgeons. At the bottom of the picture is the man's heart, pulled from his chest and cast aside. A dog is gnawing on it.

'Among the inferior professors of medical knowledge', Samuel Johnson had written in *The Idler* in August 1758, 'is a race of wretches, whose lives are only varied by varieties of cruelty; whose favourite amusement is to nail dogs to tables and open them alive; to try how long life may be continued in various degrees of humiliation, or with the excision or laceration of the vital parts.'

In their 1843 critique of Bransby's biography, the *Quarterly Review* wrote of Astley's first animal experiment that the issue was not whether vivisection itself was valuable or justifiable. The issue was whether a young man of twenty years old, a youth whose apprenticeship was not halfway complete, should have been teaching himself experimental physiology in such a manner. Astley's professional colleagues, speaking of the incident, give it as evidence of his ardour for knowledge and his desire to understand things at first hand. But even in 1787 Britons were deeply worried about cruelty to animals, and concerned over the effect such cruelty had on the characters of the people who exercised it. Haighton, the Guy's Demonstrator and physiology lecturer, won such notoriety for his own experiments that he appeared in fictional guise as the 'Merciless Doctor'. The morals of vivisection were a matter of great contemporary concern, particularly to religious Dissenters and those attracted to radical politics, yet Astley never commented on them.

When he had made his decision to train as a surgeon rather than an apothecary, he had done so after watching a man being cut for the stone. He had been accidentally stabbed in the face by one brother and had watched his foster brother John Love bleed to death after falling under a cart. He had seen his sisters die from tuberculosis, he had suffered from the disease himself, and he knew it might kill him with little warning. In such a world, working in hospitals and mortuaries where the sick sometimes rotted away even more uncontrollably than the dead cadavers, how was one to view physical pain?

A letter from Astley's mother during this academic season gives a pungent taste of her prose style and of her sensibilities:

> You seem to have improved every moment of your time, and to have soared not only beyond our expectations, but to the utmost height of our wishes. How much did it gratify me to observe the very great resemblance in persona and mind you bear to your angelic sister! The same sweet smile of complacency and affection, the same ever wakeful attention to alleviate pain and to communicate pleasure! Heaven grant that you may as much resemble her in every Christian grace, as you do in every moral virtue.*

In reality Astley was not particularly concerned with alleviating pain. He wanted to discover new ways to cure disease, and he expected others to share his broad indifference towards any suffering incurred along the way. His sentiments were widespread but far from universal. When a visiting French anatomist bought a greyhound and nailed its paws and ears to a table in order to slowly dissect away its face, tracing the nerves as he did so, the act drew enough criticism to be mentioned in Parliament. 'I have, all my life,

---

* Geoffrey Keynes, the twentieth-century surgeon, bibliographer and younger brother of John Maynard, commented: 'This picture of a simpering young prig does not correspond [with reality] . . . [he] only became repulsive when translated into the terms of his mother's sentimentality.'

had a natural horror for experiments made on living animals, nor has more matured reason altered my feelings with regard to these vivisections,' said the Edinburgh anatomist Dr Knox. Towards the end of his career, in 1839, Knox argued in *The Lancet* that vivisection was both cruel and needless. He was amongst a small number of contemporary clinicians and researchers who felt that animal experiments were morally questionable and of little use. He is remembered, however, as the man happy to buy the corpses of men and women who had been freshly murdered specifically for his dissections by the notorious Burke and Hare. 'Burke's the butcher, Hare's the Thief,' went the nursery rhyme afterwards, 'Knox, the man who buys the beef.'

The majority of people had few qualms about believing that animal experiments were a useful means of discovering truths of natural philosophy. Such experiments also had other advantages, more relevant to a world in which anaesthesia had neither been discovered nor even imagined. It was necessary for a surgeon to operate boldly when called upon to do so. Like military combat, surgery was a skill that needed to be put into practice under painful conditions, and got right the very first time it was done. As in warfare, there was a problem of how men were best prepared. No amount of theoretical knowledge could replace practical experience, and in a world where operations had to be carried out swiftly there was a limit to how much a teacher could take a beginner slowly through a procedure. So how could you train someone in such a way that they would perform correctly, under appalling conditions, on their very first attempt? The great sixteenth-century Italian anatomist Vesalius, the man who had single-handedly dispelled the medieval belief that anatomy should be learnt by looking at books and ignoring bodies, had completed each of his courses of human dissection with a triumphant animal vivisection or two. The idea was that a surgeon started with the dead, moved on to living animals, and was then as prepared as possible to cut into suffering humans. If the sacrifice of a few dogs might save a human being or two, in a world that had fun watching them die in public entertainments, was that not reasonable?

My childhood experience of cruelty to animals was limited. At the age of about seven I went into the garden with a friend and collected some snails. We put them at the top of a glass window, expecting them to race. It was probably not a pleasurable experience for the molluscs, but it would be stretching a point to view it as tormenting them. (The snails seemed gloriously unaware of the direction of the race, or even its existence, and wilfully kept still or inched their way around in slimy circles, frustrating our plans.) A little later I fed the berries of different garden plants to my younger brother and, once, a chilli to my baby sister. My motives may have been partly experimental.

At university I took other courses before medicine. I encountered a few pots of fruit flies, given to me in an effort to drum some genetics into my unwilling head. The ghost of my maternal grandfather, once a fruit farmer, stood over me approvingly while I applied too much chloroform and painlessly killed the lot of them. Afterwards came my Master's research. My thesis sounded gruesome and sadistic, a study of how chimpanzees coped with crippling injuries. But the wild chimps I studied had all been injured long before I met them, laming themselves accidentally in the traps that Ugandan locals put down to snare antelope. My research consisted of standing beneath large fig trees all day, craning upwards. The chimps were overwhelmingly fond of stuffing themselves with unripe figs, despite the torrential diarrhoea they invariably got as a result. I spent many long hours standing beneath twenty or thirty screeching chimpanzees, bending my neck painfully backwards and trying to collect data while dodging the torrents from up above. The chimps slobbered, spat, and passed unstinting amounts of urine and semi-liquid faeces. They possessed a glorious lack of concern over who or what might be underneath. If there was any cruelty to fellow primates involved in my research, it was inflicted by the chimps on the bipedal ape standing beneath them.

My medical degree demanded that everyone training as a doctor undertake live animal experiments. But the rule was largely empty propaganda, and most of the experiments actually just involved watching a video, made many years before. There were two exceptions. One was a guinea pig, anaesthetised and flat on its back. We stroked it between injections but it was insensible to both. At the end of the session the demonstrator cut the animal's belly open with scissors to show us the living guts. A few of us were shocked at that, but it was hard to blame it on anything other than squeamishness. By law the guinea pig had to be killed at the end of the experiment, in case having repeatedly to undergo anaesthetics made its life miserable. It was completely anaesthetised during the time we spent with it, and cutting apart the abdomen neither caused it pain nor changed its fate. Guinea pigs are one of the animals that humans bred for food for the longest of periods, and it is dishonest to argue that they suffer more when being expertly anaesthetised than when prepared for a traditional barbecue. None of us were vegetarians. After the guinea pig, at the very end of our course in pharmacology, there was a cat. Once more it was anaesthetised before we arrived, and this time none of us was allowed to touch it at any point: we were told a personal Home Office licence was needed for that. A large group of us watched the experiment. I forget completely the nature of the drugs demonstrated, only that the cat's legs started to twitch towards the end. The movement was involuntary, explained our demonstrator, who nevertheless seemed amused by our anxiety. It was the muscle relaxant wearing off, he said, not the anaesthetic. He appeared to take great care that the cat was free of suffering, but at the same time it clearly gave him a shot of sadistic satisfaction to see us squirm with the mistaken fear that the cat was conscious.

Years later I went to help with the killing of a pig in a French farmhouse. Given my appetite for ham, pork and bacon it seemed reasonable to see what was involved and be willing to get my hands bloody. I fed the pig a pumpkin the night before and petted it, admiring its snuffling enjoyment of the fruit and convinced that the next day's experience was likely to leave me spending a joyless life as a vegetarian. The following morning we tied the pig's hind leg to a post, which it detested, and shot a bolt into the front of its head. It fell onto its left side, a hundred kilos of unconscious pig hitting the floor with a thump, and lay insensible while a French butcher slit its throat. It was an attractive pig, and there was a general air of sadness that it was no longer there, but I thought it died without suffering and without fear.

So I have no experiences that directly allow me to feel what it must have been like for Astley to begin his vivisections. In a way that gap has been a useful prod, keeping me puzzling over Astley's apparent indifference to the pain of the animals beneath his fingers and his knife.

What I do have the experience of, though, is causing pain to other humans. I was shy of it to begin with, embarrassed about approaching people with needles and scalpels. That wore off slowly as a medical student, then very quickly as a working doctor. Particularly in a Casualty Department, it does not do to be too tender of causing people distress and discomfort. There is something wrong with forcing treatment on someone before they are ready, but prevaricating out of personal fear is no better. Early on in my career I saw a frightened six-year-old who had slipped and torn his lower lip widely apart. He sat in his mother's lap, scared and suffering, with his father standing helpless and anxious behind him. Injecting local anaesthetic, I explained, would hurt more than the single stitch he needed. The needle for the anaesthetic was bigger than that of the suture, and the drug itself would sting painfully for a second before working. We explained things to the little boy, but he remained silent. I could feel my own panic building, and if it had not been for the sensible and very experienced nurse in charge, I would have found some cause for delay. But three nurses pinned the boy down on a bed, and there was nothing to do but approach him with my needle and thread. His eyes followed me, trying to see what I was doing, and he lay completely still and uncomplaining while I closed the wound quickly and easily. Afterwards he cuddled his mother and seemed relieved. It amazed me, and made me recognise how much my own fear had been making the situation worse.

Then there were the adults, also willing to take pain in their stride. An old woman came in after a fall. She had toppled onto the stone edge of a garden wall, gouging an enormous part of her face away. A huge flap of skin and muscle hung down from her left forehead and ear, obscuring her nose and mouth. We moved it back into place, covering up the exposed bone, and she remained warm and friendly the whole time. It shook me to find that faces could be so easily torn apart and reassembled, and to see the depths of equanimity that people possessed. A little later an old man came in having put his hand into a lawnmower. He held it out towards us as he entered the department. The white ends of amputated bones and the torn tendons of his severed fingers were on full view, but the man's greatest pain was his shame at bleeding all over the hospital floor. He apologised to us repeatedly for wasting our time, obviously upset with himself for his moment of clumsiness. After that I was never quite so sympathetic with the people who violently pulled their arms away and screamed when a needle came near, sending bloody syringes and dirty scalpels flying across the room. I learnt that anyone who began by telling you about their high pain threshold was going to go on to complain about an apparently minor problem. I learnt that it is impossible to admire people who make an effort to bear pain bravely without also learning to feel differently about those who make no effort at all. It may not be possible to cope with physical distress, but it is possible to try.

Around midnight one weekend a screaming three-year-old came in, her

right eye sliced open by broken glass. I helped to hold her down and pull
the lid open while another doctor looked at the damage. We both saw a
large shard gleaming wetly back at us, sticking out of the surface of her
eyeball. While my colleague called the ophthalmic surgeons I got on with
seeing the next patient. He was a large man, half drunk but swaggeringly
pleased with himself, and he lectured me in advance about his needle
phobia and the steps I needed to take to coddle him. There was a substantial gash along the length of his forearm. As I got a trolley ready, collecting
the suture set and the local anaesthetic and the skin disinfectant, he
explained that he had picked up a pane of glass and smashed his wife over
the head with it as she held their daughter. He was rather proud of it, as
though it had been a show of strength and manliness. The glass had shattered, and it had been a piece of that which I had seen poking out of the
little girl's pierced eye.

The whole time I was sewing him up I could hear the screams and sobs
of his daughter a little distance away. He seemed not to notice them at
all. After a long time I finished putting his arm together, and he left the
department thanking me profusely and exclaiming about how painless it
all had been. He patted me on the back and called me 'doc' as though
we were drinking buddies.

Astley expected people to cope with pain. He also believed he had
the right to inflict a very large amount of it on animals, both for research
and purely for the restricted benefit of his own education. I feel sure
that he was sincere in believing that vivisection was of vital importance,
although being sincere is not necessarily the same as being correct. I also
suspect that Astley's attitude drifted over occasionally, although probably not often, into cruelty and even sadism. My belief comes partly from
having observed the effect on myself of growing used to causing pain. I
can do it easily now, very easily, and I have no doubt that if I worked
without anaesthetics and with a daily habit of vivisection, it would have
a corrosive effect on my sympathy for the pain of other people and
animals.

I used little anaesthetic on the man who was so pleased with himself
for hurting his daughter. The procedure was painless because he was drunk.
That night, as I drove home, it was clear to me that his lack of suffering
had almost upset me.

*

Sir Thomas Lawrence's portrait of Astley Cooper, now hanging in the hall of the Royal College of Surgeons of England.

Richard Horwood's map of Regency London. Jeffries Square is in the top right hand corner.
The Church of St Andrew Undershaft can be seen at the corner of St Mary Axe and
Leadenhall Street. Astley's route to the Borough was due south along Gracechurch Street,
where his second wife Catherine's father had a pharmacy. South of the river, Guy's is visible
in its modern location; St Thomas's has since moved to opposite the Houses of Parliament.
The main burial grounds for both hospitals were located just off the page, to the south.

Guy's Hospital, with the statue of Thomas Guy adorning the front quadrangle.

Henry Cline, from a bust in the possession of the Royal College of Surgeons.

John Horne Tooke.

John Thelwall.

Gillray's caricature of John Thelwall lecturing to a mob.

The church of St Andrew Undershaft. Behind it the Swiss Re building occupies the site of what was Jeffries Square.

Benjamin Harrison, junior.

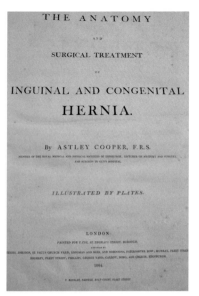

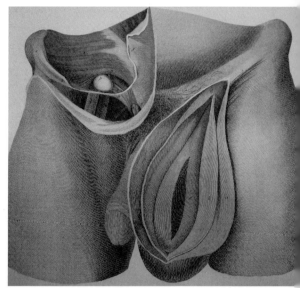

The title page of Astley's first book.

A dissection showing a mature left inguinal hernia, in which part of the abdominal contents have pushed down towards the left testicle. The right side of the body is opened to demonstrate an incipiently symmetrical hernia.

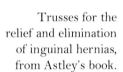

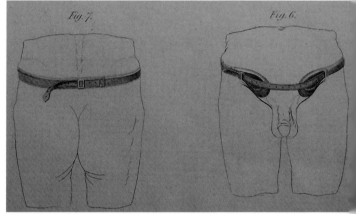

Trusses for the relief and elimination of inguinal hernias, from Astley's book.

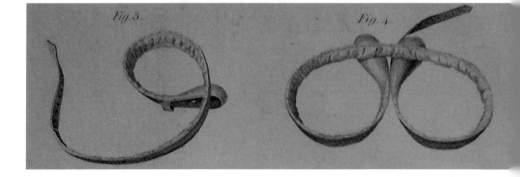

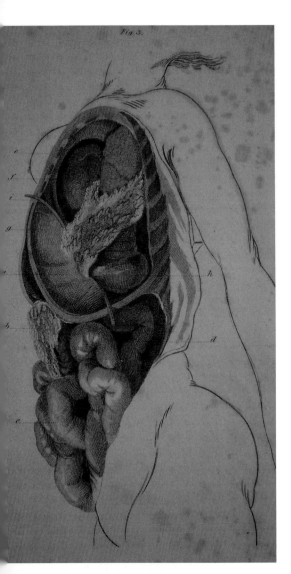

A dissection showing the herniation of abdominal contents up into the chest. The stomach (at the anterior or front of the chest) has slipped upwards, compressing the lungs and heart.

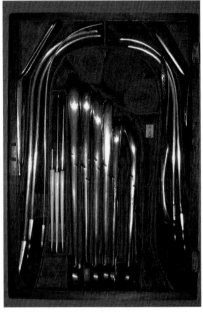

Astley's lithotomy instruments, now in the Royal College of Surgeons.

Bransby's tools for amputation.

Astley Cooper before he was made a baronet. The crossed thigh-bones in the background are a heraldic reference to Astley's distant descent from Isaac Newton.

At his father's request, in the spring of 1787 and towards the end of Hunter's lecture series, Astley went to visit a condemned man in Newgate Prison.

Benjamin Gregson was awaiting execution. Having been found out in a forgery he had appeared in Yarmouth in early 1786 under an assumed identity. His charm and lavish lifestyle won him friends, amongst whom were Astley's parents. Yarmouth society was astonished when Gregson was arrested while dancing at a local ball. As he awaited trial (making a great show of getting his iron fetters polished) he seduced the jailer's daughter, and with her help escaped. He travelled from Yarmouth to Holland and then Russia before settling in France. There he began another affair. When the lady's husband discovered the affair and something of Gregson's history, he left with his wife for London. Gregson followed, and the husband had him arrested. In April 1787 he was finally sentenced to death at the Old Bailey for his original forgery.

Sometime in the next few weeks Astley visited him. He found Gregson ill, suffering from one of the many fevers that infested the jails. Such fevers were widely believed to be contagious, but they were one of the many risks that Astley was used to facing in his normal medical studies. They did nothing to put him off continuing to meet with such an interesting man, in such an unusual place. But when Astley came home one evening after such a visit and felt unwell, he knew enough to be worried, and to seek help immediately from Cline and his family. Over the following days the fever worsened, and Astley became seriously ill.

During the worst days of the infection, Astley stayed at St Mary Axe. The Clines cared for him, unsure whether he would live or die. For fit young men to be struck down with a fever and go to their graves was nothing out of the ordinary. Letters went back and forth between London and Yarmouth, and the Clines nursed their patient, while the convict Gregson not only survived his own illness but managed to escape once again. (Later he was recaptured and, this time, hanged.)

Cooper survived. Once the worst had passed, however, the hospital season had finished. Weak from his illness, but out of danger, he retreated back to Yarmouth for a long convalescence. That August he turned nineteen. He had acquired his own ideas about the best way to learn about the world and the moral imperatives for doing so. The values of Henry Cline and the methodologies of Cline and Hunter had impressed him deeply. His convictions had been strengthened by a consciousness of his qualities: a sharp mind, a confident ability with people and ideas, and a taste for hazards. He had discovered his relish for hard work, and had no doubts about the best outlets for his efforts. Cline's circle was full of men ambitious to see change in the world, and surgery had as much to offer in that regard as politics.

Of all of Cline's democratic friends Astley became closest to John Thelwall, an impressively accomplished journalist, poet and political lecturer. Now in his early twenties, Thelwall had been born in July 1764 to an unsuccessful but indulgent silk mercer. After a childhood schooling characterised by physical beatings and rote learning, he became an apprentice tailor at thirteen. This first attempt at a career failed miserably, but during it Thelwall discovered a love for learning and spent his evenings reading Shakespeare and memorising the *Iliad*.

Giving up on tailoring, Thelwall tried the law, but he lacked the wealth to go in at a rewarding level, and the training jobs he was able to get were menial and dispiriting. For a long while he persevered, until abruptly withdrawing three months before qualifying for the Bar. It appears to have been disgust that finally put him off. He found the law to be unjust and dishonest, and he wanted no part of it. Instead he turned to writing, publishing *Poems upon Various Subjects*. It was only a moderate success, but it widened his acquaintance and encouraged him to persist with a literary career. It brought him into contact, amongst others, with a Dr Hawes, who had founded the Humane Society to try to rescue and resuscitate those who fell or threw themselves into the Thames. Hawes introduced Thelwall to Henry Cline.

Thelwall shared Cline's interest in politics, and their beliefs were similar. Thelwall had started out conservative, a solid 'Church and King' man who thought an absolute monarchy was preferable 'to such a republic as would grow out of what we call a British House of Commons'. But through the influence of public debating societies – whose speakers came from a comprehensive range of social and political backgrounds – Thelwall's views changed. The societies gave him a taste for vigorous free speech and for thinking for himself: exactly the influence that made them a horror to repressive governments. With an asthmatic wheeze and a disabling nervous stutter Thelwall took to public speaking with difficulty. But the appeal of it drew him along, and gradually, with determined and persistent application, he became a confident public speaker and a proponent of democratic change. At the same time he continued his writing. He wrote an epic poem intended to aid the campaign against slavery that was never published, but was later seized by the government as evidence of his dangerous views. As a boy he worshipped the authority of the 'heaven-born minister'; as a man, repulsed by corruption, arbitrary taxation and the oppressive use of power, his views altered. A striking man with a direct gaze and an aquiline nose, Thelwall looked like a Regency poet crossed with a Roman senator (and with a small touch of wild horse thrown in for good measure). In the evenings he and Astley sat together at Cline's fireside or drank together in the nearby taverns. They were good company for each other, both young and ambitious, both fired by the injustices of disease and politics.

Astley knew, however, that he needed to broaden his education and enlarge his experience. His apprenticeship in London was at the heart of his plans: it was in this city that he saw himself building up a career. But to do so with as much verve as possible, with as wide a view and as full a range of qualifications and experiences as he could get, he wanted to visit another capital, to see how science was practised and life was lived. Political and scientific change were hotly pursued in London, but that was partly due to the strong influence of men who had trained in Scotland.

In October of 1787, his strength fully returned, Astley travelled back to London. He spent a few days with the Clines and met up with his friend Holland. Then he left for Edinburgh.

6

Edinburgh

In Edinburgh a Physic Garden had been founded near Holyrood Palace in 1670, and in 1685 two professors of the Theory and Practice of Medicine were appointed to the university. But it was not until Alexander Monro took the first chair of anatomy in 1720 that any formal teaching began. Anatomy was joined in quick succession by chairs in botany, chemistry, materia medica (the equivalent of pharmacology) and midwifery. By 1726 Edinburgh University possessed a full School of Medicine, largely by virtue of knowledge and ideas brought back to the city by those who had studied abroad (often at Leiden). The hospital that was founded with six beds the same year, and expanded to 228 in 1741, provided material for teaching, and it was this organised use of real clinical material that set the university apart from anything else in the British Isles. John Rutherford, the Professor of Medicine in 1746, described his methods:

I shall examine every patient capable of appearing before you, that no circumstances may escape you, and proceed in the following manner: 1st, Give you a history of the disease. 2ndly, Enquire into the Cause. 3rdly, Give you my Opinion how it will terminate. 4thly, lay down the indications of cure that arise, and if any new Symptoms happen acquaint you with them, that you may see how I vary my prescriptions. And 5thly, Point out the different Method of Cure. If at any time you find me deceived in giving my Judgement, you'll be so good as to excuse me, for neither do I pretend to be, nor is the Art of Physic infallible. What you can in Justice expect from me is some accurate observations and Remarks upon Diseases.

So in some respects Edinburgh was an obvious choice for Astley. It had a great tradition of medical teaching, ahead of anywhere else in Britain. For all that many discoveries had taken place in the city of Oxford, those early breakthroughs and researches had in fact had very little to do with the university. They occurred in the environment of an informal gentlemen's club rather than an academic institution. Medicine in Edinburgh, on the other hand, had an international reputation. Of the 160 men who graduated between the school's foundation and 1827, only fifty were Scots. Forty-six were English, thirty-six Irish, and the rest from North America, the West Indies and elsewhere. At the same time many of the great figures of the profession in London – William and John Hunter in particular – were Scottish in origin. There was a refreshing lack of insularity. The Scottish Enlightenment was the product of a concentration of gifted men with wide interests, but had also come about from Scotland's links with the wider world, particularly the traditional relationship with France. 'We look to Scotland for all our ideas of civilisation,' said Voltaire.

Part of Astley's decision to go to Edinburgh, perhaps, was a young man's desire to travel, but as well as the city's practical advantages, the decision was also motivated by politics. The university was a haven for those whose religious beliefs barred them from the conservative Anglican establishments of Oxford and Cambridge, and in Edinburgh, as in so many places, Dissenting religion went along with liberal thinking. For centuries science had been held back by the need to conform with the opinions of the previous generation. With Nonconformist religion came non-conformist thought, and time and again those who held novel views in religion drove forwards free thought in science. Edinburgh's openness to religious dissent and new ideas made it welcoming to foreign influences. Many of Edinburgh's own medical graduates went on to attend universities or hospitals in France and returned enlivened by Continental ideas.

On his way to Edinburgh Astley made a significant stop. He went to Staffordshire, to visit Wedgwood's potteries. Josiah Wedgwood was a Dissenter and one of the members of Birmingham's Lunar Society, along with the physician-poet Erasmus Darwin, the Dissenting minister, philosopher and chemist Joseph Priestley, the great steam engine manufacturers

Matthew Boulton and James Watt, and the polymath doctors Williams, Withering and Small. All three of the medical men had trained in Edinburgh, testament not to coincidence but to their shared intellectual engagement with research and innovation. Traditionally the Lunar Society met on moonlit nights, the better to be able to stumble their way home afterwards. Wedgwood's pottery was a phenomenally successful experiment in the industrialisation and mass production that were soon to dominate the world. The pottery at Etruria had opened in 1769, Wedgwood calling it after the Etruscan style of the vases that had made his name. It was the promise of modernity. Physically it was a 'manufactory' on the new scale of mass production, seven acres of land sloping down to a canal-side bank. There was a village purpose-built for the employees and a grand house – Etruria Hall – for Wedgwood and his family. But along with the sheer size of the place was a spirit that declared radically modern values. During the rebellion of the American colonists, the sympathetic Wedgwood had produced medals for those who wished to show their support: the design was a coiled rattlesnake with the motto DON'T TREAD ON ME. For the anti-slavery movement the snake was replaced with the figure of a chained man, and surrounding him were the words AM I NOT A MAN AND A BROTHER?*

Cooper attended the potteries with a passport to the heart of this new world. It came in the form of his friendship with Holland, whose wife was Wedgwood's niece. There was something compact and pungent about the new world of liberal thinkers. In a Britain of only seven or eight million people, such links were easier to forge. But it was the excitement of shared aims, and the knowledge of an often indifferent, uncomprehending or frankly disapproving wider world, that gave them heat.

Holland and Cooper travelled north together, stopping first at the Wedgwoods' house in Staffordshire and then moving on to Holland's home in Knutsford, Cheshire. From there they ventured to Manchester, one of the new industrial cities of the north. They toured the factories, impressed with their scale and with the masses of human lives now tied up in manning them. Living with Cline and his democratic friends, both men were vividly aware of the building political pressure in such places,

---

* 'If there be an object truly ridiculous in nature,' wrote one of Wedgwood's friends, furious at the hypocrisy, 'it is an American patriot signing resolutions of independence with one hand, and with the other brandishing a whip over his affrighted slaves.'

these new provincial towns whose people and industry had little or no representation in Parliament.

Cooper arrived in Edinburgh in November 1787, with the winter academic season already under way. He was handsome and confident and came with a host of letters of introduction. In Yarmouth his father was friends with the local Member of Parliament, and through him Astley had warrants to make the acquaintance of Edinburgh's leading men. There was Adam Smith, the newly elected Rector of the University, whom Astley praised as 'good-natured, simple-minded, unaffected, and fond of young people'. He met Henry Mackenzie, a natural introduction for the son of the novel-writing Maria Susanna Cooper. Forty-seven years old and sharing her Tory views, he was known as the 'Man of Feeling' after the title of his most successful romance. Astley also bore introductions to two lawyers, both of whom would become Lord Advocates. Alexander Maconochie, later Lord Meadowbank, was 'a sharp man', according to Astley, while Charles Hope, the politician and judge, 'was a man of reading, a gentleman, and digni-fied, and very eloquent'.

Even medical men amongst Astley's new acquaintances often had other interests. William Cullen (who, like Adam Smith, was in the last few years of his life) had lectured on chemistry for many years before becoming a professor of medicine. 'Never shall I forget the veneration with which I viewed Cullen,' said Astley, despite feeling free enough to criticise other Edinburgh teachers as pig-like, selfish or abusive. Cullen's enlightened ideas in both fields – distinguishing acids, alkalis and salts, understanding the utility of precise pathological description in an effort to comprehend the causes of disease – combined with his gifts as a teacher to draw students to Edinburgh from across the world. 'It will only be when the languor and debility of age shall restrain me that I shall cease to make some correc-tions of my plan or some additions to my course,' wrote Cullen. It was a view reminiscent of John Hunter, and the connection between the two men was more than just intellectual. John's older brother William had been Cullen's apprentice and lived in his house for three years. Cullen worked alongside James Gregory whose succession to his father's chair of medicine at the age of twenty-three was an apt demonstration of what might be achieved by young men. 'Gregory's lectures on clinical medicine were admirable,' commented Astley, 'yet he thought most highly of his physiology, on which he enlarged in his evening lecture on therapeutics. Having on one occasion been confined to my room by illness, I expressed my regret to Dr Gregory at losing his clinical reports, but he said, "Sir, that does not signify, but you have lost my therapeutics."'

The chemist Joseph Black, friend and teacher to the Lunar Society's James Watt, was another of Astley's new teachers. Calcium carbonate, Black had discovered, could be treated with acid or heat to produce what he called 'fixed air', a substance denser than normal air and unable to sustain either flames or animal life. His description of carbon dioxide was part of a scientific life that included strikingly original explorations of thermodynamics (the notion of latent heat came from Black) and the elemental nature of magnesium. In person Astley found him imposing but friendly. 'Sir,' said Black, upon meeting him for the first time, 'you will speak to me after [the] lecture if you do not understand anything. Have you fixed upon a tailor or a shoemaker? I can recommend you to one and the other.' Astley, fashionable and well dressed, took one look at Black and recoiled. 'Seeing he might carry his furnaces in his shoes, and that his coat was probably like that worn by Noah in the ark,' noted Astley, 'I thankfully declined. He was a kind easy man. He used to lecture from his notes made on little scraps of paper, in a most unaffected style.' Despite Black's prestige and original discoveries, Astley was pleased to find himself able to keep up. 'Dr Black's lectures were clear, and I knew enough of the subjects he treated upon to understand them.'

Black had discovered that there was another component of air that extinguished both flames and life, even when his 'fixed air' had been removed. He gave the problem to his student Daniel Rutherford, who investigated it further and named the substance 'noxious' or 'phlogisticated' air. Rutherford had discovered nitrogen. His interests ran from chemistry to pathological anatomy, and he lectured to Astley and other students as part of his possession of the Regius professorship of botany. Being a polymath was almost the norm.

Cooper stayed for seven months, living in a room on Bristow Street, near the old Infirmary in High School Yards. For a shilling a day he dined at the house of a Mrs Mackintosh, nearby in Buccleuch Place. He walked the hospital wards, dissected and attended lectures. Chemistry, moral philosophy, anatomy, botany and physic were all on the menu. And in the evenings there were clubs, always more clubs. Cooper joined a student society dedicated to standing up to perceived oppression by the professors (and got himself elected president before his visit finished). On the first day of December he was elected to the Royal Medical Society, whose debates he attended over the following months. The knowledge of anatomy he had acquired from Cline, and the novelty of the views he had absorbed from Hunter, made him a successful member. From London he had brought surgical instruments not yet seen in Scotland, one of them a tool designed by Cline. He was given the promise of taking a turn as president of the society, should he ever return to Edinburgh.

Courtesy of his introduction to Charles Hope, Astley now joined another debating club, the famous Speculative Society. Founded in 1764 this was wider-ranging than Guy's Physical Society or Edinburgh's Royal Medical Society and had a traditional link with the law – Peter Holland's son Henry (who became a famous explorer and fashionable court physician) later described it as being 'famed as a school or oratory for future judges and statesmen'. From December Astley began attending its meetings, and on 12 February 1788 he took his turn formally to address the society. 'Mr Cooper read an Essay denying the existence of matter,' recorded the society. Philosophy did not come easily to him, and this paper seems to have been his most serious and public attempt at closing his grip on the subject. He managed to achieve at least the appearance of some success, the president of the society concluding kindly at the end of the debate that 'Mr Cooper has himself proved the falsehood of his doctrine, for there was much good matter in his own paper'. By March the society was out of philosophy and into politics, with Cooper taking part in a debate on the impact to Britain of her 'territorial possessions in the East Indies'. Whatever socialising happened outside of the hospitals, the dissecting rooms and the societies, little trace remains – other than his nephew's later comment that Cooper always spoke highly of Edinburgh women.

The city was sunny but still cool by mid-April. Although he had arrived late, and the season was not yet over, Cooper had seen enough of formal learning in Edinburgh. Alexander Monro *secundus*, second in the famous line of grandfather, father and son who all held the chair of anatomy, seems particularly to have aroused Astley's contempt. 'Old M— grunted like a pig', he recorded:

> He was a tolerable lecturer, possessed a full knowledge of his subject, had much sagacity in practice, was laudably zealous, but was much given to self and to the abuse of others. I gave him two instruments, Cline's gorget,

and an instrument for scratching the capsule of the lens, and the next day he said, 'Gentlemen, Mr Cooper has given me two instruments, one for scratching the capsule of the lens, which may be useful: the other, a cutting gorget, and it is curious I myself invented this very instrument twenty years ago.'

Astley much preferred Monro's assistant, a man called Fyfe – 'a horrid lecturer, but an industrious worthy man, and good practical anatomist'. The city's reputation was more than it deserved, Cooper concluded, even if the fame of some of the teachers was entirely merited.

I was glad I went to Edinburgh, because I learned that distance enhances the character of men beyond their deserts. Cullen and Black and Dugald Stewart, however, were great men, and being near them did not diminish the importance I had been led to attach to them from their public character. Dugald Stewart was beyond my power of appreciation – metaphysics were foreign to my mind, which was never captivated by speculation.

Dugald Stewart had begun as a professor of mathematics, but by the time Astley arrived he had become professor of moral philosophy, not only lecturing on metaphysics but also giving progressive lessons on political philosophy and the theory of government. The peripheral attractions of such men as Stewart were not enough to overturn Astley's view that the days of Edinburgh's surgical pre-eminence were over.

After seven months of hard work in a foreign city, Astley felt more confident than ever before of his own abilities. But for now what he wanted was a holiday, and he felt he had little more to gain by staying until the academic year closed. So he packed his bags, threw a lavish party for the friends he had made, and, hiring a servant and buying himself a pair of horses, prepared to set off on a tour of the Highlands. Samuel Johnson's successful 1775 travel book *A Journey to the Western Islands of Scotland* had highlighted both the foreignness and the attractions of such a journey.

He thought the horses were underpriced and insisted on paying more than he was being asked for. There may have been an element of youthful extravagance, but there was also an element of principle to his actions: he was a young man conscious of his privileges in life, and London friends

94

had commented on his inclination to pay above the odds whenever he thought he was getting an unfairly good deal. While his motivation may have been good, however, his budgeting was not. The mountain scenery was wild and uplifting, but did nothing to fill his pocket. Astley had lived carefully in the city, but as soon as his holiday began he forgot his caution and asceticism. His funds lasted him through the Highlands and stretched to a trip around the Western Isles. But on his way home, somewhere in the north of England, they ran out.

He discharged his servant, sold one of his horses, and pawned his watch. The miscalculation pained him, and he found it enough of a lasting humiliation to make him more careful with money in the future. But he was young and resilient, and the experience did not dent the optimism and self-confidence with which he was so well supplied. By the end of the autumn of 1788 he was back in London, safe once more in Cline's house at St Mary Axe.

7

Marriages

As 1788 gave way to 1789, the Thames froze over, a frost fair on the solid surface of the river bringing a chaotic carnival atmosphere. In the St Thomas's dissecting room, Astley spent an increasing amount of his time teaching the other students. They had need of him, since there was still little on offer from Haighton except for bad temper and abuse. But although Haighton was unwilling to put much effort into teaching himself, he resented seeing Astley doing it in his place. The two men, both regulars at the Physical Society, increasingly disliked each other.

Haighton shared the society's feeling that experimental physiology was the duty of medical men, the mark of those who were trying to make the world a better place. To that end he privately pursued vivisection on a grand scale. But to one of his experimental subjects he became emotionally attached: a favourite spaniel. His fondness for it had built up over a series of long experiments and drawn-out recuperations. Haighton had cut one of the dog's Achilles tendons to see how it would heal, and opened up one of its legs and sutured shut a femoral artery. He had also cut the dog's recurrent laryngeal nerve, destroying it as it looped up near the thyroid gland in the neck. The recurrent laryngeal is the nerve that controls speech in humans, and does the equivalent for dogs. Haighton may have cut it in the spirit of experiment, but others whispered that it had been done only to keep the dog quiet whilst the knife went in. But everyone agreed that with the experiments long completed, Haighton had a soft spot for the animal. He brought it with him to the Physical Society, leaving it outside with a servant while the meetings were under way. One Saturday that winter he fell into argument with Astley. The precise subject of their disagreement was not recorded, but a physician in the room remembered what happened next. Haighton 'called loudly to his servant, and ordered a pet and favourite spaniel to be immediately brought into the room'. He then invited Cooper to inspect the dog, 'to notice his bulk, his healthy aspect, and his good keeping, and this done, put a period to his existence in a moment. He then at once demonstrated the results of a most careful and rigid operation to which the unfortunate animal had been subjected some three or four years preceding.' The dog was worth sacrificing without a moment's thought, and presumably with a pocket-knife, to help him make his point – whatever that point may have been. Astley lost the argument as a result. Onlookers recalled him being cross at losing but amused at the dog's sudden death, and curious to peer inside its warm body. At least one other member of the society, knowing Haighton's fondness for the dog, was horrified.

The collision with Haighton did nothing to subdue the self-belief Astley had brought back from Scotland. But the abrasive debates of the society punctured the worst of his youthful arrogance. 'Big with my own importance,' Astley straightforwardly admitted, 'I became presumptuous.' The feeling was swept away by society arguments, and although the experience of being argued down to size was painful, it was also valuable.

At St Mary Axe there was a new arrival. Edward Coleman was three years older than Astley. He had completed his seven years' apprenticeship with a provincial Gravesend surgeon and come to London to study under Cline. He was warm, kind-hearted and hard-working. He also had the odd but memorable habit of vomiting involuntarily whenever he ventured into the cold London streets too soon after dinner.

In the evenings Cooper walked to Leicester Square alongside Coleman, as he had done before with Holland (who had now returned to Cheshire to set up his own surgical practice). Astley was attending Hunter's lectures for a second season, thirsty to hear again the ideas on which he increasingly felt he could build his professional and intellectual life. He was confident enough now to talk to Hunter after the close of each talk. 'We used to talk to him after lecture – Coleman and myself – and he would not brook the least doubt or objection to his opinions. He manifested on such occasions the greatest impatience, by clasping his hands over his head, and moving about in his chair; yet he always treated us with great kindness.' As they strolled back afterwards, along the Strand and past St Paul's, following the curve of the Thames, they planned their next steps. They plotted their experiments.

Neither man was rich. The animals they used were mostly stolen, neighbouring cats and dogs that paused for a moment to be stroked and patted by the young men and found themselves carried helplessly to St Mary Axe. Cline took no part in their investigations, but he was aware that they were going on and seemed content.

The chief operator was Cooper, who found himself the superior anatomist and practical surgeon of the two. Coleman had a better grasp for theory, particularly as the evenings of Hunter's lecture series swept by and he was exposed to the ideas that Cooper had already had a chance to hear. Both men found the partnership profitable, and on the basis of that mutual self-education their friendship deepened. They wanted new knowledge, and they sought it out in Hunter's Leicester Square home and in their own vivisections. Hunter had boasted the year before of how his knowledge changed too rapidly to justify note-taking amongst his students. This time around, the point was made with more force. Astley, listening closely, was surprised to hear Hunter stating an opinion completely at odds with one he had given the year before. He put his hand up and pointed it out, asking if Hunter had really meant to do such a thing.

'Very likely I did,' replied Hunter, 'I hope I grow wiser every year.' And he returned to talking about the animal experiments and surgical practice by which he did so.

The profit from Coleman's and Cooper's vivisection was twofold. Coleman was interested in asphyxia and had believed that death in hanging and drowning was caused solely by a mechanical blockage, that it was an obstruction of the windpipe that killed. At the expense of a great many animals (enough dogs to fill up Houndsditch, Astley joked) they discovered that there was something else, some change in the blood. It was a phenomenon they were able to observe and to comment upon, but they knew that they had failed to understand the nature of it. Oxygen (then called dephlogisticated air) had been isolated and described in 1774 by Wedgwood's fellow Lunar Society member Priestley, but an understanding of cellular respiration was still too far away.

Coleman took most of the credit for their researches, writing *A Dissertation on Suspended Respiration, from Drowning, Hanging, and Suffocation* (published in 1791 by the well-known radical publisher Joseph Johnson). But Cooper's star was also rising. The private experiments he was now carrying out on the domestic pets and strays of London gave him authority when he spoke in the Physical Society. His standing in the dissecting room was also high, the product of his knowledge and his willingness to teach. When Haighton resigned in 1789, abandoning his surgical career to take a physician's degree, Astley was engaged in his place. It was an exceptional appointment for a man whose own apprenticeship was still three years away from completion. But unlike Astley's first seat on the Physical Society committee, it was based on hard work rather than nepotism. He had been filling the post informally for some time, and doing the job well.

There was another new arrival at St Mary Axe at the same time as Coleman. Taylor – his first name goes unrecorded – was a clever man with his own ideas about life, and refused to have anything to do with the experiments of his house-mates. It was not only the work that put him off, it was the filth and dreadfulness of it all. He had better things to do, and while his studious house-mates were making their regular walks to Leicester Square they saw the carriages come calling. Taylor, said Astley, was 'much sought by the ladies of the west-end of the town'. That sort of high society was where his pleasure lay, and also his future.* Taylor's social achievements advertised to Astley a little of the world that lay outside the dissecting rooms and wards.

In 1789 he turned twenty-one. He was still an apprentice, and by tradition a man held off marrying until his apprenticeship was complete. But there was nothing to stop him courting. As his master, Cline might have discouraged him and urged him to focus entirely on his studies. Instead he continued to behave more as a father than a superior. At weekends, when Cline went visiting, he took Cooper with him. Some of those visits were Sunday trips out to Tottenham, then a rural village to the north of London. A distant relative of Cline's named Thomas Cock had retired there, finding a comfortable home for himself after a successful life as a merchant in Germany (where he had family).

The chief lure for Astley was one of the occupants of this country estate. Ann Cock, Thomas's daughter, was an attractive young woman.

---

*Taylor went on to marry into the aristocracy and to receive a comfortable civil position from Pitt for his troubles.

Her 'sweetness of manner, amiable disposition, and natural feminine modesty' existed alongside good looks, resolute boldness and a taste for independence. But Thomas Cock, a somewhat irritable man of frequent bad tempers, found Astley very much less eligible. The young surgeon had good looks and a happy gift of charm, that much was apparent from the effect he had on Ann, but those were no qualities to impress a hard-headed father. Astley's apprenticeship was not even close to being finished and his prospects were uncertain in a profession with no real history of being particularly lucrative or prestigious.

Cline's intervention – and his personal example of what worldly success a surgeon could achieve – were sufficient to prevent Astley's being banned from the Tottenham estate. The young man's visits increased, and he began to travel out by himself, hiring a horse rather than relying on Cline's carriage. It was clear where the visits were leading.

In the summer of 1789, another of Astley's sisters, Marianne, died of tuberculosis. She had married (a clergyman) only two years before. Astley knew that he was under the shadow of the disease as much as anyone in his family, but if the uncertainty of life's lease had any effect on him at all, it was to make him more urgent. There is no record of when Ann and Astley became formally engaged, but the letter from Astley's mother telling him of Marianne's death asked him to send maternal regards 'to my beloved Miss Cock'. In the eyes of their families, then, by 1789 they were an estab-lished couple who were expected to wed.

It was a bold move for Ann, and a romantic one, to accept this appren-tice with such shadowy prospects. She had chosen a tall and handsome young man with no other promise than his character and no appeal besides that of his own person and the world he seemed intent on creating for himself. Ann Cock shared her fiancé's political passions and understood his professional ones, and she looked forward to the Sunday visits and the sound of his horse's hooves.

In July that year, the people of Paris stormed the Bastille. The event was celebrated wildly as an intoxicating blow for freedom.* In Britain too the

---

*That the old regime had been planning on demolishing the Bastille anyway was cheerfully ignored. So were other details, like the Bastille's tiny population of prisoners (seven men) and the inconven-ient fact that the Bastille's commander, promptly lynched as a brutal tyrant, had surrendered peace-fully to the crowd in preference to firing on them with the cannon he commanded.

initial reaction was feverish approval for an uprising of the people against oppression.

Events across the English Channel fired Cooper, but did not distract him. He was storming the citadel of ignorance, pulling down its walls with long hours in the dissecting room and with ever-increasing experiments on stolen cats and dogs. He attended the Physical Society, devoted himself to his post as Demonstrator, and in the evenings socialised with Cline and other democratic friends. Only at the weekends did he have time to ride out to Tottenham. His labour and his absorption rewarded him, feeding his enjoyment of his work and his feeling of its worth. They also confirmed him in his pre-eminent position amongst his peers. In 1791, after two years as Demonstrator, his career took an even bigger step forwards. Still unqualified, still an apprentice, he was offered a position as lecturer.

The offer came from Cline, who had been sufficiently impressed with his student to wish to go into business with him. Lecturing was an entrepreneurial activity with teachers receiving no salaries except the fees of the students that signed up. They had to attract an audience. Having a position at a charity hospital gave a surgeon reputation and the use of the hospital theatre to lecture in, and some sway in deciding which lecture courses counted as valid towards a student's qualification. But although conditions were biased against the students, there was still a large degree of free choice. Courses of anatomy at private schools outside the hospitals were often popular, and were frequently accepted as valid for a student's progression. Even lectures that were wholly extra-curricular, like those of Hunter, could draw a sizeable fee-paying crowd if the speaker was good enough. Cline proposed to keep the ownership of the lectures to begin with, starting Astley off at a flat rate of £120 per annum in return for delivering a portion of Cline's surgical lectures. It was common practice for one lecturer to start, generally the one whose name brought in the subscriptions, and then for an assistant to take over as the course progressed. Cline agreed to increase Astley's fee each year until the two men were splitting their profits evenly. The offer immediately accelerated Cooper's career, over the heads of those who were fully qualified and had been waiting for just such a position for years. One of those was Haighton. 'The superior age and standing of this gentleman,' noted Astley's nephew Bransby, 'and the keen susceptibility of his temper at the slightest disrespect to his abilities (which he believed to be peculiarly fitted for the advancement of anatomical and surgical science), could not fail to make him regard this sudden elevation of the young pupil to the lectureships, with jealous feelings; and these he was of a nature too unbending and abrupt to conceal.' Cline's respect for Astley had other manifestations. For some time Cline had complained of pain while eating ('I have a spasm in my mylohyoideus muscle,' was the dinner-table comment), and eventually reasoned out why. 'I have discovered the cause of the uneasiness and spasm under my tongue,' explained Cline, after self-diagnosing a stone in the salivary duct at the floor of his mouth. Astley put a finger into his master's mouth and was able to feel the impression of the stone to one side and underneath his tongue. Immediately the two men agreed to an operation. Another resident pulled back Cline's cheek with a blunt hook and pressed a finger underneath his jaw to push the stone upwards. Astley made a cut underneath Cline's tongue with a curved blade, exposing the stone enough to pull it free with another smaller hook. It took a week for Cline to recover.

In taking on Cooper, Cline was tying his own future income to his student's ability. It was a mark of confidence as well as friendship, and it may have also been something of a promise to Thomas Cock, a paternal show from Cline of his young charge's prospects. Flushed with pleasure and excitement, Astley took advantage of Cline's offer to push a plan of his own. In preceding years Cline, like other lecturers, had always given talks that mixed anatomy and surgery. It was the traditional manner. Cooper felt they were better separated, that the new generations of surgeons required a different kind of knowledge to the operators before them. It was no longer enough to have the mastery of a small range of procedures. There was more to a grounding in surgery than a knowledge of anatomy. Pathology, embryology, physiology and therapeutics all had to be understood separately in order to be related correctly to one another. Surgery, in Cooper's imagination, was no longer the realm of the skilled craftsman, the man with a strong arm and a knack for a couple of practised operations. It was a science, and those who were qualified in it needed to be qualified in all that related to it. He wanted to make his own lectures as revolutionary as those of Hunter, while making them more intelligible and more popular.

Overcoming Cline's reluctance, Cooper persuaded him to adopt such a new method. During his evening lectures, it was agreed, Cooper would devote himself solely to what was termed surgery. That included pathology – the study of the processes of disease and of healing – as much as it included operating. It was a bold move to make a lecture course so novel.

It was widely believed that Hunter's audiences and income had been greatly limited partly by the off-putting novelty of his ideas.

One of the friends with whom Astley was able to share his good news was John Thelwall. By now, despite his original stutter, Thelwall had made a name for himself as a successful debater. He had added to that enough professional achievement as a journalist and man of letters to haul himself firmly into the middle classes. In 1789 he had met and fallen in love with Susan Vellum. In July 1791, on his birthday, he married her. The newly weds took a house near the Borough Hospitals and Thelwall began to attend lectures, both at Guy's and St Thomas's and also at the Leicester Square home of John Hunter. He was educating himself in science and medicine and hovering on the edge of a medical career. In the meantime he was able to advise Astley on oratory.

The lecture theatre was next door to the dissecting room. Five rows of seats were placed in an ellipse around a central rotating table. A small door in the west wall was the only way in or out. Beyond it there was a small lobby from which opened a room, eight feet wide, where the lecturers and their anatomical exhibits waited before the talks. Above the five rows of seats there was a gallery, accessible by a different entrance and with no access to the theatre below. This was so close to the ceiling that the taller men could not stand straight. Set in the middle of the ceiling, above the rotating table, was a skylight. But the lectures were evening ones, and beyond the glass was only the darkness of the London night.

From his earliest days, Astley had been a successful speaker to a domestic audience. Surrounded by vociferous siblings and with parents who preached and moralised for a living, he had all the childhood advantages an orator could wish for. He was an experienced teacher, and had had considerable practice talking to the Physical Society and the bullish members of agitating political clubs. It all suggested he would be a superb lecturer.

Instead, he was a failure. He made a forceful attempt to communicate the spirit and ideas he had learnt from Hunter, but adopted too much of the older man's wandering philosophy. In the age before germ theory and effective microbiology, pathology (literally, the study of suffering) consisted of pathophysiology and pathological anatomy, the forms of physical disease as they could then be discerned. Such a focus seemed strange and unimportant to his audience. The students could not easily relate it to their ambitions to become the sort of men who could walk confidently through hospital corridors, approach with courage a patient strapped to an operating table, and command high fees from rich patients.

Astley's Norfolk accent, although obvious, was not the cause of his failure. London survived and swelled on the back of mass inward migration, and regional accents in the capital were common, like that of Joshua Reynolds who spoke with a Devon burr despite being president of the Royal Academy. People took offence at Hunter's obscurities and originalities, but his strong Scots tones caused little concern. Astley's thick regional lilt stayed with him throughout his life, and there was never any sign that it hampered him. Nor did the early lectures fail because of lack of effort; he laboured hard at them. He was able to bring to them more experience of hospital surgery and experimental physiology (meaning vivisection) than many older men. But his audience's reaction disappointed him, as he saw how much he bored them. Since the students paid the fees in advance, this meant no loss of income, but it was worrying.

By the time Astley's lectures started in the autumn of 1791, Thomas Cock had little thought to spare for his future son-in-law's new post. He was too distracted by his own illness, which now left him too weak to move further than his own garden.

During his visits to Tottenham Astley began to spend as much time attending to the father as to the daughter. Thomas Cock seemed grateful for the attention, and with Astley's apprenticeship due to finish at the end of the academic year, and his own health starting to fail, agreed to the marriage. Allowing Ann to marry an unqualified tradesman with few prospects was bad, but dying and leaving her alone and free to marry without paternal approval was unthinkable. The date was set for Monday 21 November. In anticipation, Mr Cock bought a house in London's Jeffries Square, a cul-de-sac conveniently situated off St Mary Axe, for the newly weds to live in.

As the wedding approached, he grew more and more ill. Astley began to see him daily, now as much as a doctor as his future son-in-law, and the wedding was postponed. By Saturday 19 November 1791 the old man knew he was on his death-bed, and said so. He remained conscious, but two days later, on a cold cloud-ridden day, he died. It was the very date the marriage was due to have taken place.

Astley was impressed with Thomas Cock's final days. 'His life had been so perfectly moral', he wrote, 'that he looked back with pleasure and forward without the smallest fear.' Maria Cooper, noting her son's phrasing, took care to correct him, despite never having met the person she spoke of: 'I must add that I think Mr Cock must have been not only a *moral* but [also a] *religious* man, to have sustained so exemplarily the several duties of life, and the last awful scene of it. At least he must have acted up to his idea of duty. How useful are such scenes!'

But although Astley may have been convinced by his mother's eye for domestic drama, he did not defer to her beliefs about what made life worthwhile. It had been Thomas Cock's morals, in Astley's eyes, that vindicated his occasional bad temper and the pain of his death. You didn't buy your way to heaven through turning up at church, you earned it through the life you led. 'Whatever is a man's pursuit in life,' he wrote, 'it is knowledge and moral character which give to him his real rank and position.' It was the kind of comment that his mother felt treated too lightly the sacred matters of religion and breeding. Astley's friendships with Henry Cline and John Thelwall had bitten deep. His values had become those of the Dissenters with whom he now spent his life.

Cline stepped in after Thomas Cock's funeral, ushering Ann and Astley into marriage. The bereavement, Cline pointed out, was not sudden, and there was nothing disrespectful in going ahead with the wedding before the year was out. It was, after all, what Thomas Cock had been expecting, and what he had bought and furnished the London house for.

Subdued, the couple agreed. The wedding went ahead under the quiet auspices of a Cline family christening in mid-December of 1791. Astley and Ann accompanied the Cline family to church, walking the short distance southwards down St Mary Axe to the church of St Andrew Undershaft (the odd name coming from the maypole that had stood near it until the sixteenth century) on the corner of Leadenhall Street. After the christening they stayed behind and were wed. It was a cold day, not much above freezing and with the rain beating down. There was no public celebration, and that evening Astley delivered the routine lecture that had been scheduled long before. Afterwards he went home: not to Henry Cline and St Mary Axe, but to Ann and Jeffries Square.

As well as the house and his bride, Astley had come into possession of the vast sum of £14,000. Like other male members of his family, he had married well. It was enough money to reduce a young man's efforts significantly if he had been aiming simply at securing his position in life. But Astley's idealism remained, and the money had quite the opposite effect on him. It gave him the space and time to develop his career in ways that seemed likely to be most beneficial rather than simply most profitable.

Neither Ann nor Astley planned to remain continuously at Jeffries Square in the short term. They had married boldly and they intended to live in the same manner. As the winter season drew to its conclusion they made their plans for taking an extended honeymoon, a working one. Both labour and pleasure were fitting parts of life, and so they would pursue both. 'As neither Mr nor Mrs Cooper had ever been on the Continent,' wrote Astley's nephew Bransby, 'they determined to visit Paris.' Friends 'were well aware', he added, 'to how great an extent the attraction of this journey was increased by the tendency of his political feelings'.

Parisian surgery and Parisian democracy were both models of the bright new world that seemed to be dawning. The revolution across the Channel drew forth boundless optimism from the democrats and idealists of Britain. To even contemplate visiting France at such a time was to share in the general desire to see at first hand the great events that were filling the English newspapers. Thelwall longed to visit France, but lacked his friend's newfound financial freedom. 'The French Revolution', said Cline, 'was a glorious cause for a man to shed his blood in.' Correspondingly, the visit was 'a subject of extreme anxiety and regret to [Astley's] parents'. Their son did not hide his views, but on his visits to Great Yarmouth 'not only espoused with much warmth the cause of the democratic party and their tenets, but was also most active in opposing all those who differed from them in opinion'.

By the time the academic year had finished in May, Ann was pregnant. To plan the trip all the same made it clear that they were not visiting Paris as tourists, to gawp and to holiday. Their trip was the choice of a couple who had aspirations, and who felt the tide of history buoying them along. They were going to Paris to consecrate their new lives, and to bless the one that Ann was now carrying. It was not a tour; it was a pilgrimage.

8

The French Terror

When Pitt gave his budget speech in February 1792, he shared some of the popular optimism about the revolution in France. 'There never was a time in the history of this country,' he said, 'when, from the situation in Europe, we might more reasonably expect fifteen years of peace, than we may at the present moment.'

Astley, for his part, expected something more profound than peace. The light in France was a golden dawn. Ann and Astley crossed the Channel from Dover and arrived on the French coast towards the end of May. It was a simple matter to change £22 into a few hundred French *livres*. They celebrated the first day of their Continental honeymoon with some claret at lunchtime and beer in the evening. The next day came the business of arranging for travel to Paris: Astley bought himself some new boots, splashed out a considerable sum on purchasing a cabriolet carriage and two horses, and engaged a servant for the journey. The cabriolet proved troublesome – breaking down as they entered Amiens and needing costly repairs – but a few such difficulties did nothing to dull their excitement. Each evening there was a reliable supply of burgundy or claret to cheer the young couple on.

They reached Paris six days after landing in Calais. They found a hotel and bought smart new French clothes. Astley invested in a three-cornered hat, bought some fabric to have a coat and waistcoat made up, and commissioned a hairdresser to attend on him daily. He recorded in detail the costs of the hair powder. Ann – he referred to her as 'Mrs Cooper' in his journal, perhaps as much from the novel pleasure of it as from formality – had her own hairdresser and her own new clothes. They had money in their pockets and enjoyable excuses for spending it. A French tutor and a Parisian servant completed their expenditure for the first week.

On 20 June a large crowd, initially attracted by the idea of planting a symbolic tree of liberty, gathered in the grounds of the Tuileries. To get carried away with the emotion of an event, to act in a theatrical and melo-dramatic manner, was becoming the essential token of sincerity in the increasingly histrionic capital. Even better was to publicly declare a willingness to die for the cause of the revolution – and preferably follow it by shedding someone else's blood. Inside the palace, the crowd found Louis XVI largely unprotected. Brandishing their swords and pistols in his face they demanded that he give up the royal right of veto he still retained. Someone waved a pike stuck with a dripping animal heart, threatening violence. Louis, cowed but calm, took the red hat of liberty that the crowd offered him, placed it upon his head and proposed the health of the French. His sincerity was sufficient to defuse the tension of the afternoon, but it was only a momentary piece of self-possession. Louis remained too impotent and indecisive to halt the country's slide into chaos.

Not even the most exhilarated of English natural philosophers conceived of their work in terms of a religious crusade. They might talk of it in a visionary way, but always with a healthy touch of reason and humility. Astley's devotion to politics and to surgery was wholehearted, but in the English manner it demanded no hysteria to demonstrate his conviction. If he had put his hand to his breast, in a meeting of the Physical Society, and sworn to lay down his life for his beliefs, no one would have taken him seriously. Passion was all very well, but it was no replacement for British pragmatism. The atmosphere of revolutionary France was unlike anything Britain had to offer.

While Ann shopped and saw the sights, Astley worked. His French was good and getting better, enough for him to be able to attend both political meetings and medical talks. He signed on for a series of hospital lectures at the Charity Hospital and the Hôtel Dieu, for dissections with Chopart at his Académie d'Anatomie in the rue Saint Martin, and went back repeatedly to hear the heated addresses of the National Assembly. The words of the surgeons Pierre Joseph Desault and François Chopart were mixed up in his days with the oratory of Danton, Marat and Robespierre.

Desault struck Astley as the model of a successful old-fashioned surgeon, embodying everything that was both good and bad in that tradition. He knew his anatomy, he could operate proficiently, but he did not know how to think. He could neither observe nor experiment. Astley thought he lacked the 'higher scientific principles' necessary to be humane, useful and innovative. Astley watched one operation in cold fascination: a boy had come to Desault suffering from a series of diseased lymph glands in his neck. Desault began to cut the first one out, proceeding with skill and precision. He had just started to remove a second when his assistant interrupted him, disturbing his concentration to inform him that the boy had died. Desault had not noticed.

The next day the boy's body was dissected on the same operating table. Desault proudly showed his audience that he had damaged none of the great blood vessels in the neck. In Astley's eyes it was a triumph of technical skill over any understanding of human need. The dangerous operation had been conducted with an admirable amount of manual skill, but it had been murderously pointless. There had never been any need to cut away the glands in the boy's neck; the effort had all been made for the benefit of the surgeon rather than the patient. There was a hollowness to Desault's technical skill. 'This was a most unscientific operation,' said Astley of the boy's death, 'for to remove important structures . . . [when it is not essential to do so] . . . cannot effect any useful result.'

In the evenings Astley and Ann threw themselves into the opportunities that Paris still so amply offered for food, drink and conversation. By early July they were confident enough in the language to enjoy the theatre and even, occasionally, the opera. Astley's notes on their expenditure slipped slowly from English into French. They had spent over £100 already; a significant sum, but one they could easily afford. Many had travelled to Paris to greet what they saw as the start of a more democratic and fairer world. Astley's diary records that he 'paid Mr White for nine days lodgings' on 6 June. Given his outstanding democratic connections it is likely that Mr White was not a randomly chosen hotelier, rather another of the so-called English Jacobins. But the bright start of the new republic became increasingly tyrannical and bloody, and the optimistic feelings that many English people had arrived with grew ever more conflicted.

As the summer wore on, Paris became more militarised and more on edge. Patriots flooded to the city, many of them armed. In the Assembly the arguments continued, shuttling between those who wanted a constitutional monarchy after the English style and those who wanted a republic.

It was an inflamed situation, not helped by moderation being widely seen as a badge of treacherousness. On 29 July the Coopers made an expedition out of Paris to tour Versailles, now empty of the kings who had lived there. The next day a detachment of five hundred guardsmen from Marseilles arrived, singing the new anthem that was immediately named after them. Four days later the Duke of Brunswick, at the head of a Prussian army on a mission to rescue the French monarchy, declared that any further intrusion upon the royal sanctuary of the Tuileries would lead to an 'exemplary and unforgettable act of vengeance' against Paris.

The duke's declaration was aimed at destroying the morale of the people; predictably, it had the opposite effect. As far as the majority of the Republicans were concerned, the duke had helpfully clarified the situation. There was no room for negotiation, no space for a limited monarchy: democrats needed to realise they were at war. Those in Paris who were still in favour of the Crown immediately appeared to their compatriots as traitors, taking the side of an invading army. The royal family, marooned in the Tuileries, became ever less safe.

By the start of August the Coopers still found the streets comfortable enough to travel around. Astley bought a dictionary on the 1st and began making his diary entries entirely in French, recording their joint consumption on clothes, coffee, ice-cream and entertainments. The temperatures were high, over $80°$ Fahrenheit (about $27°$ centigrade). Nevertheless the Coopers took in an opera on 3 August and settled their impressive wine bill the following day before heading out to the theatre. On the evening of 5 August, they went to the Théâtre français. Armies were approaching from the east, others were organising themselves on the capital's streets. In the face of this tumult, Astley's journal entries came to a virtual close. With the world on the brink of what threatened to be catastrophic bloodshed, there seemed little reason to worry about accounts. Only his list of temperatures continued, gradually increasing, a daily reminder that the world was getting hotter. As 9 August passed over into the 10th, the tocsin, the bells of the churches that indicated alarm, began to ring. They sounded throughout the night.

In the morning, hearing the bells, the royal family fled. For protection they went to the rooms of the Legislative Assembly, the technical government of the day. They left behind them the two thousand troops serving as their personal bodyguards, half of them Swiss. The National Guard entered the Tuileries believing that it had been surrendered, but nobody had told that to the defenders. Seeing the lines of armed men marching towards them, the royal bodyguard opened fire.

It was interpreted as a deliberate ambush, a premeditated trap. The people's response was outraged and savage. The militant republicans from Brest were killed by their comrades because their red uniforms looked like those of the Swiss. Astley was watching Chopart operate when he heard the cannon fire begin. He rushed from the operating theatre, racing to discover the cause for what sounded like a civil war. From the Pont Neuf he could see part of the Tuileries across the River Seine, the Swiss guards firing from the windows at the mob that poured towards them across the bridge and swarmed up along the quay of the Louvre. 'The streets were all confusion, from persons running, and others coming out of their houses to shut up their shops, and falling over each other. I ran back to the hospital, but the surgeons had all fled.'

France began killing its own citizens on a grand scale only from the latter half of 1792, but ever since the Bastille came down in 1789, Paris had been a city of summary bloodshed, stringing people up from the lamp-posts or butchering them on the cobbles, the mob deaf to pleading or entreaty. Astley needed to cross the river in order to get back home, but the Pont Neuf was impassable. He struggled upriver with the intention of crossing the Seine at a point well above the scenes of whirling violence. As he went a woman pointed at him, screaming to those around her: 'There is an aristocrat!'

'I'm English,' replied Cooper.

'Ah! My God!' she exclaimed, taking his defence as an admission of guilt. 'Then you are for sure!'

The streets were too exposed. As the danger of his situation pressed in on him, Astley tried to flag down a hackney coach. But he was dressed that day in black, and it was known that the court was in mourning. The coachman refused to stop, declaring roughly that he would have no aristocrats in *his* carriage. Astley was forced to continue on foot:

After crossing the bridge, the scene was terrific, – cannon firing constantly, – volleys of musketry in every direction, – the tocsin sounding from every turret, – women crying, – litters conveyed along the streets, bearing the wounded and the dying; but at last I reached my hotel, in the Passage des Petits Pères, in safety.

Back at the hotel he found his pregnant wife, terrified. They sat together at the window watching the events outside. Men and women passed by carrying the trophies of their day's work: parts of the men that they had killed and torn apart: heads, fingers, hands. Soon after they saw a Swiss guard, fleeing for his life, 'chased, like a hare, along the street'. He escaped out of view but others followed who were not so lucky, and the Coopers looked on as they died. General Money, an Englishman from Norwich, was also staying at the hotel with them and had spent the previous night by the side of the French king. 'We were particularly alarmed,' wrote Astley, as 'we expected on his return to us that he would be followed by a mob.' But General Money managed to be discreet, and the mob never appeared.*
When Money returned he was able to report that the commander of the 5th battalion of Paris Volunteers had spoken with pleasure of his part in killing the Swiss Guards. 'The unhappy men implored mercy,' Money remembered him saying, 'but we did not regard this. We put them all to death and our men cut off most of their heads and fixed them on their bayonets.'

In the evening, despite the risk, Astley left the hotel. He wanted to go to the Tuileries, to see for himself the after-effects of the events that had thundered about him all that day. Fires were still burning when he got there and people were picking over the corpses. There had been almost a thousand Swiss Guards and hundreds had died, along with a smaller number of attacking French. Triumphant patriots were everywhere, while 'the gardens of the Tuilleries were full of dead men', wrote Astley, 'and there they lay naked, having been stripped of all their clothes by the mob'.

The following day Astley returned, and this time Ann came with him. On their way they passed through a large crowd, in the midst of whom were Louis XVI and Marie Antoinette. They were on their way to prison.

In the Tuileries the bodies were being piled up and burnt, but there were still enough lying around to show what the crowd had done. Limbs had been hacked off, abdomens slit open, extremities cut away with scissors. Genitals had been fed to dogs or stuffed back into the gaping mouths of the people whose bodies they had been ripped out of. And among it

---

* General Money was an English eccentric who had travelled to France with the principal object of waging war. 'Colonel Money', he said of himself before receiving his higher commission on 19 July 1792, 'does not mean to assign any other reason for serving the armies of France than that he loves his profession and went there merely to improve himself in it.' Hilaire Belloc, in his short essay about Money called 'A Norfolk Man', comments approvingly on this statement: 'Spoken like Othello!'

all, like Astley and Ann, thronged those who had come to see. Another Englishman in the crowd described the 'many beautiful ladies . . . walking arm in arm with their male friends . . . contemplating the mangled naked and stiff carcasses'. The Coopers watched as the woodwork of the barracks and the furniture of the palace were piled on top of the corpses, the fires crackling the flesh of the dead. A story went around that some of the women who watched the pyre pulled out an arm or a leg here and there and tasted them. Some who saw the ways in which the corpses had been mutilated found it easy to believe.

Astley wrote that the temperature was 85° Fahrenheit (29.4° centigrade), the hottest day of the summer.

The massacre at the Tuileries brought no immediate change to the couple's routines. Astley continued to attend the wards of the hospitals, sporting a democratic cockade out of genuine belief as well as wary tact. The 2nd September saw another round of killing. News came of a defeat for the armies of the republic at Verdun; the duke's forces were closing in. The rhetoric of paranoia demanded revenge, and the revolutionaries turned on the inmates of the Parisian prisons. In what became known as the September Massacres almost 1,500 people were slaughtered. It was enough, for the first time, to alter the Coopers' plans. They still believed in democracy, but they no longer believed in Paris. They wanted to leave.

By now it was no longer easy to come and go, nor even to remain in safety. The slaughter of the Parisian prison population marked the beginning of Terror on a new scale. The machinery of a police state was fully in place. Murder was the order of the hour and it was no longer an amateur business. When the streets seemed more dangerous than usual Astley stayed in the hotel with Ann. On most days he continued to attend the hospitals. The violence made the city streets no place for holiday-makers, but it also made the wards more profitable. To the normal accidents of daily life were added instructive doses of gunshot wounds, stabbings and other forms of violence. Astley was gathering much of the experience of a battlefield surgeon.

As he did so, the storm-clouds of popular suspicion began to veer towards the English. They were all aristocrats, people whispered. They were the enemies of the people. It was a small step from being the subject of a rumour to the object of a lynching. Some of the English believed their only chance for escaping a slaughter lay in offering their services to the revolutionary government, forming a 'légion britannique'. Others, like Astley, who might once have willingly volunteered to defend the republic, now wanted nothing more than to leave it. A historian of Guy's suggested that it was only Astley's democratic connections in England that kept him safe. And fortunately for the Coopers, their passports were granted before the situation grew any worse. The passports were documents of their times, picturesque summaries of the state of the revolution. 'Live free or die', they were headed, the legend supported by two female figures. On the right was Minerva, goddess of wisdom, but in place of an owl she held a pike with a cap of liberty slung over its sharpened point. On the left was the female personification of the French Constitution, sitting upon a lion. In one hand she held the French Constitution – with 'The Rights of Man' as its subtitle – and in the other she had the royal crown. Beneath the two women was printed 'La Nation, la Loi, le Roi' – 'The Nation, the Law, the King'. Someone had taken a pen and crossed out 'le Roi' and the crown above.

The Coopers fled Paris in the company of an eccentric English travel writer named Richard Twiss. He claimed to have travelled to Paris in the hope of being able to witness a bloody counter-revolution and visit the capital's famous gardens at the same time. Disappointed in the first and finding the second increasingly impractical, Twiss was doing the best he could by writing up his trip anyway. Having walked around the Tuileries on the same day as the Coopers, he was happy to swap stories with them. For a man who viewed himself as a modern – he took a special interest in admiring the 'cabinets of natural history' that were still on display along the road from Paris to Calais, the museums of animal and human specimens – to travel with a surgeon was a gift. In return for Astley's stories of the state of French hospitals and French science, Twiss was able to tell them more of the horrors that were the staples of Parisian life. He told of hearing how a man had been dragged before a judge in the Tuileries, accused of theft and found not guilty, then killed anyway, the crowd lying him on his back in front of the judge who had acquitted him, and, over the prolonged period of a quarter of an hour, hacking off his head with a serrated scythe. At a provincial stately home where Twiss had stopped on his way to Paris, he tried taking the Coopers to admire the collection of hundred-year-old carp that he had seen swimming in the garden's ponds. They had all been eaten.

Astley took back with him a horror of the violence he had seen, but also the knowledge that he himself had survived intact and with his democratic ideals preserved. 'A revolution may sometimes be a good thing for posterity,' he reflected afterwards, 'but never for the existing generation, for the change is always too sudden and violent.' However nightmarish the events of Paris, however badly the French Revolution had turned out, democracy itself was not dirtied. Disillusionment with France did not equal disillusionment with the dream of building a fairer society. Nor had surgery lost anything of its appeal. To see it done well was inspiring; to see it being done badly was even more so. The promises of surgery and politics were as bright then as ever. Astley returned with relief, ready to work. And he brought back to Britain with him not only new knowledge but also the physical cargo of some human remains – a parting gift from the French surgeon Chopart, a collection of anatomical dissections.

Human remains were not the safest cargo to try to carry out of revolutionary Paris. But then Astley was not in the business of being safe. He savoured those risks that seemed to him to advance the things he loved – and one of those was surgery.

Desault died suddenly of fever in 1795, having survived arrest and imprisonment during the Terror. He had helped to care for the orphaned son of the king, who, normally silent and unresponsive in front of his captors, had clung to Desault and wept when told that the surgeon's visits would no longer be allowed. There were allegations that Desault had been poisoned, and these persisted even after his friends could find no evidence of poison at their post-mortem. Chopart, who had been helping Desault care for the Dauphin, died within a day of his friend. His wife, at least, was in no doubt that the two men had been deliberately killed, and she blamed their deaths upon a dinner they had attended a short time before at the Committee of Public Safety – the body at the heart of the French revolutionary police state.

9

Showman Surgeon

By the end of September the Coopers were back in London. Ann, now eight months pregnant and growing easily tired, stayed at Jeffries Square while Astley whipped briefly northwards to Yarmouth to reassure his parents that they were both safe.

Mary Wollstonecraft, the radical author of *The Rights of Woman*, had done her best to get to France for the early days of the revolution. Her friends had prevented her, and she reached Paris only in December 1792. After her return to Britain she suffered from depression and made serious efforts to kill herself, on one occasion jumping from Putney Bridge into the Thames. Horace Walpole, one among many who found both her character and behaviour repulsive, called her a 'hyena in petticoats'. She met the philosopher William Godwin (a friend of Thelwall's) in 1791, and irritated him immediately. When they met again some five years later she produced a different effect, and the couple fell in love and married in March 1797. Their daughter, the future Mary Shelley, was born on 30 August 1797, and in the days after the birth Wollstonecraft sickened. She suffered from precisely the same disease that brought down many anatomists, a streptococcal wound infection. But whereas surgeons usually contracted the germ by accidentally inoculating themselves with tiny parts of the dead, with her it was by giving birth to the living. Her placenta did not fully come away. The part that was left, dead now that it was no longer nourished by the uterus, became a source of infection – effectively a piece of cadaverous flesh lodged inside her. The raw lining of her womb became infected and Mary died unpleasantly over the following eleven days.

The point of the tale is that it is only a modern fashion to speak of 'delivering a baby'. 'Delivery', originally, referred to the woman rather than her baby. Birth was dangerous, and the job of the attendant was to deliver a woman from that danger. It often proved impossible.

In his first winter of attending the Physical Society, Cooper heard the case – explained after dissection – of a woman whose womb had burst whilst straining to give birth to her child. The baby had passed through the tear in the womb and into the cavity of her abdomen, where it had died amongst the loops of her bowels. As it decomposed it gave rise to the same process of internal infection that killed Wollstonecraft; the mother died after almost a week of suffering, and when her abdomen was opened 'the Child was perfectly putrid'.

That had been the woman's ninth birth, and she had been unfortunate. Of all births, it is the first that is the most dangerous. The uterus and pelvis are untried, the labour longer and the outcome more uncertain. The Coopers were painfully aware of this. It was common knowledge, after all, and a professional involvement in medicine is not calculated to reduce awareness of awful possibilities. Astley grew increasingly anxious, recording his fears and worries in private notes.[*]

Back in London, the routine start of the academic year came against the backdrop of this uncertainty. The Coopers had been deeply attracted by the promise of a new world in France, only to be disappointed by its lies and violence. But democracy itself was untarnished in their mind – what they had seen and been repelled by was something different – and there still seemed pregnant prospects of new worlds, both in Astley's work and in Ann's body.

In the mornings Astley rose early, dressing carefully and receiving the daily attentions of his hairdresser Searle before leaving for the hospital to get in some private dissection before the day started. For a while he was taking a break from having corpses at home. Once the quiet hours were over he left the dead-house and ate a quick breakfast before the students arrived around nine. Then it was back into the dissecting room, now crowded with the living, for his duties as a Demonstrator. Increasingly that

---

[*] The existence and contents of these notes are recorded by Astley's nephew Bransby, but he gives no details and the documents themselves are now lost.

meant not only teaching the students anatomy and the technique of dissection, but helping them prepare their material in such a way as to show up particular structures – injecting blood vessels, delicately stripping out nerve fibres, exposing anatomical or pathological oddities in the most revealing way possible.

After lunch came the first lecture of the day. Astley spoke on anatomy from two o'clock until half past three, finding it relatively easy. There was still the labour of preparing his thoughts and getting his notes ready, but beyond that there was no difficulty. He knew anatomy thoroughly, and the subject required no conceptual innovations when it came to communicating it.

In the spare time between teaching and preparation came hours on the wards and in the hospital theatre, collecting experience, making notes on particular patients and their fates, and acquiring the practical skills that had to be learnt on the living. Then on alternate evenings came the second set of lectures, the ones on surgery. They had gone badly the previous year, and as a result the benches of the lecture theatre were mostly empty each time that Astley came in to speak. The disappointment hurt him, and he struggled to understand and fix it. The first week of October shot past with all of the concentrated mayhem of the start of the year. There was no sign yet of Ann's going into labour, but as far as the couple could calculate the baby was most likely due towards the end of the month. On Saturday evening of 6 October Astley left his heavily pregnant wife at home and made the familiar journey over to the Borough, the autumnal streets still bathed in daylight.

It was the first meeting of the year for the Physical Society. After the greetings and the public business of cases and theories, experiments and reports, the bureaucracy took over in earnest. There were elections to get out of the way. Astley was voted in as one of the society's six rotating presidents for the coming year, while his friend John Thelwall was brought onto the society's management committee. At the end of the meeting the two of them, along with a handful of others, retired to a nearby tavern to finish the evening together. There was much to talk about in addition to science and surgery. Both John and Astley were newly wed and with advancing careers. John was matching his pursuit of science with an ever more successful role as a public speaker, but his Society for Free Debate, like many similar groups, was under the suspicious surveillance of the Government. Astley's first-hand experience of the French Revolution gave him immediate allure among his band of democratic friends, and they heard him recount both his horror and his continuing belief in democratic principles. Acting as president of the Physical Society in the autumn of 1792, Astley was reprimanded for breaking the rules when he awarded a £5 prize offered for the season's best dissertation to a paper that had been handed in late, excusing his leniency on the grounds of the exceptional quality of the work. His action was overturned by the other members, who felt he had overstepped the powers granted to a president. The dissertation had been late, held the society, and was therefore disqualified. The society voted to take back the £5 but in its place, with full constitutional authority, award a special and separate prize of £10. What seems pedantic was an attempt to combine cold laws with warm justice, to offer a constitutional solution of a kind that the country as a whole was struggling, and failing, to find.

In addition to his hospital duties, Astley was now seeing significant numbers of personal patients for the first time. He was doing it out of charity, devoting a couple of hours a day to patients who could not afford to pay. They came to Jeffries Square and received their treatment for free, accompanied by gifts of whatever medications they might need. Such *pro bono* work was widely seen as being standard good manners for physicians and the higher ranks of surgeons.

Ann's £14,000 dowry was being invested in Astley's career, giving him the time and the means to acquire the best possible training. His duties in the hospital brought in very little, and patients added nothing. But at the same time as he provided a service that they would otherwise have had no access to, these patients gave him experience, a way of expanding his knowledge and enhancing his skills. He was conscious of practising on the poor in preparation for selling his skills to those with enough wealth to pay, but he saw no reason why that should trouble him. He had finished his surgical apprenticeship and was fully qualified. When he consulted for free he was not poaching a patient from someone with more experience, nor stealing them away from some alternative health care. He was a beginner, and he knew that that made him less safe, but how could he be endangering the poor by offering them his services? Such abilities as he had were better than nothing. Cooper's relations with his impoverished patients were both self-interested and generous.

At the weekends there were sedate carriage rides out to Tottenham to visit Ann's mother. The first few weeks of the academic season passed.

Then, as October came to a close, there were signs that Ann's labour was finally at hand. For all the fear that had gone before it, for all of the anxieties and terrors that Astley had confined to his diary and tried to hide from his wife, it was almost a relief that the moment had arrived. At least the uncertainty would soon be over.

The child was born early in November. She was healthy and vigorous, and her birth caused no great problems. Ann rapidly recovered from her labour and, a few days after the baby's entrance into the world, the couple named her. Anna Maria Cooper had arrived into a country that everyone agreed was trembling on the edge of a revolution. On 28 November the President of the French National Convention, the revolutionary government, welcomed messages of goodwill from democrats in London with the response that 'doubtless the moment is near when Frenchmen will bear congratulations to the National Convention of Great Britain'.

If revolution came, Ann and Astley would have to hope that it would be less bloody than the one they had already witnessed. Until then, there was nothing for it but to get on with things with as much energy as possible. Astley turned his mind to his lectures. The cause for their failure, he realised during the early days of Anna's life, was their abstraction. He himself had attended Hunter only after some years of medical training, and he had felt enlivened by the wider science and philosophy, enthralled by the animal experiments. Most of his own students were newer to the subject and more practically minded. They had less interest in what seemed abstruse and distant. They needed to be shown what was real and immediate.

In the evenings Astley sat with Ann, watching her and their daughter with fascinated astonishment. He was absorbed by the sight of Anna at her mother's breast, by the child's constant cries, her repeated calls for attention, and by his and his wife's answering feelings of love. Here was something even grander than the body's ability to heal, here was its capacity to grow from a physical act of love into an entirely new person. For an anatomist who continued to dissect babies, and a surgeon who operated on them, it was a particular pleasure to watch Anna's healthy development.

Astley's lectures suddenly became something quite different. He understood how to make them vivid. It was not enough to present Hunterian theory and expect people to be able to take an interest. They had to be won over. So he began to take the cases he found in the hospital wards, or the poor patients who came to see him in Jeffries Square, and to use them to tell stories. Only once the story had gripped his audience did he move on to theories of underlying pathology and recommendations for treatment. The students were faced with far less abstract theory or general statements. There was still a little, but it was quickly replaced by more graphic and memorable material. Lectures might begin with the general:

> *The danger attending these injuries of the brain arises principally from two causes: viz., inflammation, and the formation of fungus. 1st, Inflammation; and 2nd, Fungus; both of those may be conquered by prompt and scientific measures.*

but they swiftly moved on to the individual:

> *John Dent, a boy, aged eleven years . . . received a severe blow from the kick of a horse . . . The same evening he was brought into St Thomas's Hospital in a state of stupor, with a considerable tumour under the scalp. A longitudinal incision, to the length of two inches, was made, when immediately a portion of the brain made its escape, about the size of a small hazel nut . . . During the operation, small quantities of brain were escaping continually with the blood . . . Every depressed portion of bone being now sufficiently elevated, the wound was dressed superficially, and notwithstanding the great degree of stupor and insensibility he laboured under prior to the operation, his senses returned . . .*

Cooper used an ever increasing number of props, courtesy of the specimens that he laboured to acquire. So when he talked about fungus arising from a wounded brain, he held up an example. When he discussed sabre wounds to the skull, he could display parts of his previous patients. It was show *and* tell. Where Hunter had passed around only a handful of body parts during his entire lecture series, Astley began to do so at every opportunity.

Despite the attractions of home life, Astley continued with a demanding schedule of work, made more intense by his role as one of the Physical Society's six presidents. It was a troublesome time to have acquired such a post. In January there was a noticeable drop-off in attendance, and the stauncher members agitated for something to be done. Thelwall made the proposal that a committee be set up to examine the options, and, for his pains, was promptly elected to lead it. He too was busy attending a number of societies, and when the report of his committee was due he was unable to attend, sending a note explaining his conflicting engagement 'at a meeting of the Society of the Friends of the Liberty of the Press'. Thelwall's Society for Free Debate had been closed down by the Government as part of its campaign against any possible democratic uprising. The London Corresponding Society, however, founded in January 1792 by the shoe-maker Thomas Hardy, along with Astley's friends Thelwall and Horne Tooke, was flourishing. At the start of December 1792 Pitt's government had passed an act that mobilised a British militia, troubled both by the success of home-grown democratic societies and by the threat of an inva-sion from overseas. On Monday 21 January 1793, the French sent their king to the guillotine and sliced off his head.

At the end of the same week, on the Saturday, Astley listened as Thelwall presented a paper to the Physical Society. Thelwall spoke on the subject of 'Animal Vitality'. It was a debate about the nature of life, the problem with which Hunter began his lecture series. The relish with which the society anticipated Thelwall's delivery brought an unusually large audi-ence to the chilly January operating theatre. Thelwall's national reputa-tion as an orator was well known.

The talk turned out to be the most popular in the society's history. It was not only the manner of Thelwall's delivery, it was also what he had to say. The talk was a working-through of what it meant to be alive, of what was known about the property that differentiated animals from vegetables, or living creatures from those that had died. Hunter had dealt with this topic before, but with more caution. Radical enough when it came to great swathes of natural philosophy – of human and compar-ative anatomy, of dissection and vivisection, physiology and pathology – John Hunter remained conservative in some key areas. To a correspon-dent who wished to bring a French friend to see his museum, Hunter wrote, 'If your friend is in London in October (and not a Democrat), he is welcome to see it; but I would rather see it in a blaze, like the Bastille, than show it to a Democrat, let his country be what it may.' Equally, Hunter clung tenaciously to a belief about vitality that was part exper-imental but partly based on a literal interpretation of the Bible. Thelwall took him to task for this. Hunter said blood was the stuff of life, and he believed that the evidence lay in the words of Moses. Had not Leviticus proclaimed that 'the life of all flesh is in the blood thereof'? It was the coagulation of the blood, held Hunter, that marked the departure of an organism's vitality. As long as the blood was still fluid, a creature was not yet truly dead.

In a manner that Astley wholeheartedly approved, Thelwall's political radicalism led him to argue that eminent authorities were no guide to truth. The fact that Moses said something did not make it true; God might be all-knowing and all-powerful, but the men who spoke for Him had human flaws. The fact that Hunter was a great genius did not mean he was also infallible. Had Hunter not himself taught that the reputations of men were poor guides to the truthfulness of their beliefs, untrustworthy compared to what came from thoughtful experiment?

If Hunter was correct then the public were right to be horrified at human dissection, for blood was sometimes still liquid when a body was opened up. Perhaps these people were in some way still alive, maybe even retaining some sensation or awareness. Nobody might yet understand the means to restore them to health, but at least potentially they could be saved, just as some of those who were pulled limp from the Thames could be resuscitated. Thelwall argued against this notion of Hunter's. Was not the life of eggs destroyed, he pointed out, when they were frozen and then thawed, and had not Hunter's early belief that human life could be suspended and restored by such freezing and warming been proven false? Yet blood could be frozen and thawed without losing any of its fluidity or its ability to coagulate. It was true that blood was essential to the physical economy of an organism, but so were air and water to the life force of a plant, and that did not make either air or water themselves 'alive'. Hunter could transplant the testicle of a rooster onto the liver of a hen, and see it kept alive by the hen's blood, but that suggested nothing more than did the transplantation of a plant from one bit of soil to another. Blood was essential to life, but so were hearts and livers and muscles and guts. If any one organ was to get priority as being more essential than any other, Thelwall suggested it should be the brain.

He was even more categorical in rejecting the philosophical side of the argument: that there was a non-physical 'vital principle' that accounted for life. These beliefs of 'vitalism' went back past Aristotle to ancient ideas about spirits, but in their modern form they dated from seventeenth-century attempts at defining chemistry. The Frenchman Nicolas Lemery in 1675 had divided compounds up into animal, vegetable or mineral; just over a hundred years later Lavoisier combined the first two but kept Lemery's crucial idea of organic materials being qualitatively different from all others, that difference explained by a 'living principle'. What was this 'principle', Thelwall asked; was it a 'soul'? Thelwall argued the mechanist viewpoint, that life was inherent in the physical organisation of a body. Someone who spoke of a 'soul' or a 'living principle', as meaning a kind of superadded property, was merely being obscure. If a property had been added to a body, Thelwall said, then it was part of the body and a materialistic explanation was still the only comprehensible one. The only things that existed were matter and vacuum, something and nothing. Spirit, if the word meant anything at all, had to refer either to something or to nothing, to matter or to vacuum. There was no place for a soul that was defined as being neither and could be located nowhere. This was literally a non-sense, and so it was meaningless to talk about it. Nouns like 'spirit' that had been constructed from verbs were misleading. They were mental traps, pieces of verbal garbage, endlessly vague, behind which people could hide. Thelwall's challenge was to religious as well as scientific tradition.

He ended his talk with the physiological problem of respiration. It was clear that blood needed to pass through the lungs in order to maintain its nourishing properties. What was going on when it did so? What was it that was being transferred between the blood and the atmosphere, that changed the blood's colour? It was exactly the problem that Cooper and Coleman had investigated on so many dogs and cats. Thelwall was excited by the possibility that the answer might be 'electricity', the substance that Galvani had shown to have a miraculous vivifying power, that could return movement to the amputated leg of a frog.*

After Thelwall finished his presentation the society continued to discuss it, both for the remainder of that Saturday and for the following four weeks. Such was the impact of the first scientific paper of the man with whom Astley passed his Saturday evenings, whom Coleridge thought to be 'intrepid, eloquent and honest', and whom Wordsworth called 'a man of extraordinary talent'. For the next month the Physical Society discussed Thelwall's thoughts on the physiological basis for life. While they did so, France and Britain declared war.

At home, Astley's little daughter Anna Maria was doing well, and both

---

* The fact that Thelwall turned out to be so clearly wrong about electricity suggests something of the success of his overall argument. By tying his conception of the vital principle to a physical property, Thelwall made a statement that was precise enough to be tested. Precision was no guarantee that a statement would be correct, but it was a warrant that it would be sufficiently clear to allow thought and investigation the opportunity to reveal, in time, whether it was true or false.

her successes and her setbacks were a source of warm interest to her father. He noticed how much her constant little illnesses made her even more precious to both him and Ann. Along with his flourishing career, his concern for little Anna left less time for the politics that had been such a part of his life for the past six years. His beliefs were unchanged, but there is an absence of any comment by his friends or family on political activity around this time. In the years before Anna's birth it was something that his parents and their conservative friends often complained about. With a young child it was increasingly difficult to get to the evening meetings of the debating societies.

Thelwall, less encumbered, continued his political activities. According to the new *Oxford Dictionary of National Biography*, ' "Citizen" Thelwall quickly became the most prominent and articulate member of the reform movement, calling in his speeches for universal suffrage and an end to the war with France.' His language was seditious but he took care to say by implication what it was dangerous to say outright. He spoke about a cockerel lording it over a farmyard dunghill in such a way as to make the target of his analogy clear, but when the Government eventually tried a prosecution for seditious libel against Thelwall's publisher Daniel Eaton in February of the following year, 1794, Eaton was found 'not guilty'. Thelwall mocked the Government's members for having themselves said that they thought a pompous and tyrannical chicken was an obvious reference to the king. But not all threats came via the courts, and Thelwall took the precaution of reinforcing his hat to make it cudgel-proof and always walking down the middle of streets, the better to avoid whoever might be hiding in the shadows.

By the 2nd March Astley's baby was four months old and doing well. The Physical Society had finally finished its extended discussion of Thelwall's paper on the essence of life, and had voted him their formal thanks 'for his excellent and very valuable dissertation . . . and the instruction which this institution has received from his assistance on the debates thereon'. To hold that the soul had to be either something or nothing, that the difference between life and death could be determined by physiology rather than theology – such views were materialism. But the society voted Thelwall its praise nonetheless. It was the first time the society had ever issued such a declaration of admiration and gratitude, and it strengthened immensely the position both of Thelwall and of his friend Cooper, the president who shared his radical beliefs.

With Jeffries Square forming an increasingly attractive centre to his life, Astley began to spend more time there. The hospital dissection room was once again reserved chiefly for teaching, and he returned to his habit of taking his work home with him. Human corpses began to fill some of the house's more secluded rooms. The servants were instructed to bring in what dogs and cats they could, and other small animals – rabbits, snakes, frogs and chickens – were added to the growing menagerie whenever they could be bought or stolen.

The obvious horrors of the French Revolution made life difficult for those in Britain who advocated democratic change. Nothing undermined their position more than the example of what was happening across the English Channel. The cry of 'Liberté, Egalité, Fraternité' was inspiring but its practical results were proving murderous. The very word – 'revolution' – changed its meaning. Gone was its implication of a return to an idealised original state, some kind of primitive freedom, some honest and mutually beneficial relationship between men and their government. In its place was the spectre of something fiery and destructive. As the British Government cracked down ever harder on those who pushed for change, both sides saw the real possibility of discontent bubbling over into political action. The question of whether there would be a second English revolution was undecided.

In May 1793, as the academic season drew to a close, little Anna's frequent illnesses had taken on the appearance of something more than the normal run of an infant's coughs and colds. Her parents began to worry about her. Work, politics and every other activity of daily life took second place. Astley had been well trained, and he could see that Anna was beginning to struggle, even if he wasn't sure why. His suspicion of contemporary medications and his belief in the body's natural capacity for healing were the hard-won products of self-education and strenuous experiment. His daughter's health was failing, but neither ignorance nor desperation were going to drive him into seeking refuge in useless potions or damaging treatments. He rented a cottage in rural Pentonville, then a village to the north-east of London. Every morning after breakfast, while Astley continued his London studies, Ann and Anna took a carriage out to their little cottage, often accompanied by Cline's sister and her own infant son. The countryside in summer was to be Anna's therapy. Her parents rested their hopes on the healing powers of fresh air and peaceful, clean surroundings.

10

The Physical Society

Standing by the lecture theatre's rotating table, with benches full of students rising up on all sides of him and even the gallery crowded with faces, Astley had reason to feel a flush of pleasure. Autumn 1793 brought twice the audience of the previous year. The success was the result of the talent he had displayed the year before. Surgical sciences had long had an exciting grip upon his own mind; now in front of him were the attentive faces that testified to his ability to communicate that feeling. When Astley was pleased his face showed it, and the students at his first lecture could see his excitement.

His own abilities had summoned this audience into being, but another post came through patronage. Not long before the academic season started Astley had been invited to lecture at Surgeons' Hall. The previous incumbent had resigned after only a month, choosing idleness and leisure after marrying a lady of fortune. Astley, having made a similarly advantageous marriage himself, felt differently.

The Company of Surgeons was ambitious, sensing the rising fortunes of the profession. They began construction of Surgeons' Hall in 1747, with the demolition of a group of houses in the Old Bailey next to Newgate Prison, but it was delayed by endless arguments over the designs (the initial plans had been drawn up by the surgeon Cheselden, but these were amongst many that were subsequently rejected). Since it had no premises, the company had to forgo its corporate privilege of concentrating legal dissections and anatomical demonstrations in its own buildings. From 1748 the way was open for private schools to fill the enormous gap in the market. By the time Surgeons' Hall was completed in 1753 it was too small and too late to suck the business away from all the thriving private anatomy schools. It had to be content with remaining the architectural and symbolic centre of the profession's ambitions; a statement of intent. Astley's appointment as one of the most visible members of the company was prestigious, particularly given his age. He may have merited it, but he owed it to the benign intervention of Henry Cline and William Cooper (who was once again showing signs of familial friendliness). Both men were on the Court of Examiners, the ten-strong group of surgeons that effectively ran the company. The court met monthly to examine the fitness of candidates, with a particular focus on providing surgeons for the navy and army. The appointment of Astley as a professor was part of the company's efforts to reinvent itself as an active teaching institution. The value for Astley in the appointment – there was no wage – was in the publicity it gave him. He was already licensed for private practice by virtue of having completed his apprenticeship: this was his chance to attract some custom. Surgeons, like physicians, were forbidden from advertising for custom. It was a long-standing rule, an effort to mark themselves out as professionals rather than tradesmen, and it necessitated alternative approaches to self-promotion. Astley's new job was a fine way of exposing himself to a wider circle of his colleagues and making his name known in high society. His duties consisted of a small number of very public lectures. Surgeons' Hall had been built alongside the Old Bailey for the sole reason that it was the lecturer's job to dissect the bodies of hanged criminals. Such lectures, cheerfully obliging an audience with both voyeuristic gore and scientific interest, were terrifically popular.

When Astley stepped out in front of London's fascinated high society, he took part in the grand public theatre of trial, verdict and punishment. For the hanging itself the condemned's head had been covered with a hood. On the table of Surgeons' Hall the face was on full display. Before he began opening the corpses up, Astley could point out the livid and swollen face, the engorged ears and lips, the blue and swollen eyelids and the bloodshot eyes beneath them that projected forwards and were sometimes forced halfway out of their bony cavities. Bloody froth often covered the lips and nostrils and the room frequently smelled of the urine and faeces of the dead, expelled through terror or the physical convulsions of dying.

Against this gruesome background there was something winning about the sight of this healthy young surgeon, tall and confident, as he went about his work. He revelled in his qualities of showmanship, taking the bodies apart without a trace of hesitation. Nothing repulsed him and no ignorance made him pause. He took pleasure not only in showing off the anatomy, the normal structure of the human body, but also in displaying what was particular. The purplish-blue face, so horribly swollen, was evidence of the mechanism of death: a slow strangling, the arteries still able to pump their blood upwards through their deep and powerful channels around the spine, while the slacker veins could drain nothing away. He could point out all the details: the yellow crust of atherosclerosis inside the sliced-open tube of the aorta, the badly set old fractures of bones, the swellings of aneurysms and cancers and the evidence of hidden disease.

For each dissection the theatre was crowded, and Astley's performance was laced with round after round of applause. His words and his knife moved with equal wit, and the audience relished him. Old William Cooper watched and was delighted, quite forgetting his simmering anger at Astley's continuing democratic beliefs. Even Henry Cline, habitually terse with his encouragement, spilled over into compliment. Astley was elated. He recalled it all with evident joy. 'I was appointed Professor of Anatomy to the Company of Surgeons, and gave lectures on executed persons, which were received with great éclat, and I became very popular as a lecturer. The theatre was constantly crowded, and the applause excessive. My uncle was quite delighted, and Mr Cline complimentary, which he seldom was.'

Henry Cline probably had a shrewd idea that too much flattery would have a bad effect on his young protégé. But there was no immediate danger of Astley becoming self-satisfied and complacent; life was too uncertain for that. Baby Anna continued to grow, but her daily trips out into the countryside had not restored her to full health. She remained a sickly child. And outside these family circles the war with France rumbled on, contaminating the talk of politics and the wider world.

Thelwall wrote of how he had walked through Kent during the previous summer of 1792, dazzled at the sight of the white cliffs of Dover, excited both by the beach below and the cliffs above, by the English coast and the view across the narrow Channel that separated him from French liberty. He climbed up and down, eventually stranding himself somewhere halfway up the side of the cliffs. There he perched, 'though my heart beat an audible alarm . . . with all the calmness I was master of, beneath the hanging precipice, and contemplated the beautiful serenity of the spangled sea'.

While his description of his heart beating 'an audible alarm' had an emotional meaning, it also had a very peculiar physical one. For Thelwall's heart had the odd property of beating so loudly when he was excited, that it could be heard for a considerable distance. A man once crossed the street to ask him about the sound. His wife had been woken from sleep by it, believing the noise to be someone hammering at the door. Thelwall's heartbeat was the perceptible knocking of mortality; ever-present, everthreatening, a constant uncertainty. Long life in the late eighteenth century was a piece of striking good fortune, not a part of reassuring normality. Thelwall promised Cooper the post-mortem gift of his own heart, should he suddenly die. In the meantime, towards the end of October, both men sat and listened as the Physical Society discussed another heart of great interest to both of them. It belonged to John Hunter, and had stopped beating just three days before.

It was not the first time that Hunter's heart had stopped. Hunter had himself reported that it seemed his heartbeat would cease in response to violent exercise. He had prophesied the possibility of his sudden death and had even, the morning when it finally happened, predicted that his scheduled meeting with colleagues at St George's Hospital might bring it about. In those days St George's Hospital stood facing Hyde Park, not having yet made its move south of the river towards Tooting. In the board-room beneath the operating theatre, in the midst of a violent argument over whether to admit two students who had not formally completed the new apprenticeship requirements, Hunter collapsed and died.

The proximate cause was clearly the energy with which he had been speaking, an energy that had characterised his life. A more mediate cause, the Physical Society heard, was the physical degeneration of the structure of his heart. The valves were mineralised and stiff and Hunter's aorta had begun to stretch and dilate. He had not died from a burst aneurysm, but the evidence of the disease was there.

Hunter's post-mortem was an elegant demonstration of the state of science and society in 1793. He had specifically requested that his body be examined once he had died, and it was publicly opened in his own dissecting room. Hunter's students and colleagues peered inside his body as intently as they had followed his difficult lectures. The dissection itself was carried out by Everard Home, Hunter's brother-in-law. Just as relatives had surrounded Hunter in his profession, so they now did in his death. But Home, even as he cut Hunter up, showed a peculiar delicacy over his corpse. He refused, despite his brother-in-law's recorded wishes, to remove and preserve the parts of Hunter that the old surgeon had thought to be of public interest. Hunter had wanted his heart, so long a source of trouble to him, to be preserved, along with the Achilles tendon that he had accidentally torn and self-treated in 1766. Home followed neither of these wishes.

He also failed to identify exactly the ultimate cause of Hunter's death. What Home and his colleagues in the Physical Society lacked was knowledge and technique. They could not examine tissue with the stains and microscopes necessary to understand the microscopic damage caused by atherosclerosis. They could neither see nor imagine the streptococcal bacteria that damaged so many contemporary hearts during bouts of rheumatic fever. The exact cause of death escaped them.

Hunter died in debt and left his family in poverty, having spent his fortune on his experiments and the museum he built to house them. The Prime Minister Pitt refused to buy the specimens for the country, protesting he had no money even to buy bullets that might fend off the French. Hunter's servant was left topping the pickle jars up with alcohol, keeping faith with the floating relics of his dead master's work in the hope of better days.

As the sunshine of autumn faded, anniversary celebrations were held for Guy Fawkes night and the Glorious Revolution. Both events combined religion and politics. The Catholic Guy Fawkes had tried to blow up Parliament, the seat of the country's Protestant government, while the Glorious Revolution marked not only William and Mary's rescue of the country from the supposed threat of Catholicism, but also their acceptance of the terms under which they had taken their thrones. In 1789 revolution societies throughout the country celebrated the hundredth anniversary of the monarchy's agreement to be bound by Parliament and the people. Many saw the rosy promise of change across the Channel and looked forward to further revolutions at home. By 1793 it was clear that the French Revolution was something darker and different, but the anniversary of the Glorious Revolution was still a rich symbol for those who felt power in Britain had once again grown too concentrated and self-serving.

In London's Crown and Anchor tavern a celebratory dinner was held to mark the landing on English shores of William of Orange. The 5 November 1793 was a Monday, and one of the stewards of the revolution society holding the dinner was the twenty-five-year-old Astley Cooper. 'He went a step beyond the whiggism of those days,' a friend explained, meaning that his attachment to democratic reform had not abated.

Five days later and Astley was back in the Guy's operating theatre, his regular Saturday evening haunt. He told the other members of the Physical Society about a man he had once seen in Yarmouth, a patient of his old apothecary master Mr Turner. Astley could recall how strong and vigorous the man had appeared, and how, despite it all, his penis had swollen and become painful. Over the course of a few weeks the skin and then the flesh beneath broke down, and the inflammation spread down to the man's scrotum and into his testicles. His penis rotted open over the urethra within, and urine trickled out through the resulting holes, running into the open flesh of his scrotum and turning the little bit that was healthy into a rotting sore.

It had been agony, and the man had begged Turner to operate, to cut away what remained of his genitals. Turner had refused, explaining to both Astley and the man that he believed the disease to be cancer. The condition was fatal, and to operate would only be to needlessly inflict further pain.

The man listened but was not deterred. The pain had grown too awful for him to tolerate it any longer. He begged Turner, so insistently and with such earnestness, that the apothecary and self-trained surgeon finally agreed. He took out his instruments and removed the remnants of the man's penis and testicles. Astley continued the story:

The symptoms now abated, the wound soon put on a healthy aspect & in six weeks entirely heal'd – The orifice of the Urethra situated on the Perineum was extremely small & contracted in such a way as to direct the stream of urine over his left shoulder. These inconveniences however were not sufficient to induce him to submit to the introduction of a Bougie.

In other words, the man had nothing left between his legs save for a tiny constricted hole where his urine spurted out. That caused him trouble, but not enough for him to be willing to let the surgeon force a dilator into the hole to tear and widen it.

After Astley's presentation, a colleague began a discussion of what the function of a spleen might be – and tentatively suggested, on the basis of his own animal experiments, that it might serve as a reservoir for blood. Next came a discussion of what would now be called Munchhausen's syndrome: two cases in which women had arranged to have themselves cut for the stone. One had inserted pebbles in her urethra, eventually blocking her bladder entirely. Another had repeatedly placed stones in her chamber pots and reported urinating them out. Even Thelwall, although not a clinician, contributed a case at the close of the meeting: he described his experience of dog bites.

These apparently unconnected and meaningless cases, these gruesome stories of pain and deformity and disease, all told within the close atmosphere and spluttering winter lights of an operating theatre in central London, were a serious business for the men involved. Astley could appreciate this now, in a way that he had been unable to achieve on his first student visits. The pain that the society members spoke about was real, and they were the ones that the suffering turned to for help. They were required, on a daily basis, not just to hand out hope and health, but also to prognosticate: to give out their judgements as to whether an operation was worthwhile, or life likely to continue, or whether there was nothing left any longer but despair and death. The members of the Physical Society took themselves seriously, and whether they understood a case or not, whether they were ignorant or ineffective, they were right to do so. They were right not because they were all virtuous and worthy, and not because they possessed a full understanding, but because they were taken seriously by those who sought out their help. It was their life's work to provide the best treatments and explanations that they could – even if the treatments scarcely worked and the explanations rarely explained. They were the best that was available, and they knew it. The knowledge drove them to try to become better. So they spent their Saturday evenings in Guy's Hospital, clustered around the lamps in the theatre, surrounded by the cold dark English nights and the deeper darkness of ignorance.

11

Winter

On the evening of 14 December 1793, Astley made his way across London Bridge and into the Borough. It was coming up for six in the evening and the city sky was dark. The day had been cloudy and fretted by showers and by four o'clock the dusk had settled in.

As he saw the lights glinting back from the water of the Thames, Astley had two reasons for looking forward to that evening's Physical Society. Tonight the rotating presidency was his, giving him the running of the meeting, and the main business of the evening was to be another paper by Thelwall, whose name was now national property. The London Corresponding Society was the most successful of all of the English working- and middle-class democratic clubs, and he was its chief speaker. Only the Society for Constitutional Information held similar sway, and it did so by drawing its audience and membership from higher social circles.

Out of doors it was cold rather than freezing, a fine temperature for a brisk walk, and inside the hospital operating theatre it was not much warmer. The men of the Physical Society gathered at about six o'clock, milled around making their greetings, then took their seats. Astley called the meeting to order and the business began. After the mix of case histories and anecdotes, Astley introduced the main paper. It was a continuation of the theme that Thelwall had spoken on so successfully before. 'On the Origin of Mental Action explained on the System of Materialism' was ambitiously modern, and intentionally radical in its efforts to understand the physiological basis for life. Thelwall stood up to speak, assured and confident. He was well used to much larger audiences and more threatening atmospheres.

When he had finished, the discussion was surprisingly heated. Then for the next two weeks no one spoke about it, and Christmas and New Year passed peaceably. But at the end of a short but beautifully sunny day in early January, the discussion was taken up again at that day's Physical Society meeting. It should have lent relief from more anxious issues. Outside Guy's the country was sliding towards civil strife, and as the short days of January passed, events pressed in. On 20 January 1794, at the Globe tavern, Thelwall met with other members of the London Corresponding Society and discussed their next moves. The Government was becoming increasingly dictatorial. Citing the threat to national security, its members were arguing that English freedom was too open to Terror to be allowed to continue without restriction. The right to free speech needed to be judiciously curtailed while police and government powers had to be heavily increased. Critics were defamed as unpatriotic and threatened with prison if they continued to speak out.

At the end of their meeting the London Corresponding Society decided they should stand ready to call a 'General Convention of the People'. They meant something modelled on the meeting that had brought revolution to France. Thelwall was able to explain to Astley and the other democrats at the Physical Society that they had agreed to be very specific about the conditions under which they would take such an inflammatory step. They would call a General Convention only when all hope of milder measures was lost. They set out the specific criteria by which they would judge that the monarchy had betrayed its people and set itself up as a dictatorship: if Pitt and George III broke the agreements of the Glorious Revolution and landed foreign troops on home soil, if martial law was imposed, if the right of assembly was removed, or if habeas corpus – the Act preventing the Government from holding its citizens without rapidly bringing criminal charges – was suspended.

Astley's daughter was fourteen months old, and her health showed no signs of improving during the winter weather. At the Physical Society, with the world in uproar all around, the discussion of Thelwall's paper on the physiology of the brain continued for several weeks. Finally, towards the end of the month, some people had had enough. On 25 January, the presidency having rotated to Astley's old enemy Haighton, a motion was put that angrily blocked any further discussion on the subject. After stormy argument it was passed by thirty-nine votes to nineteen. Thelwall and three supporters immediately resigned from the society in protest. The meeting was cut short in disarray and not resumed.

To suggest that the mind was the function of the brain, that there was no superadded and invisible quality that could be called a soul, was certainly a radical idea, and accepting such a materialist view of life clearly carried other implications. Materialism implied atheism, and if there was no ineffable difference between man and animals, might it be that there were no similar differences between classes of men? Some physiological arguments removed problems that had seemed philosophical or theological. This one did the opposite: if the order of the world could not be unquestioningly assumed to be ordained by God, then Church and King conservatism lost its firmest foundation.

Thelwall's exploration of the physiological basis of life had made up the earlier paper for which he had been so warmly applauded, just as it now constituted the one for which he was shunned. In the space between those two talks neither he nor his arguments had significantly changed. What had changed was the ability of men to tolerate ideas that had fascinated them a short time before. Suspicion and paranoia were triumphing over open speech and free thought. 'He attempted to explain the elementary phenomena of the mind', wrote Thelwall's wife Susan, 'and . . . he followed precisely the same train of ideas as were pursued in the preceding paper, [but] nothing could surpass the fury of opposition with which he was assailed.' She felt that the change in her husband's reception at the Physical Society was clearly the result of wider arguments raging in English society. It was also, she complained, directly due to government propaganda against him, to 'thunders of ministerial denunciation . . . levelled at his head'.

The same week that Thelwall resigned from the Physical Society, the king ordered German mercenary troops to disembark on the Isle of Wight and at Portsmouth. It was a breach of the agreement by which the monarchy had existed since 1688; a *coup d'état* by the monarchy and the Government over the constitution they were meant to uphold and the people they were meant to serve. The Physical Society met again as normal the following week. This time their subjects were more circumscribed. Chiefly they discussed the nature of cold, then focused on whether or not parasitic worms might perforate through from the rectum into the blood. Afterwards came a discussion of the sex lives of plants. Astley remained a member, walking weekly across the Thames to talk of other matters than revolution, and returning late at night to his wife and his sickly child.

In March, at the age of sixteen months, Anna Maria Cooper died. She had been weak for some time, but the death itself still seemed sudden. Astley arranged for a post-mortem, but felt unable to take personal charge of it. The cause of death, his friends told him, was an accumulation of water in Anna's head. It was one of the many afflictions that doctors were able to describe without being able to understand or effectively treat,* and it is not clear what caused Anna to suffer from it. After the autopsy Anna's body was taken out to Tottenham and buried in the family vault with her maternal grandfather's.

Nothing had prepared Astley or Ann for the grief that came once their daughter was dead. The young couple retreated into a bereavement that swallowed up other feelings. The strength of Ann's feelings came as no surprise to her friends and remaining family, but they were struck by the reaction of her husband. Contemporary England was desperately familiar with infant deaths, and had little of the later mild distaste for open emotion. The stiff upper lip was a Victorian trait and in 1794 an outward appearance of indifference was not a badge of manliness. The degree of Astley's grief, nevertheless, made his friends worry about him.

On the evening of 13 May men were waiting in the street for Thelwall when he left his house. He had been expecting them. He knew that the secretary of the London Corresponding Society, Thomas Hardy, and Daniel Adams, his counterpart at the Society for Constitutional Information, had been arrested the day before and taken to the Tower of London. As the news had spread, friends and colleagues thronged to Thelwall's house. Hardy's wife was saying that the men who had arrested her husband had

---

* A smaller but still significant number of diseases are still described and named not for their causes but in terms of their pathological appearances. It continues to be a sign of medical ignorance over the underlying process that causes them. Asthma, named from the Greek for 'panting', is a common example.

spoken of treason. It was not a report that anyone took too seriously, since they knew the Government would not bring such a charge. Treason was a capital crime. Mrs Hardy must have misunderstood. The charges could only be those of sedition.

Thelwall knew that if Hardy had been taken, he was likely to follow. He left his house that evening hoping to deliver a lecture, but was arrested almost as soon as he was out of the door. He refused to give any information other than to correct the Government's spelling of his name and was taken to the Tower. The men who arrested Thelwall also took his papers: his letters and his notes, his essays, his poems and his journals. Prime Minister Pitt sat waiting with a secret committee, ready to examine the trawl of stolen documents. None were ever returned.

As soon as the arrests of the country's leading democrats had been made – twelve men including Thelwall, Horne Tooke and Thomas Hardy – Pitt went before Parliament to demand the suspension of habeas corpus. 'This great guardian of personal liberty', in the words of Charles James Fox, Pitt's political opponent, was suspended by the Commons at the Prime Minister's request. 'The Constitution itself being in danger,' Pitt said, 'the suspension ought to be acquiesced in by every man who loves the Constitution.' Those who loved freedom, he argued, ought to submit to its being restricted. His freedom-defending Government could now imprison its own citizens whenever it pleased, for as long as it pleased, without bringing charges against them.

With no pressure on them from the law, the authorities moved slowly. June found the prisoners still in the Tower and still without charge. Henry Cline visited regularly, providing medical care and encouragement to Thelwall and the other democrats who needed it. Horne Tooke's prison diary records Cline's visits on an almost daily basis, usually along with the terse note 'passed a bougie'. Clearly Tooke had some problem with his excretion, but there is doubt as to whether it was urine or faeces. (A bougie was most often placed to help with the discharge of urine, but after Tooke's first admission to the Tower there was a significant gap before Cline's visits began. If the flow of his urine had been completely obstructed then the delay would probably have been fatal. It is possible that Tooke's bowels, like the opium-poisoned ones of Coleridge, required some physical assistance.) There are no records of whether Astley also visited. On 6 October Thelwall learned that the Government was finally bringing charges against him. To his disbelief he was told that the early rumours were true: he was to be tried, along with his colleagues, for treason. The charge meant that if they were found guilty, they would hang.

For Pitt and the Government, the charges against the democrats were only a first step. Any reform, they feared, would lead to revolution. All opposition had to be obliterated. Once Horne Tooke and Thelwall and the others had been executed, a precedent would have been established. The Government would have shown itself able not only to imprison British subjects without charge, but also to manipulate the courts to hang those people it viewed as a threat. Pitt had a list of some two hundred names drawn up for surveillance and future consideration. It included such men as Coleridge and William Godwin.

In late October an anonymous article appeared in the *Morning Chronicle*. It argued that the prosecution brought by the Government made no legal sense. The Treason Act limited the crime to outright rebellion and regicide; to preach dissent or to campaign for change was something quite different. Free speech was a right. There was nothing treasonous about arguing for reform, or criticising the Government. The *Chronicle*'s article on the Treason Act, soon republished in pamphlet form, shaped the line that the defence lawyer Thomas Erskine took throughout the trials. He would act for each of the arrested men in turn. Along with trying to discredit the spies and informers that formed the bulk of the prosecution's evidence, opposing the Government's interpretation of what constituted treason seemed the defendants' best hope. But with the Government able to play a decisive role in choosing the juries for the trial, hope seemed slight.

Crowds gathered quickly and in force to see the prisoners moved from the Tower to Newgate to stand trial. From then on a mass waited around the gates outside, unable to see the action within but staying to hear news of it.

First to come to court was Thomas Hardy. At seven in the morning on the last Tuesday of October he was brought to the Old Bailey. The following Saturday, Erskine finished a major speech and was applauded loudly within the courthouse. The crowd waiting outside heard the applause and began to celebrate prematurely, believing that only an acquittal could have given rise to such warm approval. When Erskine left for home on the last day of the trial, which continued until half past one on the Monday morning, he found a crowd of supporters waiting. The *Morning Post* reported that 'wishing to express their sense of his extraordinary and brilliant exertions upon this day [they] immediately took the horses from his carriage and drew him home'. A few short days later, and to general amazement, the crowd got to do the same for Hardy when he was unexpectedly acquitted. The 'not guilty' verdict was received 'with a murmur of Joy' within the courtroom and by raucous appreciation outside.

The first case had been won. The second was that of Horne Tooke. Once more the Government tried to pack the jury. 'My God!' exclaimed a horrified Erskine to Tooke, after seeing the first nine selections. 'They are murdering you!' But he had underestimated both his own ability and the jury's sense of justice. Tooke too was acquitted.

Thelwall was the Government's last serious chance. It needed a conviction if it was to continue with the trials: the publicity surrounding the acquittals was too damaging. With his youthful legal training, his gift for public speaking and his strong sense of having committed no crime, Thelwall wished to defend himself. He had already written his final address. 'I'll be hanged if I don't plead my own cause!' he protested to Erskine. 'You'll be hanged if you do,' the lawyer retorted.

On the first morning of his trial, Thelwall sat in his cell at Newgate and composed a sonnet to steady himself. He called it 'The Crisis':

> It comes – the awful hour! – compatriots dear,
> Who oft, confiding in my honest zeal
> And keen attachments to the public weal,
> Bent to my artless theme the partial ear;
> Now search my breast with scrutiny severe:
> That breast which, frequent in the swelling pride
> Of youthful ardour, the stern threats defied
> Of distant danger: mark if now base fear
> Palsy its boasted future – or if now
> (Forgetful of the truths so oft upheld)
> Abject beneath the imperious foot I bow
> Of terror-vested power – suppliant! – depressed!
> Or one emotion feel, but what the breast
> Of Hampden or of Sidney might have swelled.

He felt he was representing people whose lives or choices prevented them for standing up for what they knew to be right. Those 'compatriots dear' were men like Astley, men whose love for democracy and desire for reform were strong, despite their reluctance to stand up for them. Thelwall was willing to die, and he knew there was a good chance that he would. He had no contempt for those who shared his views but not his prison cell; he understood that other men made other choices.

Court hearings lasted for four days and included an appearance from Henry Cline as character witness. Although the records of the trial are incomplete (a full transcript was not taken), it is unlikely that Astley was called – compared to the older and far more senior Cline, he was a less impressive witness. The judge summed up in favour of the prosecution and the jury retired to consider their verdict. Just under two hours later they returned and announced their verdict: they found Thelwall not guilty. The Government's campaign collapsed, and the charges against the remaining men were dropped. The prosecutions had failed, and the men of the two societies walked out of Newgate alive. No second wave of indictments took place. William Godwin, author of the anonymous article in the *Morning Chronicle* that had aided Erskine's defence, had unwittingly helped keep his own neck safe.

Ann retreated to the countryside, just as she had done when her daughter had first fallen ill. In Hornsey, to the north-east of London and a bit beyond Pentonville, Ann rented a small cottage. There she went to escape from city life, and in the evenings her husband rode out to stay with her, bringing his London news with him.

During the summer of Thelwall's imprisonment, Ann's grief showed little sign of easing. Astley distracted himself with his work: he had been elected once more to lecture over executed criminals at Surgeons' Hall, and though it took up little time it was an addition to his already heavy load. Ann for her part sought relief in the life of the village around her. She made friends with a working woman who had a toddler daughter, about the same age as Anna would have been. While the mother laboured, Ann increasingly looked after the little girl. Her name was Sarah.

In September the Coopers took a short trip to Yarmouth. When they returned Ann once again helped to look after Sarah. The child's mother was frequently ill, and Sarah stayed with Ann increasingly often. Nothing made Ann as happy as the presence of the little girl. For Astley, whose own youth had rested on the care of foster families, it was no great difficulty to join his wife in her growing involvement in Sarah's life.

Ann's attachment to the toddler who spent so much time in her lap grew rapidly. With it came a return of her spirits. The hours that she spent with Sarah were happy, and she was aware of the effect that the child was having on her. As Sarah's mother grew more ill, the hours Sarah spent with Ann turned into days. The two adult women agreed that Sarah should stay with Ann for as long as her mother's illness lasted – 'nor was there any difficulty anticipated in inducing the father, a man of dissolute habits, to accede to the proposal'. Within a short space of time after the agreement was reached, Sarah's mother died. The child was to stay permanently with the Coopers, to be brought up by them as their own. Astley's gift for fitting into families also ran to creating them.

The next few years passed as smoothly for Astley and Ann as they did tumultuously for the country as a whole. In 1795 Astley developed a curved aneurysm needle that became a standard piece of operative kit for over a century. Ann spent some of their wealth differently, subscribing to novels like Maria Illiff's two-volume *The Prior Claim*, to *Artless Tales* in three volumes by Margaret Hurry and to George Smythe's five-act comedy *The Generous Attachment*. The war with France rumbled on threateningly. Thelwall, shaken by the experience of his trial, retired for a while from the fight for freedom. By the end of 1795 he returned, his oratory and his passions recovered, his voice once more inflamed and inflammatory. He never rejoined the Physical Society, and for the time being his medical interests were put to one side. On 26 October he spoke to vast crowds at Copenhagen Fields in Islington. The organisers claimed that more than two hundred thousand attended. Three days later, driving in his coach from St James's Palace in order to officially open Parliament, George III was attacked by a mob. A carriage window was smashed – some said by a stone, others by a bullet – and a member of the rioting crowd pulled open its door. According to the Government, the king's life was only saved by a company of the Life Guards spotting the commotion and galloping up to his rescue. Arrests were made but no charges were ever brought, and the incident was probably a piece of propaganda constructed by the Government. But even if the attack had been invented, it demonstrated that those in power felt that the threat against them was real. Pitt dwelled on the possibility of sharing the fate of Louis XVI, predicting that if he lost his grip on office he would lose his head within the following fortnight. George III wondered privately if he was likely to be the last king of England.

An Act for the Safety and Preservation of His Majesty's Person against Treasonable and Seditious Practices and Attempts was presented. It formally expanded the definition of treason to include any incitement against the monarchy or the Government: to include, in other words, all forms of political opposition. The Act to prevent Seditious Meetings and Assemblies banned any meeting of more than fifty people if the purpose of that meeting was to press for reform. Anyone who ignored the ban would be liable to the same penalty as someone found to be treasonous – death by hanging. Having found himself unable to hang whomever he chose, Pitt simply changed the law to make sure he would have less difficulty in future. He argued that the attack upon the king's carriage had been the direct result of the London Corresponding Society meeting at which Thelwall had spoken. A royal proclamation was published, declaring that the attack upon the king had been part of a deliberate plot by the society. It was pointedly released on the first anniversary of the 1794 acquittals.

This time round Pitt won. His Bills became Acts and the Acts became laws, reaching the statute books a few days before Christmas. Membership of the two societies immediately fell away. Thelwall was forced from the stage, the Government having made it death to be either a speaker or a member of the audience. The best that Thelwall could do in response was to tour the country lecturing on classical history. Now when he spoke of tyrants and of republics, the names he used were Caesar and Brutus, Greece and Rome, and so the meetings were not technically treasonous. All the same his message was clear, both to his audience and to the authorities. The meetings were often violently broken up by Government-organised mobs. Thelwall took to carrying a loaded pistol about with him, using it to defend himself against the mobs and against the Government agents that attempted to press-gang him into the navy and out of the public eye.

The 1794 trials that had taken place in the Old Bailey had been for a capital crime. Astley, the lecturer of Surgeons' Hall, must have wondered if, in the event of a guilty verdict, he would find himself publicly dissecting his friend. Thelwall had come a whisker away from making inadvertently good on the offer of allowing Astley to examine his brave and strangely audible heart.

12

Surgeon to the Dead

With Sarah as her adopted child, Ann grew happier. She moved back to London, to the couple's home in Jeffries Square. Private dissection and vivisection at home started the day off for her husband. After that he dressed for the day, still with care, and received his morning's visit from his hairdresser. The effect was impressive. A colleague described him at the time as having 'decidedly the handsomest, that is, the most intelligent and finely-formed countenance and person of any man I remember to have seen. He wore his hair powdered, with a queue, then the custom, and having dark hair, and always a fine healthy glow of colour in his cheeks, this fashion became him well.' After breakfast, he spent an hour or two seeing poorer patients for free. The rest of his day was mostly taken up by the hospital.

Medical and surgical care was often lengthy and ineffective. The number of patients entering and leaving the charity hospitals was far below what we would expect today. In the 1790s the London Hospital in Whitechapel, probably the busiest in the capital, saw only about fifty outpatients a week. The number of new patients admitted onto the wards was about half that. (By comparison Guy's and St Thomas's today see a combined total of three quarters of a million patients a year.) Data from the end of the twentieth century in Britain showed that around 160 per 1,000 people were admitted as inpatients each year, while enough people had outpatient appointments to render the yearly average more than 1,000 per 1,000. In Astley's time the average *combined* figure for both out- and inpatient attendances was closer to 2 per 1,000. The wards themselves were still often overcrowded, but only because each patient's stay was extended over weeks or months. There was plenty of time within a surgeon's schedule for research, teaching and private practice. Astley, partly by choice and partly because he lacked the position as senior surgeon that would make him sought after, had very little of the latter.

The summer of 1796 saw an unusual respite from the normal routine. Astley was asked to provide surgical help to a man engaged to fight a duel. Both parties were British, but as the law forbade duelling they planned to fight in Hamburg. It was a slightly half-hearted business on the part of Lord Valentia, upset at the relations between his wife and a Colonel Gawler. The piqued lord was encouraged to duel by his relatives, but having already begun a legal action against the colonel he protested that he could not challenge him physically at the same time. So a quarrel was arranged with the colonel's brother instead, and it was this Mr Gawler who retained Astley's services.

It was an opportunity for Astley to visit some of his wife's German relatives, and too intriguing to pass up. He travelled by packet with Gawler's party and spent a few days in Hamburg. When it came time for the duel the two men, their seconds and their surgical attendants all decamped outside the city. Facing each other at twelve paces distant, they exchanged shots. 'I am hit!' exclaimed Lord Valentia, staying on his feet. His second asked him where he was hurt and Valentia opened the top of his coat. Blood covered his neck and ran down the shirt beneath. Mr Gawler was uninjured.

Although he was there to take Gawler's part, Astley hurried to help Lord Valentia. His Lordship's own surgical attendant melted away beside the enthusiastic skill of the London surgeon. With Valentia's clothes pulled away from his neck, Astley could see that the ball had entered his chest immediately below his collar bone. He pushed his finger into the wound in Valentia's chest, feeling for any metal within. With his finger shoved in to the knuckle he could feel nothing, only the ball's track curving around the line of Valentia's second rib. Mr Gawler, watching, assumed he had inadvertently killed Valentia and took to his heels, fleeing on foot to the Danish border and getting lost on the way. Despite his rapid departure he proved to be both the better shot and the kinder man: it later turned out that he had deliberately filled his gun with only half the normal amount of gunpowder in an effort to avoid killing his opponent.

Astley continued to probe Valentia's wound until he announced himself satisfied that the ball had simply glanced around the rib and cut its way out. Valentia survived, Mr Gawler eventually found Denmark, and on the way home Astley – for what seems the first time in his life – grew so frightened that terror unmanned him. 'Not the riches of the Indies,' he announced once the boat had safely reached England and his seasickness had worn off, 'should ever again induce me to make a longer voyage than from Dover to Calais.'

It was back to the altogether more homely environment of the ward, the operating theatre and the mortuary.

Thirty years before, in 1765, the Derby artist Joseph Wright had painted *Three Persons Viewing the Gladiator by Candlelight*, a scene of men admiring an illuminated model of the Borghese gladiator. It drew applause at that year's meeting of the Society of Artists. But the following year he caused even more of a sensation. In his 1766 painting, *A Philosopher Giving that Lecture on the Orrery in which a Lamp is put in place of the Sun*, a sage old man addresses a small group. Three children press close in fascination while two youths admire and take notes, and an adult gazes upwards towards the philosopher. At the centre of the scene is an orrery, a mechanical model of the solar system, and the light shines out from the lamp that serves the place of the sun. The youngsters look at the illumination coming from the centre while the grown man looks at the light being spread by the philosopher's words.

Science, Wright was saying, was not only worthy of the same interest as art, it was potentially as profound, as capable of potently lighting up the world. Two years later, Wright painted *An Experiment on a Bird in an Air Pump*, a picture of a philosopher asphyxiating a bird. It is recognisably a related scene with a similar crowd. But there is horror on some of the faces, and even the ones that watch in fascination are sombre and earnest. What looks like a human skull in a glass jar sits, brightly lit, at the centre of the painting. To study the mechanisms of life is to study the advance of death, and the cost of looking into the abyss is hanging everywhere in the air. Wright was speaking to his audience about the mysteries of air and breath that somehow made up the unique quality of being alive, but he

146

was also making sure his audience had a long uncomfortable think about the ambiguities and ambivalences of vivisection and the tools for exploring these new worlds of knowledge.

The public were right to worry that equipping surgeons to operate also made them capable of cruelty. In order to anatomise the dead and cut into the living, one needed at least a working indifference to pain. Astley ignored the protests of his patients once an operation had begun. When they instructed him to stop, he carried on regardless. How could he have done his job otherwise? He admitted that he had little sympathy for bodily pain, but to a large extent he managed to keep many of his sensibilities intact. When he was presented with a posthumous letter from a favourite student who had committed suicide, he wept convulsively. In front of another student, he once prepared to carry out one of the most trivial of all his operations: removing a mole. The sweet-looking young boy who was his patient walked into the room and looked up at the surgeon with a trusting smile. Astley burst into tears.

The academic year of 1797–8 brought change. Astley's lecture work increased: he was engaged by the Company of Surgeons to speak on comparative anatomy. His experience in vivisection and in exploring the anatomy of the dead qualified him for the job, but his knowledge fell short of the comprehensive grasp of zoological anatomy that he needed for his talks. The amount of work required was monumental, and he knew he would be unable to manage it by himself in addition to his other duties.

Meanwhile, Henry Cline was leaving the house at St Mary Axe where Astley had lived for so many years, and moving to Lincoln's Inn Fields in Holborn. In the same year the Company of Surgeons, with which Cline continued to be heavily involved, moved its headquarters from Surgeons' Hall by the Old Bailey to a new building at 41 Lincoln's Inn Fields.* In September 1797, Cline offered Astley his old house. Astley wrote:

Mr Cline is going to the other end of the town, and has left me his house in the city, which I feel myself strongly disposed to take. It is well

---

* The new property cost the company £5,500. Adjusting for inflation that is the rough equivalent of £330,000 today: the fact that the same property in Lincoln's Inn Fields would today sell for many millions of pounds is an illustration of the difficulty of converting currencies across the centuries. Adjusting for inflation underestimates the change in buying power.

*calculated for private practice, and has also a large warehouse attached
to it, which will make a most admirable dissecting room. I already,
prompted by fancy, figure to myself the effect of our united labours in
this most convenient place.*

Astley was writing to John Saunders, a young man who had come to
the Borough Hospitals after finishing a five-year provincial apprenticeship. Saunders had made his way through two further years of London
hospital training, and his abilities had impressed people. He not only
worked hard and dissected well, he had an artistic gift for understanding
and explaining complicated three-dimensional structures that inspired
both Astley's admiration and his jealousy. In the middle of an argument
the student was able to grab whatever material was to hand – a piece of
half-burnt wood from the fire, its end acting as a charcoal nib – and draw
the relations between physical objects with such precision and accuracy
as to trample over any incorrect opinions. Astley wanted Saunders to get
the Demonstrator's job at Guy's, but in the meantime he wanted the
younger man's help in preparing for the lectures on comparative anatomy.
He offered Saunders a wage along with bed and board at St Mary Axe.
'I live in a plain economical style,' he warned. 'You are only to expect a
joint of meat and a pudding.' Not put off by the lack of a fish course,
Saunders accepted.

So in the autumn of 1797 Astley moved back into the large and imposing
house where he had lived as apprentice. This time he was master of the
place, and he had Ann and Sarah with him. He converted the warehouse
into a dissecting room, painting over its windows for privacy, and made a
large portion of the spacious loft into a menagerie. The yard in front of
the house left plenty of room for carriages to draw up with visitors or
discreet deliveries. Some of the reception rooms were used for patients,
either as places where they might wait in moderate comfort, or be examined, undergo small operations, and recover afterwards. Occupying Cline's
house also brought in some of the private patients that had attended him,
although Astley's private work remained small – around £200 a year. Most
of his labour was still in learning, but he was confident about the future
'because, if no stroke of adverse fortune prevents it, my income must be
yearly improving'. Soon after he moved into St Mary Axe he was hastily
summoned back to his old house at Jeffries Square by the alarmed owners.
A viper had emerged from the fireplace during breakfast. There was no

cause for alarm, Astley reassured them, it was merely one of the many animals he had kept for experiments, and it must have somehow escaped in a previous year and hid in the fireplace for its warmth. There is no record of whether the new residents of Jeffries Square were reassured by such an unusual explanation.*

In general, Astley's neighbours were remarkably tolerant. They were aware of what he did, but eighteenth-century London was not short of eccentrics, and if you kept your odder activities behind closed doors then most people were willing to let you be. Society as a whole, however, was less inclined to ignore the practice of body-snatching. As the nineteenth century loomed, the number of anatomical schools and surgical trainees in London began to increase. The price of bodies went up accordingly. And there were markets beyond the anatomical schools. 'I do not think', said a professor of anatomy at Trinity College in Dublin, 'the upper and middle classes have understood the effects of their own conduct when they take part in impeding the process of dissection . . . very many of the upper ranks carry in their mouths teeth which have been buried in the hospital fields.'

Not that the benefits were restricted to cosmetic ones. Astley described vividly to his students the horror of watching surgeons operate when they had insufficient knowledge of anatomy. With the patient strapped down, fearful and in pain, everything would stop whilst the surgeon tried to work out what exactly it was that he was about to slice into. Since operations were few, far between and generally well attended, there were usually plenty of people whose opinions could be polled if the operating surgeon felt some doubts about his procedure. 'Hence,' said Astley, 'the frequent pauses in the operation and the hesitating appeals to the judgement of the bystanders, [as to what] . . . the membrane immediately under the knife is or is not.' Accurate and profound anatomical knowledge was essential. How could it be acquired in a country whose scaffolds, laden as they often were, bore less fruit than was required?

John Collins Warren was a young American, over from Boston in the late 1790s to study at the Borough Hospitals. Edward Warren's biography quotes from a letter home:

---

* 'I had kept many snakes, vipers, and frogs, to watch them through the winter,' said Astley. Animals that were cold-blooded, or actually hibernated, were particularly intriguing to those trying to understand the nature of life, and how bodies that were cold and motionless might be brought back to warm animation.

149

Dissection is carried on in style: twelve or fifteen bodies in a room; the young men work on them in different ways. The people called resurrection-men supply us abundantly. An odd circumstance happened some time since. A hungry beggar got some bread and ate it with so much avidity as to suffocate himself and fall down in the street. One of the resurrection-men, passing, immediately claimed the man as his brother, took him to the dissecting-room of St Thomas's, and secured a good price.

The resurrection-men had many names: body-snatchers, exhumators, lifters or grabs, sack-'em-up men, resurgam homo. And their commodities were also blessed with a range of euphemisms: things, subjects, stiff 'uns, corpses, bodies. Adults were called 'larges' and children 'smalls'.

It was a boom time for the Lord's humble labourers in the vineyards of the dead. The number of surgeons was increasing, and the extra live bodies needed extra dead ones. New workers flooded into the grave-robbing field. For men who made their living as porters or grave diggers, as sextons or thieves or irregular unskilled labourers, there was an astonishingly attractive amount of money to be made if they could get hold of 'something for the surgeon'. And as the theft of bodies began to rise and became more notorious, so did public opposition. Some of it took a practical and immediate form: high walls covered in broken glass and hidden spring-guns in dark graveyards. There were sextons with cudgels and firearms, standing guard or at least demanding to be bribed. There were body-snatching colleagues, ready to steal or inform, keen to guard their own turf and the ripe treasures beneath. And surrounding it all was the dangerous prospect that any group of passing people might suddenly transform, when news or suspicions touched them, into a mob. Grave-robbers were beaten and whipped to death, their families assaulted, their homes destroyed.

Unsurprisingly, such men were not the most straightforward to deal with. The hospitals and surgeons faced the danger and difficulty of dealing with those who operated in the shadows, who lived on the wrong side of the law's sharp edge. With their fluctuating prices and promises, the body-snatchers could destroy an anatomical school by not supplying it. And along with their frequent drunkenness and unreliability, many were also violent, strong and reckless.

Years later, in 1831, when a London body-snatcher called James May was arrested on suspicion of having murdered a boy in order to sell his corpse, he was open about one part of the business. He cheerfully admitted that he had smashed in the boy's jaw. 'And what does it amount to? I did use the brad awl to extract the teeth from the boy, and that was in the regular way of business.' The boy was dead anyway, May argued, and they had been about to take his body to Guy's. A dentist was happy to testify that May had sold him twelve fresh-looking teeth. They still had bits of gum attached.

What normally happened to a body after death was important. The corpse had to be laid out in the correct manner. The final offices – straightening the limbs in the right manner, closing the eyelids with coins until rigor mortis had sealed them shut, tying up the chin – mattered greatly to many. Bodies were washed, their orifices plugged. Food and wine might be consumed, sometimes with the specific purpose of taking away from the dead the sins they had committed in life. Correct burial was important. Part pagan and part Christian, practices varied. Bury the body with the feet facing east. Wrap it in linen, for Christ was buried in linen. Sit with it until burial to protect the soul from evil spirits.

Official religious views were divided on what a body required after death. Some worried that a body which was marred as a corpse might not return whole after the resurrection. As late as 1942 the British philosopher Isaiah Berlin sat in a New York Jewish religious court and listened, impressed, as the judges dealt with just such a case. An old man's leg had not been returned to him after the operation to amputate it. The thought of spending the rest of his life without it did not terrifically trouble him, for he knew he was old. What he found appalling was the prospect that, on the day of resurrection, he would still be hobbling – that if his leg were not buried with him, he would spend all eternity without it.* Others felt that the Almighty, able to bring the dead back to life, would not be troubled by such details, and that a reincarnated spirit would as easily find its bones in a museum as in a tomb. Modern concerns over the medical profession's secretive and illegal retention of human organs do not relate solely to the

---

*The judges eventually settled on ceremonially burying a token piece of the man, something like a fingernail, to stand in for the leg, with the conclusion that God would respect their efforts enough to make good with a whole limb when the Day came. Berlin was moved by the decision, feeling he had witnessed judicial power being exercised with genuinely good intentions.

offensiveness of the practice. The same feelings – that the integrity of the corpse is in some way essential to a person's afterlife – are still present.

In the eighteenth century those who died on the scaffold had a pressing reason to wish themselves safe after death from the surgeon's knife. By the twentieth century hanging was supposed to be a quick death. The drop and the jerk were designed to dislocate the joint between the first and second vertebrae in the neck – the 'atlas' on top, supporting the weight of the head, and the 'axis' below. A bony peg rises up from the axis, allowing the head to rotate about it on the column of the spine. A prompt dislocation between the first two vertebrae, particularly with the presence of the bony peg, destroys the spinal cord at that level. The nerves that control breathing emerge from lower down, beneath the third, fourth and fifth vertebrae. Death is not so quick as with a guillotine, as the heart continues to pump blood to the brain. But no air moves in or out of the lungs, so life does not stretch beyond the minute or two it takes to suffocate.

In Astley's day hanging was not so precise, nor was it intended to be. Physical pain was a larger part of the world, as was the conviction that justice was there not only to deter but also to punish, harshly and publicly. Those who were hanged usually died slowly, gradually choking, their necks unbroken and their lungs in full working order. They could keep the noose from crushing their windpipe so long as their neck muscles stayed strong. That depended upon the knot and the rope, upon the drop and the jerk, and upon what reserves of vitality and terror they could bring to bear whilst they dangled. There are a great many nerve endings in the windpipe, enough that deeply unconscious or comatose patients will often show signs of distress when a breathing tube is pushed or pulled along it. Death by hanging was slow, terrifying and painful. It was also not certain. Asphyxiation could cause unconsciousness without killing. The pressure on the windpipe could be relieved by the hanged body being cut down. If the brain had not been without oxygen for too long, if the windpipe had not been crushed, it was possible to survive. It was an accident that did not happen very often, but it definitely happened. So there was the prospect that if you were cut down from the hangman's noose you might be dissected by the surgeons while you were still alive.

There was also the problem of when exactly death occurred. It was not clear precisely what it meant to be 'alive' or to be 'dead', nor could anyone be sure of the nature or location of the boundary between the two. A vast amount of thought and exploration was being poured into trying to understand the properties of life. Was the definition a philosophical one? Religious? Scientific? Could it be established through thought and logic, from scripture and divine guidance, or via hypotheses and experiments? Even the method by which the answers might be arrived at was unclear.

When it came to hanging, John Hunter was confident enough about the nature of life and death to make a practical effort to intervene. When Astley was still a boy of nine years old, running around Norfolk in a scarlet coat and with his hair falling in ringlets down his back, the Reverend Dodd was sentenced to hang. It was for forgery, a crime the Reverend committed when his taste for high living ran him into debt. In the summer of 1777, his appeal failed, despite popular sympathy and the exercised eloquence of Samuel Johnson. But Hunter was there to save him. Hunter knew how hanging killed and he knew that it sometimes failed. He had spent many years experimenting on animals and on humans, alive and dead. Like previous members of the Royal Society he had experimented to see how long hearts could beat after being removed from bodies and how animals could be kept alive by artificial ventilation. He had helped with the guidelines issued by the Humane Society for resuscitating those pulled from the waters of the Thames.

Dodd hung at the end of a noose for an hour. It was almost as long again before he was carried away from Tyburn and delivered to Hunter. Despite the surgeon's best efforts the experiment was a failure. But it seemed worthwhile to Hunter to have made the attempt, and he ascribed the failure of his efforts to the delay in obtaining the body. His lack of success did not dent his conviction that the possibility for revivification existed. And if John Hunter, the greatest experimental physiologist of the age, had such doubts and uncertainties over the borderline between life and death, how was anybody else to be certain? When the body-snatchers were also called resurrectionists, it was not just in dark jest. There was a degree of ambiguity.

It was a widely held belief that the living principle did not leave the body in an instant. In an era with no knowledge of neurophysiology, no access to understanding that human life was perpetuated by electrical activity in the brain that required a degree of continuity, this was a reasonable belief. It had been the nub of Thelwall's disagreement with Hunter. Did the living principle leave when blood clotted, when the body cooled?

Did the soul – whatever that was – stay near the body for a while after death, or depart more rapidly? Could it be damaged by what was done to the body whilst it appeared lifeless? There were rational grounds for being concerned about human dissection. Vesalius had written of removing the heart of someone who had been killed in an accident and finding that it was still beating. Might anatomists be performing their dissections in a manner that would one day seem similarly hasty?

Robert Christison qualified as a physician at Edinburgh in the early 1800s. Like Astley, he trained partly under William Cullen. In his autobiography, published posthumously in 1885, he recalled his anxieties over the dissections he had witnessed as a youth. After a death, he wrote, there was almost a competition between

> *the relatives and the [surgical] students – the former to carry off the body intact, the latter to dissect it. Thus dissection was apt to be performed with indecent, sometimes with dangerous haste. It was no uncommon occurrence that, when the operator proceeded with his work, the body was sensibly warm, the limbs not yet rigid, the blood in the great vessels still fluid and coagulable. I remember an occasion when Cullen commenced the dissection of a man who had died one hour before, and when fluid blood gushed in abundance from the first incision through the skin . . . Instantly I seized his wrist in great alarm, and arrested his progress; nor was I easily persuaded to let him go on, when I saw the blood coagulate on the table exactly like living blood.*

Astley had once assisted John Hunter in the dissection of a whale, probably one of several unfortunate enough to swim into the Thames and end up in Hunter's museum. But it may have come from further afield. Friends sent Hunter specimens, and at one stage he even managed to get his hands on a sixty-foot sperm whale. Even if the whale that Astley helped to dissect was only the seventeen-foot specimen despatched to Hunter from the Severn estuary near Berkeley by his friend Jenner, it was large enough to impress. Astley admired the old man's effort and the way in which he was willing to wade thigh-deep in a rotting corpse in order to see what it was made of. John Abernethy, a contemporary London surgeon noted in Bettany's *Eminent Doctors* described Hunter's appearance during a dissection:

... he would stand for hours motionless as a statue, except that with a pair of forceps in either hand he was picking asunder the connecting fibers of some structure ... patient and watchful as a prophet, sure that the truth would come: it might be in the unveiling of some new structure, or in the clearing up of some mental cloud; or it might be as in a flash, in which, as with inspiration, intellectual darkness becomes light.

Cutting with a scalpel was only rarely the appropriate method for parting flesh; both in the dead and in the living a surgeon wanted to separate certain structures from others, not slice regardless through whatever happened to be under the blade. Blunt dissection – pulling apart flesh along its natural lines of cleavage – was slow and painstaking but it was the only way to reveal rather than destroy. Using blunt metal probes, forceps and fingers, a good dissector worked with gentle steadiness. Cooper, like Hunter before him, was an excellent dissector, and with the older man dead, he began to take over some of his empire. Astley let his interest in acquiring unusual animal and human remains become publicly known. It occasionally brought unexpected results. The owner of a dead kangaroo, for example, sent it for a post-mortem. The valuable animal had been lying on a bed of straw in a London stable, and there had been a fire, but the kangaroo had not appeared to have been badly burnt. Its death was unexpected and unexplained. Astley was able to show that although the burns had not been extensive, they had affected the animal's genitals, resulting in its urethra being scarred shut. It died from being unable to open its bladder, which eventually burst from the pressure of the urine within it. As well as accepting such unusual gifts, Astley also arranged with the keepers of the royal menagerie, then held in the Tower, to receive whatever animals died there.

It was part of a wide-ranging effort to acquire both knowledge and specimens from throughout the animal kingdom. If unusual creatures were brought to London by fishermen or explorers, Cooper arranged to be the first to know about them. Someone brought him a woman's foot that had been found floating in a river in Canton, her bones deformed by the binding of her feet. When he delivered the lectures on comparative anatomy, the fruits of his own and Saunders's work were literally on display, and his talks were fragrant with hundreds of newly dissected, injected and coloured specimens: 'an overpowering discourse, and highly perfumed! – the preparations being chiefly recent, and half-dried and varnished'.

155

When an elephant died in London's menagerie, a message was sent. Did Astley want it? He most certainly did. So with difficulty the creature was heaved into a cart and brought through the City streets to St Mary Axe. For all Cooper's democratic tastes, for all that he was sociable and clubbable, friendly and charming in private and comfortable and assured in front of a lecture audience, he was nervous of mobs. Perhaps it was the memory of being overlooked by builders while dissecting human remains in his student bedroom, or perhaps Paris had given him a distaste for such a formless and frequently violent mass of people. Astley had the elephant covered with a large cloth during its journey, trying to attract as little notice as possible. When it arrived he did everything he could to move it through into his dissecting room in order to work in private – but the elephant was too large even to be got through the doors of the former warehouse.

He began to cut it up where it lay. As he did so, a crowd quickly gathered to watch, pressing themselves up against the iron railings that bordered the courtyard. Soon there were so many watching him that all the traffic in the street outside came to a stop. He could have chosen to perform for the crowd, to show them some of the theatrical flair he displayed so confidently and so often for the Company of Surgeons or in the theatre of Guy's. Instead, and quite unusually, his nerve failed him. He had his servants drag the elephant as far into the courtyard as possible, then had carpets thrown over the iron railings to block off the view.

In the last heated years of the 1790s, a mixed crowd of Londoners was too much for him. Even for those who had managed to hold on to democratic beliefs – perhaps especially, given the frequent violence of the conservative 'Church and King' mobs – there was something menacing about the masses.

13

Surgeon to the Hospital

For a boy who had grown up in the countryside with a love of being out of doors, the life of a London surgeon was occasionally stifling. Fortunately the city, then as now, was full of parks.

In the mornings, when the weather was warm enough to be comfortable, Astley went riding. As well as the pleasure of the exercise there was the enjoyment of dressing up. His favourite outfit at this time consisted of tall polished boots and yellow buckskin breeches topped off by a light blue coat. When a man went to so much effort over his dress, he could hardly be reproached for making sure his hair did not let him down. Searle had been hairdresser to Henry Cline's household when Astley had been an apprentice and continued to visit when Astley took over the house in St Mary Axe. He did so despite being the occasional victim of Astley's humour. The expression on Searle's face, on reaching into his powder box and finding that his hand plunged into the entrails of a monkey that had been quietly placed there, struck Astley as the pinnacle of comedy. But while his jokes were cruel, the way he treated his servants was not. When Searle died Astley looked after his young son, funding him through a medical training and helping to set him up as a general practitioner.

Curled and powdered by seven-thirty at the latest, on a summer day Astley usually ordered one of his carriage horses to be saddled and brought round. In 1798 he turned thirty. His figure was still muscular and trim – he was well aware of how his breeches and boots showed off the shape of

157

his legs – and he took pleasure in the dashing figure he cut upon a horse. To be handsome, tall and well dressed made a good impression, but it was even better if you were seated on a fine horse and could ride with grace. Astley could ride very well indeed, and was always partial to a bit of showing-off.

Not that prowess in the saddle was a guarantee of safety. In September 1798, enjoying the long summer vacation from his lectures, Astley went for a ride. The satisfaction of physical activity, the pleasure of the open air, of the tracks and lawns of Hyde Park, the delight of the company, all came to a sudden end. Astley fell, landing on his head. In a haze of concussion he was carried home to St Mary Axe. Henry Cline was sent for and rapidly arrived, his skill and his paternal presence both immediate comforts. There was no indication for an operation, since there were no shards of bone projecting out from the skull or forcing their way down into the brain, but there was clearly bleeding within. Trepanation – the drilling of a circular hole in the skull – was still in use by many English surgeons for such injuries, but Cline decided against it. Instead he visited Astley several times a day, bleeding him extensively to begin with. The young man was confused and agitated, unable to remember the events of the fall. He vomited repeatedly.

As well as the frequent bleeding, Cline gave his old student repeated purges of calomel to keep his bowels open. Senna and magnesium sulphate enemas were used for the same purpose, as were acidified drinks which were supposed to draw blood from the brain to the guts in order to keep the latter working. Mercury was used to make Astley sweat, since sweating was thought to rid the body of harmful substances. Opium was avoided for the same reason as it would be today, since the effects of opiates and of concussion are too easily confused.

The days immediately after the accident passed badly, and Astley thought that he was likely to die. Cline agreed that it looked possible. Astley told his old master that he thought his death hugely regrettable: not for any personal reasons, but because of the loss to the world. His surgical colleagues and his patients would be deprived of his skill and his future researches.

It was enough to touch off Cline's knack for bringing his protégé down to earth. 'Make yourself quite easy, my friend,' he told Astley. 'The result of your disorder, whether fatal or otherwise, will not be thought of the least consequence by mankind.'

It took five or six weeks for Astley slowly to recover. His mother, kept informed by Cline and Ann, took it upon herself to hide the news of his injury from Astley's father, but failed to explain to the rest of her household that the event was to be kept secret. Samuel Cooper was informed of his son's illness by the family hairdresser. By then, fortunately, a recovery was clearly on the way, and he thanked his wife for not having worried him with the earlier uncertainty.

Astley declined his parents' offer of a recuperative trip to Great Yarmouth. By the end of October he was regaining his strength and needed to catch up after the start of the academic year. For the first time he began to publish – a few essays and case reports in a book whose contents were culled from informal meetings and discussions amongst Borough colleagues. His expectations were still of great things. The income he received from private patients was rising. He recorded it as reaching £400 in 1798, twice the sum of the year before, but not nearly enough to support his lifestyle and his expensive programme of dissections and animal experiments. What was missing was a hospital appointment as a full surgeon. Such posts were rare and hard to come by, and it was almost always a case of waiting in line at the hospital where you worked and were known. Inheritance, one way or another, was the key.

Immediately after Christmas came bad news from home. The Reverend Samuel Cooper had suffered a stroke. It left him housebound and unable to preach, although he was able to remain in his Yarmouth vicarage whilst his curates filled in for him. He was sixty years old.

In London, his ambitious son continued to make his vigorous way through the capital's world of hospitals, streets and houses. There was something in Astley's energy that directed order to certain spheres and denied it from others. By the end of a morning's consultations his notes would be carefully arranged, as clearly laid out on the page as the memories were in his head. The room, however, would be half-destroyed. 'The organ of order was imperfectly developed in him, if not wanting,' wrote his apprentice Benjamin Travers, 'and he was essentially insusceptible of its comforts; careless, if not slovenly. This was evidence enough in his consulting-room, which presented a perfect chaos of confusion when he quitted it for the day.'

Humour, too, was approached with some of the same hasty appetite. Astley was fond of a joke but hardly cared for its finesse. His friends commented on his preference for puns that were obvious rather than original, and kindly chose to avoid recording any examples. His taste in practical jokes was not sophisticated. He tried locking an assistant in his dissection rooms one night, and put bits of corpses where people would be horrified to find them. Astley's older brother Samuel, now a married minister in Norfolk, often came to stay for a few weeks each summer. Samuel's apparent gravity was a pretence; he cracked his jokes with mock seriousness. Astley's humour, meanwhile, would come out in uncontrollable snorts and convulsions of loud laughter. He was unable to remain deadpan: inadvertent mirth burst through. On Samuel's visits his wife, Sarah, came with him. An imposingly intelligent and witty woman, Sarah's 'judgement had scarcely a sufficient control over her powers of wit and sarcasm to render her always agreeable to those against whom she was directing her raillery'. When his sister-in-law was there, Astley took an energetic delight in inviting guests likely to provoke and stand up to Sarah's sharp humour. Then he settled himself into a good chair to watch the fireworks.

As the end of the century approached, hospitals were still essentially forms of village industry: small groups of men, working as much individually as they did collectively. Despite the rapid growth of industry, 'manufacturing' still commonly referred to people making things by hand, as the origins of the word implied that it should. A man's industry was mentioned if he was a hard worker, not if he used a machine. Many crafts needed only an apprenticeship and basic tools, and for surgeons, still craftsmen themselves, the situation was not much different. Astley took what he needed wherever he went, carrying a small collection of surgical instruments, hand-made and held in a box of polished mahogany.

In the late seventeenth century and through the eighteenth, few people doubted that the pursuit of science and the practice of medicine were arts. 'Nature exhibits herself more clearly', wrote Bacon in his 1623 *De Dignitate et Augmentis Scientiarum*, 'under the trials and vexations of art than when left to herself.' When he used the word 'art', he meant the art of discovery. He meant science.

In that respect, Astley was an artist. He had immersed himself in his profession, finding a way to unite its values with those of the rest of his life. His physical charm and charisma, his energetic productivity, his teaching and his ward work, his operating and private practice, his research and experiment: all of them fitted him out as a professional surgeon. He was one of a new breed, not only of medical men but of something wider. In his road to self-made professional success he may have been in the style of John Hunter, but he was just as much in that of Matthew Boulton and

Josiah Wedgwood and Erasmus Darwin. There was no existing professional role for Cooper's life, instead he shaped one fresh to suit himself. All he needed now was the hospital appointment and it looked as though that was coming up. From 1798 came rumours that his uncle, William Cooper, senior surgeon at Guy's Hospital, was planning to retire.

Throughout 1798 and 1799 the prospect of William's retirement floated around. Many of Astley's friends assumed that the job would pass to him; not only was he the best candidate, but these things had a habit of running in the family. The treasurer of Guy's Hospital also appeared to see Astley as the natural successor to his uncle. Benjamin Harrison had moved into the large Treasurer's House at Guy's in 1785 when his father had taken up the post that entitled him to it. Although the hospital was run by a board of seventy-two governors, the treasurer took day-to-day control and his influence was often the strongest. In 1797, at the age of twenty-six, Benjamin had taken over from his father as treasurer, and although he was a young man he was strong-minded, opinionated and autocratic. ' "King Harrison" ', records one of Guy's chroniclers, Cameron, 'was at no particular pains to conciliate opposition:

> It was his task to administer Mr Guy's Hospital. Opposition to his decisions by the officers of the Hospital, he considered, was no less than rebellion and rebellion was a thing to be crushed ... If, as is very probable, there were softer and more endearing sides to Mr Harrison's nature, history has not recorded them.

Harrison repeatedly called Cooper in to discuss the possible appointment: he was sure of his power over the governors, and wanted Cooper to understand it fully. The position as surgeon was soon going to be available, and it would suit Guy's Hospital to have such a promising young man take the post. But Harrison had an objection that needed to be overcome. He found Astley's political beliefs and political friends wholly unacceptable. The Government of Britain was at war, against the armies of France and civil unrest, and it was clear to Harrison that men who took the wrong side in such struggles were not fit for appointment to what was virtually a public office. If Astley wanted the job, he needed to jettison his views and abandon his friends.

Harrison was the younger of the pair by three years, but he was already established in what was effectively a lifetime post, and his power over selecting William Cooper's replacement was clear. So was Astley's response. Faced with the treasurer's demands he refused either to moderate his views or adapt his friendships.

The end of the century approached. Astley and Ann were in St Mary Axe, their adopted daughter Sarah was now a bright and healthy seven-year-old. Astley's assistant John Saunders lived with them, spending his days toiling away at dissections in the converted warehouse whose blacked-out windows meant it was only ever lit by candlelight. There were plenty of servants to bake and clean, to care for the horses and for the minia-ture menagerie in the attic.

War with France continued. The time for a great democratic revolu-tion seemed to have passed, and those who had pinned their hopes on such an event found themselves marginalised and isolated. The demand for medical men and for medical advances, in contrast, was stronger than ever. Wars are fruitful times for surgeons.

Astley's expenses were considerable. The fine house in St Mary Axe was largely his alone – there were no crowds of fee-paying apprentices as there had been with Cline, only, as yet, the student Benjamin Travers. Nothing in Astley's professional position yet attracted them, for he was still not a senior surgeon at a prestigious hospital. The dissecting room was expensive, as was paying Saunders to staff it. Acquiring the bodies, and the live animals who generally ended up on slabs next to them, also came at a hefty price. With his wife's fortune the need for money was not pressing, but it was there all the same. The income from £14,000 was not nearly enough to pursue the lifestyle and all the researches that he wished. Hunter had died in debt despite his income of £6,000 a year. The acqui-sition of a personal anatomical and pathological museum to rival Hunter's was at least as important to the rising surgeon as to be seen in fine clothes and riding in a fashionable carriage. By 1799 Astley's income from his surgical practice had risen to £600. It was a significant amount – and was in addition to what he earned as a teacher – but it was still loose change compared to his potential earnings. Henry Cline was bringing in ten to fifteen times that amount. When Astley visited a merchant with a broken leg, he joked to Travers that his fee for the single consultation was half of his year's income.

Succeeding his uncle as surgeon to Guy's was critical. It would secure him for life, providing not only the foundation for a private practice but also the base from which to continue his teaching and his research. The importance of the position made it an intimidating opportunity; nothing similar was likely to come up for a considerable time. There were so few senior surgeons – Guy's and St Thomas's had three apiece – and they were almost universally appointed from amongst men whose social and professional position within a hospital was already established. To miss out would be potentially to slip out of the class of life which he had hauled himself into. Central London at the end of the 1790s contained many fine houses like St Mary Axe, the town residences of merchants who liked their grand homes to be close to their places of business. The *Gentleman's Magazine* described the world in which Astley lived, a world of 'stately mansions, with their quiet interior quadrangles and little patches of garden, approached through massive folding-doors from some narrow street or lane in the heart of the traffic'. Many of these mansions had been built by the nobility of the seventeenth century and kept up ever since, their splendour blazing outwards in firelight and candlelight from winter windows. Now they were starting to be left behind as the city expanded out towards the north and west. The vast residence that John Hunter had built for himself in Leicester Square was a fine home as well as a spacious museum, lecture theatre and laboratory. Astley could look around him as he walked and rode through the streets and know what it was that he wished to keep up with. But he could also contemplate the fate of Hunter's museum and realise how much his life was going to cost, and what the price of failure would be. Only in that very year, 1799, was the Government finally persuaded to buy the collection for the nation. They paid £15,000 for it and gave the keeping of it to the Company of Surgeons.

At the start of January 1800, Astley's father died. He had never recovered from the stroke of the year before. The *Gentleman's Magazine* praised the late Reverend Cooper for having, through his life and his pen, 'endeavoured to prove the unrivalled excellence' of the existing English form of government. Very soon afterwards, and perhaps prompted by the death of his brother, William Cooper finally retired. He resigned his position as surgeon and allowed the post to be formally advertised. Four men applied.

None of Astley's three competitors was particularly well qualified for the post, not when it came to the things that were seen as important. The greatest credit in one man's favour was that he was the brother of the St Thomas's apothecary; the greatest demerit against another was that having worked for recent years as an army surgeon, he had spent little time in the Borough Hospitals. The third of Cooper's rivals was the most outrageous of them all, for at no time had he ever been an apprentice at either St Thomas's or Guy's. Local loyalties were what mattered and the three men, despite all being older than Cooper, appeared to be weak opponents.

The normal ties of nepotism, however, were pulling in the wrong direction. Although William had warmed to his nephew on seeing his skill at public dissection, his feelings had settled back into cool dislike. The young man was too radical. To hold democratic sentiments even after visiting Paris, and to be intimately involved with men tried for high treason, was too much for William's family feeling to overcome. Throughout the time that Benjamin Harrison was urging Astley to mend his ways, William Cooper publicly opposed his nephew's appointment.

Even more dangerous to Astley than his uncle's disapproval was his own reputation as a radical. The 1789 spring of hope that had burst forth with the promise of benevolent democracy in France had frozen over into pessimism and fear. Harrison's demand that Cooper change his ways was a pragmatic one for a man running such a large and public institution.

As the test of Astley's professional ambitions approached, the Company of Surgeons showed what could be achieved by those who hungered for respect and prestige. By the end of March 1800 it no longer existed. In its place was a new body, dedicated by royal charter to 'the promotion and encouragement of the study and practice of the art and science of surgery'. The Royal College of Surgeons of England had been born. Their home, facing the flowerbeds and green lawns of Lincoln's Inn Fields, embodied the respectability they had so long been seeking. In corporate terms at least, the surgeons were level now with the physicians. The fine new building, so close to Cline's own house and to the ancient Inns and Courts of the legal profession, also gave them space for Hunter's specimen collection. The Hunterian Museum was rapidly established.

The Royal College of Surgeons and its Hunterian Museum still exist on the same site today, despite the damage to both following a direct hit by a Second World War bomb. Today, in a grey cardboard box in the college archives, amongst lecture notes, dissection notes, drawings, a description of a Continental tour and reminiscences of childhood, there is a short note. It is written in the loops of Astley's compressed italics and is his own copy of an anonymous letter:

To the Treasurer of Guy's Hospital.
Sir,

The candidates proposed for your choice at Guy's Hospital on Wednesday, are three gentlemen of tried abilities, who have served their king and country during the present war, and one who is a Jacobin, a friend of Horne Tooke, and an associate of the celebrated Thelwall.

By the nomination you may judge the sense of the present committees.

CAUTION.

Although the note contained nothing new it nevertheless gave Harrison the excuse to once more summon Astley in to see him. Perhaps the treasurer genuinely felt that the decision of his hospital was under some form of scrutiny; Pitt's Government was certainly making effective use of a wide network of spies and other agents.

Harrison explained his position. Astley's professional successes and long association with Guy's made him the perfect candidate. The obstacle was of his own making. 'I could not help', explained Harrison afterwards, 'feeling much hesitation and difficulty in recommending him to the Governors as a proper person to fill so responsible a situation.' He made his position even clearer when he dangled the threat of forwarding the anonymous letter to each of the governors.

What followed was described by Astley's nephew Bransby. According to him, Astley began: 'My friend Coleman, whom you know, Sir, was under the same democratical influence as myself.' He then explained how the two of them had taken a walk together earlier in the summer of 1800. As they strolled through the dappled sunshine of Epping Forest they were aware of a mutual silence. 'Instead of either of us feeling that exuberance of spirits which naturally was so common to us both, we walked along for half an hour without exchanging scarcely a word.' At the end of the silence came an epiphany. The two men, close friends ever since their days as apprentices in Cline's household, revealed to each other their growing feelings of depression.

'Do you know, Coleman,' said Astley, 'that at this moment I feel a nasty disagreeable sensation about my throat,' – he made a throttling motion to demonstrate – 'and I should not be much surprised if that is what we come to, if we persist in our intercourse with our present political set of associates. What good has it ever done us, Coleman?'

His friend agreeing, they decided, so Bransby reported, to turn their backs on their former friends and discard their long-held beliefs. 'They can never improve us in our profession,' Cooper is said to have told Coleman, 'nor advance us in its practice; we had better have done with them, and think more of paying obedience to the laws of our country than of disputing their justice and propriety.'

Harrison, delighted at what Astley told him, responded by saying that the barrier to his appointment as surgeon had just dissolved. He promised Astley his warm support. Wanting to preserve for himself the precious memory of how close he had come to disaster, Astley asked if he might make a copy of the anonymous letter. Harrison graciously consented.

Over the days following the meeting, Astley put aside his work. It was still the summer vacation, so he had no teaching duties, but he now also abandoned his surgical duties, saw no patients and did no experiments. For the first time in his life since Cline had challenged him with the arm thrown upon the table, he did no dissection. Instead he spent the remainder of the late summer days personally visiting each one of the seventy-two hospital governors of Guy's Hospital. With his newly acquired endorsement they were happy to listen to him. In October 1800 the election was made. Astley Cooper was unanimously appointed the new surgeon at Guy's Hospital, London.

The only two records of Cooper's transformation are the letter at the Royal College of Surgeons and Bransby's account. The latter derived partly from an interview with Benjamin Harrison more than forty years later. Despite the intervening years Harrison was still apparently able to remember the words of so many decades before.

Self-interest, the taste of which Harrison puts so strongly into Astley's mouth, is a possible explanation for his about-face. He had a family to think of. Then there was his own lifelong desire to be a part of things, to attach himself, to find a community and an extended family. Democratic society was fading almost into the underworld, making it no longer much of an option for a man whose fortunes hung upon his respectability. And Astley had an honest awareness of his own appetite for money, for the power it gave him to pursue his researches and live his life in the way that he chose. He mocked himself for it publicly from time to time. His professional life would not have been over if he had missed the surgeon's job at Guy's, but it would never have recovered. He would have had to move to a new city and affiliate with a new hospital – an almost impossible task for a man past his apprenticeship – or accept becoming stuck in a junior position for the rest of his life.

James Parkinson was a contemporary of Astley's and his life casts a light on Astley's decision. Thirteen years older, he had grown up in Shoreditch on the south side of the river. It was a place with a history of violence and of theatre. Hoxton Square, where Parkinson lived, had been built on a field where Ben Jonson had once killed a fellow actor in a duel. Shakespeare had lived and worked in Shoreditch, and many of his plays had been performed for the first time in a theatre nearby.

Parkinson came from a family of apothecaries, and he qualified in the same profession before attending the London Hospital and becoming a member of the Company of Surgeons. He sat with interested attention through the lectures of John Hunter the year before Astley. During the last decade of the 1700s he worked as a general practitioner while pursuing a ferociously political life: he was an early member, in 1792, of the London Corresponding Society, and became one of its better-known speakers. Like Henry Cline he appeared as a character witness for Thelwall at his treason trial. A pamphleteer, he published a long series of inflammatory attacks on the Government and the lack of freedom and justice. Then suddenly, at the end of the century, his anger and his sarcasm came to an abrupt halt. He carried on his work as a family doctor and combined it with becoming an early (and internationally known) expert on fossils. Later, almost as an aside, he published the first proper description of the disease that now bears his name.*

Parkinson began his fossil collection in 1799, the same year in which he gave up his political activism. From that point on he seemed to see more fertile ground in the soil beneath his feet than in the society above it.

Parkinson and Cooper knew one another. No records attest to it, but the worlds of London medicine and of radical politics were too small to permit otherwise. Both persisted in their democratic views despite the danger to themselves and their reputations. But by the end of the century what prospects were there for Astley's support having any positive

---

*He called it the 'shaking palsy'. His description was not widely noticed and those who knew of it soon forgot. But Charcot, the nineteenth-century French physician whose interest in diseases of the nerves did so much to establish the speciality of neurology, somehow heard of it. After much effort he acquired a copy of Parkinson's paper and thereafter referred to the disease as 'maladie du Parkinson'.

outcomes? No substantial good had come of the years before, when the world had seemed so full of promise; who could hope for it now, with Napoleon looming across the Channel and government spies and oppressive laws propping up a British police state? Thelwall had retreated, becoming a farmer amongst the hills of the Brecon Beacons, all of his gifts of oratory having done nothing to achieve the causes that both he and Cooper had believed in. Horne Tooke had rejected universal suffrage and modified his views sufficiently to attract the support of moderates. Holland was busy in Cheshire with his provincial surgical practice, his own radicalism finding outlets that were limited but practical, like providing pioneering occupational health services to local manufacturers. Cline continued with the same friendships he had always had, but Cline was a mature man whose position was secure and whose active involvement with politics was minimal.

Astley issued some sort of promise, some declaration or retraction, to the Guy's treasurer and in person to each of the hospital's governors. There is no way of knowing how closely it resembled the one that Bransby Cooper and Harrison presented years later. The friendship between Astley and Thelwall melts away at around this point, but the two men corresponded warmly in later life, a sign that Thelwall held no grudge. What seems to have happened was that Astley made a choice. He had no ability to bring about any great political change, but he had the skills and the talents to alter the world in other ways. That was the revolution he could work towards, so he did. It was a pragmatic choice, a sensible one. It was the beginning of Astley's middle age.

In September, Astley did a curious thing. He went to stay in Yarmouth with his older brother Samuel. He was greatly taken with Samuel's three-year-old son. The child was called Astley, in the family's tradition of reusing names, and Astley spoke to his brother about the possibility of adopting the toddler. The subject had come up before and Samuel had refused. But this time he agreed: his own family was growing and his living of Inglethorpe was not rich. He already had three daughters and two older sons while Astley had only his wife Ann and adopted daughter Sarah to provide for.

Astley explained to Samuel that he was not likely to have any more children of his own. There is no explanation for his conviction, but it seems not to have been due to any emotional failure in his marriage. Astley travelled back on the overnight Old Blue Yarmouth coach to London, carrying the infant on his lap, a journey of twenty-odd hours. He reached home unannounced, running up the stairs in a breathless rush to show his wife their new adopted child.

14

The Uses of Money

Astley's distinctive accent remained a characteristic of his conversation, and his students frequently commented on it. He was unable to pronounce 'prostate', noted one of them, John Flint South, perpetually saying 'prostrate' instead. He had other mannerisms, too, that people were quick to notice. When something he was saying struck him as funny he would interrupt himself with a short snort of laughter, rubbing his nose with the back of his hand in a helpless effort to subdue his own mirth. He had, said one of his most observant and articulate students, 'a joyous manner'. Benjamin Travers, whom he took on as apprentice soon after his appointment as surgeon, was of a similar opinion, later telling Bransby:

> *Cheerfulness of temper amounting to vivacity, and a relish for the ludicrous, never deserted him, and his chuckling laugh, scarce smothered while he told his story, will never be forgotten by any who were accustomed to it. Of a piece with this was an habitual air of bonhomie, and a good-natured mirthfulness of look and manner, in listening to the narration even of a stranger. He had also an irresistible temptation to perpetuate a pun, if opportunity offered, not always so original as obvious.*

Being apprenticed for seven years to a man with an addiction to bad puns was clearly a memorable experience.

Fond of his dress, at the end of the century Astley typically got himself

170

up with white silk stockings below lightly coloured silk knee-breeches. Travers was one of many people who noticed that Astley was particularly pleased with the shape of his legs, often hoisting them onto the operating theatre table to demonstrate an anatomical point to his students. The tightly fitting stockings and breeches were perfectly designed to show them to advantage. Above the waist would be a dashing blue jacket over a pale waistcoat. His face, not yet red-cheeked or double-chinned, was bright and animated. His hair continued to be the subject of great attention. Observers agreed that Astley took his work desperately seriously and laboured over it industriously. He just happened to have a riotous sense of humour and be a bit of a dandy into the bargain.

With the hospital appointment came a firmer foundation for joy. Money bought bodies. If he could get them himself, he still enjoyed doing so, although the days of being his own grave-robber were long over. Travers, only seventeen, was horrified to have his assistance required almost immediately upon moving into St Mary Axe. The two men got into Astley's gig one evening and rode to the village of Newington Green, three long miles north of London through the dark and threatening countryside. There lay the body of an old woman who had died of stomach cancer. By candlelight the two men opened her up. Travers was chief assistant at the operation, and it was his first sight of a human corpse. 'I made a strong effort to assume a part, appear *au fait*, and give all the aid in my power, undressing, and, in part, sewing up the body, and bringing away a precious, though not over fragrant, relic of the old lady's interior upon my person.' On the way back the sudden flash of a man's coat in the darkness outside alerted them to bandits; they turned around and raced to a tavern for help. An armed escort was provided to get them through to the main London road, while Travers, already shaken by the corpse, was left wondering what the robbers would have made of him had they searched his pockets and found the cancerous human stomach he carried.

But the frequency of such expeditions was falling. Money gave Astley the power to have the bodies brought to him. The King of the Resurrectionists was able to take up his throne. Deliveries could now be routed through Guy's as easily as through St Mary Axe, and at the latter he could afford a man to manage his increasingly busy affairs. Charles Osbaldeston – whose name Astley peremptorily decreed should become Balderson for ease of pronunciation – entered St Mary Axe.

Charles managed private practice appointments. 'It is worth spending any money merely to convince the public that your opinion is at all times to be obtained,' said Cooper. And with Charles dispatching messengers and carriages back and forth to preserve that public belief, Cooper often ended up spending more on making a visit than he received for his fees in return. In the long run, he was convinced, it was worth it. There was stiff competition, and Astley was happy for Charles to lie on his behalf in order to win a client from a friend or colleague. Even Cline was not immune from Astley's commercial competitiveness. Such a cut-throat attitude was generally accepted as the reasonable way to do business. One Sunday afternoon a wealthy patient, whom Charles was attempting to detain at St Mary Axe for as long as it took to track down and retrieve Astley, decided to hedge his bets and sent his own servant to see if an alternative surgeon could be found more rapidly. Astley rushed back from a visit to his brother-in-law at Tottenham to find the surgeon Sir William Blizzard attending to the wealthy patient in the lower rooms of Astley's own house. Defeated in a game he felt it perfectly reasonable to play, he withdrew upstairs without intruding.

Once he was established in the household, Charles organised the acquisition of experimental subjects. Stray dogs and cats were gathered up in multitudes, no one caring very much whether the animal was feral or fondly missed. Fetching a bonus of half a crown each, they offered a significant source of income for the servants who managed to bring them in. The animals were put in the hay-loft above Cooper's stable, up to thirty of them at a time, there to await or to recover from their appointment with the surgeon. Charles also took charge of procuring specimens from the Tower menagerie and from whatever other sources seemed promising. Taxidermists were one source, men who positively wished to get rid of an animal's insides. Fishmongers were another, and Charles became a regular at the Billingsgate market, wandering along the stalls looking for the striking and the unusual.

Although the trade in live animals was kept successfully secret, Astley was notorious all the same. His dealings with the human dead were public knowledge, and they made him infamous. All of which did nothing to harm his growing reputation as the most fashionable surgeon of his day. During 1800, the year of his appointment as surgeon to Guy's, his income doubled once more: £1,100 was only the beginning.

Having a loft with up to thirty dogs in at one time, almost all of them stolen, keeping cats and snakes and rabbits in abundance, to slice and inject, dissect and preserve: it was all an expensive business, in time as well as money. Choosing one dog he destroyed the blood supply to one of its testicles, then cut the vas deferens (the tube that carries sperm towards the penis) on the other side. Six years later he killed the animal, showing that the testicle without a proper blood supply had shrunk to nothing, while the one on the other side was large and healthy. By showing that slicing the vas deferens did not appear to damage the testicles, and that the two ends of the parted vas did not manage to join up again, he had taken a pioneering step towards the operation of vasectomy. But he had operated purely out of curiosity, with no particular practical benefit in mind. Astley still never showed any sign of worrying about vivisection, although he was aware of how repelled many people would be if they knew what he was up to. He was conscious also of his own unusual tolerance for physical pain, when it came to causing as well as suffering it. Unlike many colleagues – Hunter went white and shook with terror when an operation approached – Astley used his knife with the same cheerfully boisterous temper as his tongue. A colleague, depressed after witnessing the agony of an operation, declared to Astley as they shared a carriage home that he believed theirs to be a very melancholy profession. Not a bit of it, came the reply: 'I think ours a very pleasant life. Is it such a hardship to chat with a succession of well-bred people every morning and seal up a round sum for your banker as often as you get home?'

Astley had become largely immune to the pungent daily presence of pain. Part of it was exposure and part his natural tolerance, but a great deal stemmed also from what he took the meaning of the pain to be. To cut into an animal or attempt a dangerous operation on a person was, in his mind, to engage in something important. And when he opened up a living suffering dog, purely for experiment, he was inflicting the same experience upon it as he did weekly to men, women and children. And to an extent all surgery – all medicines even – could be viewed as experimental. There were no guarantees, only attempts that might reasonably be made. Discussing cancer of the penis, Cooper wrote in his printed lectures: 'Arsenic I have tried in these cases, but have never succeeded with it; on the contrary, it has greatly irritated and made the sore more extensive and the warts more numerous.' He concluded:

The only means by which the effects of this dreadful malady can be averted, consist in the early removal of the diseased portion of the penis. The operation is dreadfully painful, but it lasts only for a moment.

173

Pain, in other words, was essential. However horrible it was, the alternatives were worse. What should happen if the surgeon or the patient should not face up to the suffering?

The penis continues ulcerating until that part which is naturally pendulous becomes destroyed, occasioning retention of urine, and great difficulty in its discharge at other times. The urine passing in various directions excoriates the scrotum, and leads to a most painful but lingering termination of existence.

Astley's awareness of the pain of an operation, and the need for it to be tolerated, explained something of his own working indifference. He talked to his students of his uncle William, 'a man of great feeling, too much so to be a surgeon'. A patient had needed to have his leg amputated. Such an operation would be quick – a minute or two – but despite being brief would still be dangerous and agonisingly painful. William had been in no doubt that it was required to save the man's life, but his own nervousness of inflicting pain made him hesitant. The patient was brought into the operating theatre, the surgical instruments and the bandages set up in readiness nearby. The man climbed up, gazed with horror at the bone saws and the scalpels, and immediately jumped down again, hobbling away from the theatre as fast as he could go. William, rather than pursuing him and insisting that he went through with the procedure, let him go. 'By God,' he explained with relief to the audience that thronged the operating theatre's tiered sets, 'I am glad he's gone.' Astley saw this as a failure of William's responsibility to the scared and panicking man. No surgeon with a care for his patients, he said, could allow sentimentality to overpower sympathy. Compassion must never lose out to cowardice.

Like many of his contemporaries, Astley had motives that were in deadly earnest. The continents of health and disease were there to be mapped out. There was no way of knowing in advance which expedition was most likely to lead to success but there was no excuse for not setting off. Only adventurers made discoveries.

Astley believed that his vivisections were an essential part of his life as an innovative surgeon. 'I should much wish for your assistance in making experiments upon animals,' he wrote to his friend and assistant Saunders. 'I am certain that everything valuable in physiology is only to be so obtained.' He showed no indication of worrying about the effects that those experiments might have on his character. And it is hard to read through his note-books without being struck by how high-handed and callous he became in his treatment of animals. Many of the experiments he did had been done before, and their repetition could have been avoided had he not been so devoted to the idea of learning everything for himself from scratch. There is something to be said for not relying on books, but little for ignoring them altogether. Astley grew better at setting bones from having deliberately broken so many of them, but Hunter had already carried out much of that work and had written it up. When Astley tied closed the urethra of a rabbit, he was interested to see what happened, and over what period. The rabbit's bladder slowly swelled, the urine unable to escape. Eventually the pressure ripped apart the bladder's muscular wall, and the acid urine poured into the inside of the rabbit's abdomen, killing it. Tom Nero, the sadistic anti-hero of Hogarth's *Four Stages of Cruelty*, would have approved.

By 1803 Napoleon, now the master of France and beyond, had lined up a hundred thousand troops at Boulogne. Between two and three thousand ships stood by to take them across the Channel and invade England. George III reviewed the troops in Hyde Park, where Astley still regularly rode, and was cheered by more than half a million loyal citizens. It was only a short distance from where he was once supposed to have been attacked in his carriage and almost lynched. At the height of Boneyphobia, in 1804, fear of invasion gripped the country.

Free of any involvement in politics, Astley had a grand project of his own. Up to this point his reputation had been made chiefly on a personal level and his publications had been restricted to case reports. His promi-nence in the Royal Society was a good advertisement amongst his more scientifically minded colleagues, but it took little more than an amateur and gentlemanly interest to become a member. But in 1804 the first part of his *Treatise on Hernia* was published. It was a deliberate effort to estab-lish himself as a surgeon of the first rank, to advertise his knowledge to his medical brethren and to make sweeping changes in the way operations were carried out. The book was lavish in all respects, a quarto volume over half a metre (about 18 inches) in height and almost as wide. 'Cooper on Hernia' read the simple cover, while inside his qualifications appeared prominently beneath his name: 'Astley Cooper, Fellow of the Royal Society, Member of the Royal Medical and Physical Societies of Edinburgh, Lecturer on Anatomy and Surgery and Surgeon to Guy's Hospital'. The dedication was to Henry Cline:

Two reasons strongly impel me to dedicate the following Work to you. The one is, that many of the ideas which it contains have been derived from your public and private instructions:

The other, that it gives me an opportunity of acknowledging, with gratitude, the kind attention which I invariably experienced from you whilst an inmate of your family.

Illustrated with eleven engraved plates of dissections, some in colour, the book was a revelation of precision, its novelty in its clarity and detail. Along with the second volume that followed in 1807, the work cemented Astley's wider reputation as well as losing him a fortune in the printing of it: over £1,000. There was no subscription list and he bore the cost himself, a staggeringly expensive gesture, a deliberate and very successful piece of self-advertising extravagance. 'In 1804,' says a modern textbook on surgery, 'he published his classic work on hernias in which he demonstrated the anatomic defects of groin hernias, described the transversalis fascia, and defined the superior pubic ligament that later bore his name.'

In the foreword, Astley set out to explain that his precision lay in more than just painstaking dissection. He laid out the way in which he used anatomical terms, slighting others for being vague in such basics as not defining whether 'above' and 'below' referred to the depth of a structure within the body or its distance from front, back, head or foot. Hearsay, also, was a generator of confusion and something strictly to be avoided:

I have almost uniformly, in the following work, avoided quoting the opinions of other authors on this part of surgery. This I have done, certainly not from any wish to slight or undervalue the labours of some of the most excellent physiologists and practitioners that have adorned our profession, but because it did not form a part of my plan to give a history of this branch of surgery, and because I wished to confine myself to the very wide scene of observations afforded by the two noble institutions of St Thomas's and Guy's Hospitals, and to that portion of the practice of this metropolis, which I have been personally enabled to authenticate. I have therefore related no case, and given no remark, to the truth of which I cannot vouch; and for the same reason the subjects of all the plates annexed to this volume are from preparations, either in my own possession, or in the Anatomical Museum at St Thomas's Hospital, which may at all times be consulted.

Some of the plates showed the method of treating a hernia by attaching a truss. The teenage boy who had been so frightened by his own deforming hernia had grown into a man with the skill and vision to explore the problem in a groundbreaking way, and with the worldly knack to let others know about it.

The following year, late in July 1805, Mr Coppendale, a personal friend of Nelson, fell from his horse as he was riding through the Borough's tangled streets. When he reached the hospital blood was coming freely from the wound at the back of his head and he was unconscious. But he responded well to being bled from his arm and submitted to an enema. Over the following days he remained drowsy but could be roused into answering questions. He complained of pain. On the fourth day he became sleepy. Not even the ravishing presence of Emma, Lady Hamilton, could draw a response. Astley continued to treat him with bleeding and blisters to no avail. After Coppendale had died, he dissected him, tracing for the few summer students that remained the fractures in his skull and the tears in his brain.

Soon the summer was over, the academic year had begun again, and in October the Battle of Trafalgar appeared to turn the tide of war. On 9 January the following year, 1806, a young boy pressed his face against the cold glass of his window and watched a water-borne procession move slowly along the Thames. It was a windy day, and waves of over a metre high hampered a slow flotilla of more than sixty boats accompanying the black-plumed funeral barge carrying Nelson's body, preserved in brandy within a lead-lined coffin. They were taking it upriver to the Admiralty, prior to its final burial in St Paul's Cathedral.* The boy with his face against the glass was John Flint South, and his life's ambition was to be a surgeon. He watched the boats sail steadily past without knowing that Nelson was far from the only man to be brought dead up the River Thames. The

---

* Where it now lies not far from a bust of Cooper.

import of foreign corpses had boosted the supply of bodies to the capital's surgeons. It was not only the living that flocked in their masses to England's capital.

In its way it was a successful example of the creativity of the free market. By the entrepreneurial endeavours of surgeons like Astley, and the body-snatchers who supplied them, great obstacles were overcome. The harsh conditions of the market even worked in favour of the labourers, at least some of them. Astley understood that his fortunes depended on a skilled workforce, and like Wedgwood and other entrepreneurial employers in a similar position, he treated people in a way that was both sensible and humane. He supplied the grave-robbers with work for as long as they were able, and bore with them through periods of illness or extended drunkenness. Should his body-snatchers run into trouble with the law, then Astley paid for their legal representation. If they went to jail he supported them whilst they were inside and he looked after their families at the same time.

As a result, he received the best supply of corpses in London. He entered into negotiations with his colleagues – they called themselves the Anatomical Club – to try to form as much of a monopoly or cartel as they could. There was nothing unusual about that in Georgian Britain. The remarkable thing was that, if they could stay sober enough, the body-snatchers were able to do the same. Unions of workmen who sought to influence their own pay and conditions were illegal. But that did not matter to the resurrectionists. They were outside the law already.

Astley had met and admired Adam Smith while in Edinburgh. The 'invisible hand' of the free market that Smith had described in his *Wealth of Nations* proved as successful in sourcing dead humans as it had live animals.

In the first two years of the century, Astley investigated the ear. He noted that the tympanic membrane – the eardrum – was like any other drum. In order to work, it needed to have air on both sides of it. A number of people became deaf after ear infections, and if you peered inside their ears it was possible to see that their eardrums bulged inwards rather than outwards. The air on the far side of the drum appeared to have been obliterated by their infections. Astley knew that the ear behind the drum was connected to the inside of the nose through an air-filled canal. He noted that spontaneous or traumatic perforations of the drum tended to heal, and that even when they didn't, people often were not left deaf. One of his own students was an excellent flautist, even appearing in concerts, and yet had eardrums that were perforated on each side. The student, said Astley,

> gave me the following satisfactory proof of each membrane tympani being imperfect. Having filled his mouth with air, he closed the nostrils and contracted the cheeks. The air, thus compressed was heard to rush through the meatus auditorius with a whistling noise, and the hair hanging from his temples became agitated by the current of air which issued from the ear . . . To determine this with greater precision, I called for a lighted candle, which was applied in turn to each ear, and the flame was agitated in a similar manner.

So Astley undertook an experiment. He took a Gloucestershire man who came to him complaining of deafness following an infection. The man's eardrum was characteristically concave, bulging inwards in exactly the opposite way to what was natural. Astley burst a hole in it. The infection had blocked with pus the air-filled canal behind the man's eardrum, and now both air and hearing flooded back in. A full account appeared across two issues of the *Philosophical Transactions of the Royal Society* in 1800 and 1801. The operation restored the Gloucester man's hearing and made Astley a Fellow of the Royal Society and a recipient of their prestigious Copley medal. It was experimental, inspired and exceedingly painful: a characteristic combination. The famous surgeon Cheselden, half a century before, had proposed that a similar operation be tried out on criminals awaiting execution, but when his proposal was rejected he gave up on the idea. Cheselden lacked the authority to get permission to experiment on the condemned. Astley never asked, and simply used his own patients.*

Following Hunter, as we have seen, Astley had become fascinated by the body's capacity to develop collateral circulation, strings of new blood

---

* Cheselden got as far as arranging a pardon for a condemned criminal in return for participating in an experiment, but the prisoner died of fever before it could go ahead and the Government did not allow Cheselden a second attempt. 'Mr Cheselden's failure can only add lustre to Mr Cooper's success,' said Sir Joseph Banks in a presidential speech to the Royal Society.

vessels that grew from nothing to replace ones that had been shut off. In countless dogs, rabbits, cats and other animals he tied off arteries and watched the strange growth of vessels that could lead to recovery. Hunter had declared in his lectures of twenty years before that he thought it theoretically possible to close off the carotid artery in humans and for a man or woman to survive. The huge carotids, one on each side of the neck, supplied the brain with the bulk of its blood. Both Hunter and Astley had tied off the carotid artery in animals and seen them survive. Yet despite Hunter's assertion of its technical possibility, no one had ever tried such an operation on a human. The neck was too full of delicate structures that were easily damaged. The blood supply to the brain was too essential to be cut off so suddenly. Diseases of the carotid artery, like an aneurysm, were untreatable. It was best to leave them alone.

So when Cooper met Mary Edwards in 1805 he took particular interest in her. She was forty-four years old and an aneurysm of one carotid formed a pulsing swelling that took up most of the right side of her neck. Arriving at St Mary Axe one morning, she allowed Astley to examine her. He encouraged her to come to Guy's, explaining his intention of admitting her as an inpatient. She came, but after a panicked conversation with her husband changed her mind and fled home. Astley found out where she lived and went after her. The swelling in her neck was plainly getting worse quite rapidly. She would die, he told her, if nothing was done.

Subdued and frightened she agreed to return to Guy's and to undergo an operation. As she sat in a chair, Astley opened up her neck and dissected down to the swollen artery. Beneath its base he tied two tight loops, immediately stopping the flow of blood through it. The pulsations within the swelling instantly stopped. As always, the threads were left hanging out of the wound, ready to be pulled free when their inner section rotted into two.

When the operation was finished Mary stood up and began to cough. The coughing increased, growing ever more violent, preventing Mary from so much as catching a breath. Astley believed she was about to die where she stood. But just when it seemed set to choke her completely the coughing gradually began to subside. Soon Mary was breathing more easily, and she was led back to her ward

There were two great dangers to operating on the carotid. The first was that it lay near so much else that it would be catastrophic to disrupt – blood vessels, nerves, trachea and oesophagus – and the second that any

Sir Astley Cooper, Surgeon to the King.

Profile sketch of Astley in later life.

Sketch of Astley Cooper

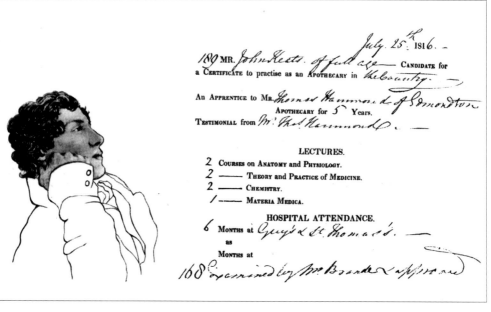

A sketch of Keats by his friend Charles Armitage Brown, along with the certificate proving Keats's qualification as an apothecary – or, as they were starting to be called at that time, a General Practitioner.

The chest and heart of a fetus, injected
and dissected by Astley.

The neck, chest and heart of a dog,
dissected by Astley.

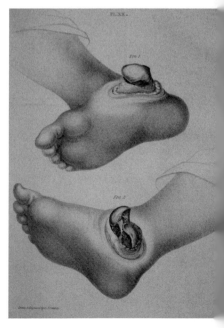

A badly set but long healed femoral fracture.
From Astley's *Treatise on Dislocations and
Fractures.*

From the same book, a sketch of an injury
that Astley discusses. The protruding bone
eventually rotted and fell away.

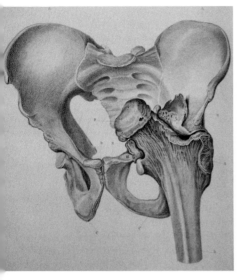

Another of Astley's illustrations of the way in which the body was capable of remodelling after injury. The ball of the left hip has pushed upwards and broken through the socket, but a new socket has grown up around it.

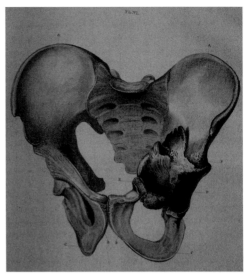

The same pelvis with the hip removed to show both the new and the old sockets. The name for the socket is the acetabulum, a classical reference to the fact that it looks like an upturned vinegar cup.

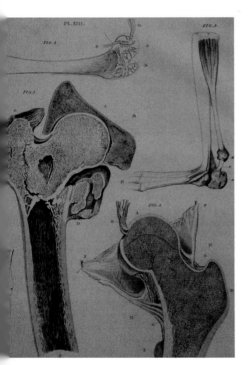

Astley's illustration of the blood supply to the head of the femur.

A patient after having had their leg amputated at the hip joint, among the most prolonged and fabulously painful of all operations.

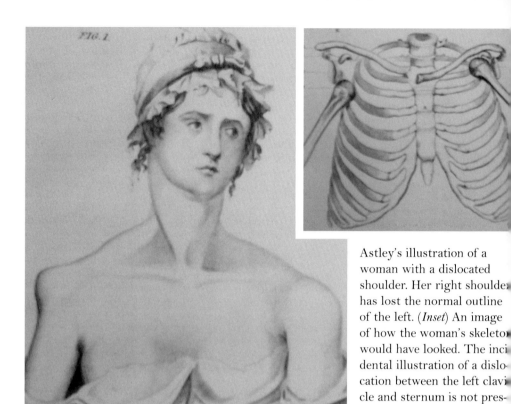

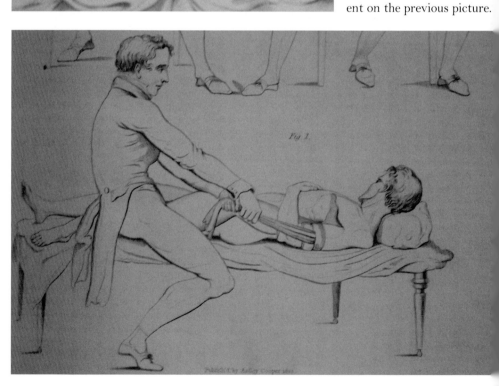

Astley's illustration of a woman with a dislocated shoulder. Her right shoulder has lost the normal outline of the left. (*Inset*) An image of how the woman's skeleton would have looked. The incidental illustration of a dislocation between the left clavicle and sternum is not present on the previous picture.

This was Astley's favourite technique for putting a dislocated shoulder back into its socket. It suited a man particularly proud of the shapeliness of his legs.

An Account of Appearances which were observed
in inspecting the body of his late Majesty
——————— June 27th 1830

The body exhibited very slight appear
ances of putrefaction

The Appearance had disappeared except
some slight remains of it upon the Thighs

Notwithstanding the apparent emaciation
of his Majestys person, a very large quantity
of Fat was found between the skin and
the Abdominal muscles

Abdomen

The omentum and
all those parts in which fat is usually
deposited were profusely loaded with it
The Abdomen did not contain more
than an ounce of Water
The Stomach and Intestines were
somewhat contracted and they were of
a dark Colour in consequence of their
containing mucus tinged with blood
and in the Stomach was found
a Clot of pure blood weighing not
less than six ounces —

Astley's notes of his post-mortem of George IV, complete with stains.

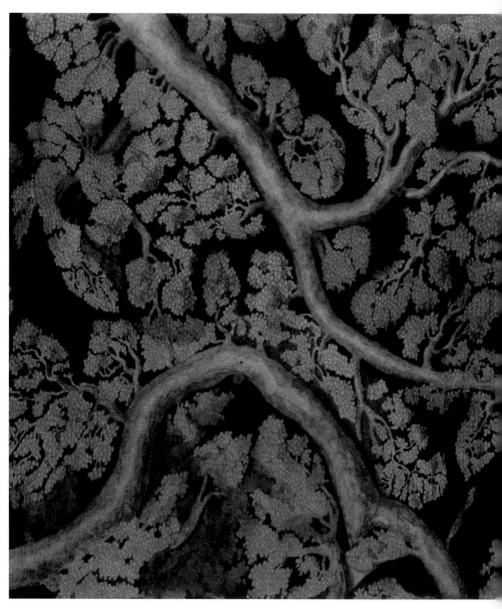

An illustration made for Astley's final book, showing the inside of the human breast. The leafy structures synthesize the milk and the trunk-like ducts transport it towards the nipple.

interruption to its flow could cause a stroke. Both dangers had been over-come. It was the first time anyone had deliberately carried out an oper-ation on a carotid artery, and it went miraculously well. That technical success was not the product of luck. It was the mark of many long hours spent vivisecting and in the dead-house. It took a practised hand to get something so difficult and so novel completely correct on the first attempt.

For the next few days Mary continued to recover. Then abruptly, a week after the operation, she lost the use of the left side of her body. It was a disaster, but at least an explicable one, since the right carotid supplied the right side of the brain and it was that which controlled the left half of her body. But it wasn't clear why such a setback should have occurred. Four days later, in much the same way that warmth had returned to the antlers of Hunter's stag, Mary found the movement of her left arm coming back. At the same time the surgical wound continue to heal well. The swelling in her neck had subsided and the pulsing had never returned.

For another week everything continued to go well. Then Mary's neck began to bloat once more. It became painful, and the wound that had closed now opened itself up from within. Pus and blood oozed out. Mary began to cough, and this time the coughing did not subside. It grew ever more constant and ever more violent until she could no longer even swallow her own saliva. Soon after that she couldn't breathe. Death came twenty days after the operation. Astley opened up her body. Mary's wind-pipe had been crushed, squashed from within by an accumulation of pus. The cause of death was 'inflammation', a sad but unavoidable risk in any operation.*

Astley was disappointed but not discouraged. The ability of the human body to withstand surgical closure of the carotid seemed to have been demonstrated. Not every operation worked; no one would dream of expecting it to. In the contemporary scheme of things, closing off the woman's carotid aneurysm had gone better than most people had believed possible. In the summer of 1808 another opportunity presented itself. 'Mr George Young, surgeon,' wrote Astley, 'had the kindness to furnish me with a case of the most favourable nature, by sending, first to my house

---

* The cause of death was actually an infection, but Cooper had no way of knowing the difference. The cardinal signs of inflammation had been known since the Roman Celsus. 'Rubor, calor, dolor and tumor' harmoniously signified that inflamed flesh grew red, hot, painful and swollen. But without germ theory, no one could distinguish inflammation due to trauma from that caused by an infection.

and afterwards to Guy's Hospital, a man who was in all respects the subject I should have chosen.' Humphrey Humphreys was a fifty-year-old porter who had an aneurysm 'about the size of a walnut on the left side of the neck, just under the angle of the jaw, and extending from thence downwards to the thyroid cartilage'. Astley tried again, feeling warranted in his attempt by the symptoms that Humphreys was starting to experience. 'The tumour affected his speech,' Astley explained, 'so as to make him extremely hoarse; and he had more recently a cough, attended with a slight difficulty of breathing, and which seemed to be the effect of the pressure of the swelling on the larynx.' Humphreys sat through the operation with such co-operative stoicism that Astley wrote admiringly of his bravery.

> The result of the case afforded me a degree of pleasure which compensated for the disappointment I felt in the issue of the former. In a professional point of view, it was highly desirable to ascertain the possibility of saving life in a case which had hitherto proved generally fatal; and I could not but feel more than common interest in the fate of a man, who, although he well knew that the trial was new, and the risk considerable, never betrayed the smallest signs of apprehension.

The procedure worked and Humphreys made a full recovery. Both men were left feeling they had reason to be pleased with themselves. Thirteen years later, when Humphreys died of an unrelated condition, Astley was swiftly informed. He despatched a team of resurrectionists to bring him back Humphreys's body.

The two operations for carotid aneurysm provided excellent meat for publication, appearing in Medico-Chirurgical Transactions in January 1809.*

*

Astley's morning routines had changed a little. At six o'clock in the morning he rose, regardless of the season. Throwing on some clothes he

---

* Humphreys died in 1821, of a bleed into the left-hand side of his brain. Astley felt that the haemorrhage being on the same side as the ligated carotid was evidence of success; Humphreys had died from the very opposite of a lack of blood. 'Account of the First Successful Operation performed on the Carotid Artery for Aneurysm in the year 1808, with the Post-mortem Examination in 1821' appeared in 1836 in Guy's Hospital Reports.

went to the dissecting suite he had had built. There he found Saunders
– also up and about at such an early hour – and the two men dissected
until half past seven or so. There were two rooms to dissect in, built above
the large stables. Bottles, tables, sinks and cauldrons complemented the
tables and slabs.

These days, only when the dissection finished was it time to dress for
the day, and to do it properly. Astley spent a good thirty or forty minutes
getting himself ready, much of it closeted with Searle. Once he had made
himself presentable to his own satisfaction he began to see his free patients.
With his private practice now increasing rapidly, the poor were squeezed
into the little time that remained before taking breakfast at home. Self-
denial at the breakfast table was something he seemed to hold as a virtue,
looking longingly at the bloaters, the lightly smoked herring sent from his
Yarmouth family, while avoiding them as dangerous to the fortunes of the
day. Instead he ate hot buttered rolls, let his cup of tea cool while he read
the newspaper ('which was likely to excite laughter') then drank it down
in one and was ready to spend the rest of the morning seeing his wealthy
private patients. They waited for him, the men in two large drawing rooms
to the right of his entrance hall, the women directly above them on the
first floor. Appointments were rare, and either the patients or their servants
were left to negotiate or plead with Charles. It was a mark of Astley's
flourishing reputation that his servant made up to £600 a year in bribes
received during the course of such negotiations – more than his master
had earned for most of his career. In the large entrance hall Charles directed
the traffic, beckoning the next patients in line from their waiting rooms
into the smaller ante-chamber immediately outside Astley's consulting
room. It was a source of frequent exasperation to Charles that Astley's
personal charms often interrupted the pace of his schedule. 'There was
more difficulty in drawing one lady than two gentlemen,' observed Charles,
referring to the challenge of separating a patient from Astley's side. The
charm was necessary, not least because it helped to hide the unpleasant-
ness of occasional visits. A patient might arrive in pain and leave in agony,
since Astley conducted a large amount of minor surgery in his own rooms,
sometimes without prior warning. Not only might a fashionable lady or
gentleman sit down without being aware that an operation was immediately pending, she or he might know nothing about it until Astley's strong
arm pressed down on them and there was a stab of pain. Surgeons, like
dentists, often sprang upon their patients under the pretence of examining

them. The house was large enough to contain rooms set aside for the recovery of those who had undergone a surgical procedure.

'Sir,' said one of Astley's surprised patients, as an unheralded operation suddenly began, 'you had no right to do that without consulting me; God bless my soul! Sir, the pain is intolerable; – if you had asked me, I don't think I should have submitted.'

'The very reason', replied Astley, 'that I considered it right to think for you.'

On a hospital day Cooper would leave the house around one, often escaping the queue of waiting patients by plunging through the back doors of his own stables and out into a nearby street where he would wait discreetly for his carriage to collect him. At Guy's a large crowd of medical students stood in the stone quadrangle awaiting his arrival. 'Tuesdays and Fridays were the days when he went round,' remembered one, 'and, as his carriage drove quickly up and stopped at the hospital steps, he was out in a moment and skipping up like a bright schoolboy. He was immediately surrounded by a crowd of pupils, amongst whom he, towering like Saul above the people, rushed – for walk he did not – up the ward staircases, the pupils pushing and scrambling so as to get near.' His popularity came from a number of sources. The students were genuinely fond of him, and his lectures and bedside teaching were highly thought of. Combined with the local infamy of his body-snatching and vivisection, was the glitter of his private practice. Aristocrats with private incomes did not become surgeons. The boys who bloodied their sleeves for the long years of an apprenticeship had their fortunes to make, and they knew it.

Diplomatic relations with patients were essential. Once Astley cut for a bladder stone a West Indian merchant named Hyatt, a seventy-year-old man who had made the journey to England specifically to have the operation. Hyatt recovered well, and when Astley went to visit him a few days after the operation the merchant asked Astley his fee. 'Two hundred guineas', was the reply.

'Two hundred guineas!' said Hyatt. 'I shan't give you that sum; *that* is what I shall give you,' and he threw his nightcap at the surgeon.

'Thank you, sir,' said Astley, putting the nightcap in his pocket and leaving.

Physicians and the surgeons who aspired to match their status trod a narrow line when it came to money. On the one hand they often had a taste for it, but on the other they were restricted by the tradition that they were gentlemen, and therefore above such things as bills and set prices, the stuff of merchants. To accept what you were given, even it was nothing, was the mark of polite behaviour; a surgeon was supposed to complain no more about being given too little than he would about being given too much. When a patient offered no fee at the end of a consultation, *The Times* recorded, as in Hyatt's case, Astley assumed he or she was unable to do so and made no mention of it.

When he reached his carriage Astley found that Hyatt had given him more than the nightcap itself; folded inside was a cheque for £1,000. It was a vast sum for a single operation, and the story became public knowledge, the kind of legend that formed a lasting impression on ambitious students. Over a hundred often waited on the hospital steps, then followed him around the wards for the half or three quarters of an hour or so that he took to walk through them. In its April 1843 review of Astley's life, *The Times* gave a glowing description of Astley making his rounds:

He was the idol of the Borough school; the pupils followed him in troops; and, like Linnaeus, who has been described as proceeding on his botanical excursions accompanied by hundreds of students, so may Sir Astley be depicted as traversing the wards of the hospital with an equal number of pupils, listening with almost breathless anxiety to catch the observations which fell from his lips upon the several cases presented to his view. But on the day of operation this feeling was wound up to the highest pitch. The sight was altogether deeply interesting. The large theatre of Guy's crowded to the ceiling, the profoundest silence obtained upon his entry, that person so manly and truly imposing, and the awful feeling connected with the occasion, can never be forgotten by any of his pupils. The elegance of his operations, without the slightest affectation, all ease, all kindness to the patient, and equally solicitous that nothing should be hidden from the observation of the pupils; rapid in execution, masterly in manner; no hurry, no disorder, the most trifling minutiae attended to, the dressings generally applied by his own hand.

To go around the wards in thirty to forty minutes was quick, even by the standards of the day. Admirers said Astley got through more work in that time than his colleagues managed in their more normal hour and a half; detractors cited it as evidence of high-handedness. Part of the explanation for such generally short rounds, however, was the relatively low workload: patients stayed for weeks and months recovering from operations, and there were few new admissions each week. Despite only leaving home about an hour earlier, Astley was famously prompt for the start of his two o'clock lecture that followed his ward round. After that came home visits of private patients until six or seven in the evening. At supper the joint of meat and the pudding were followed by two glasses of wine and a short nap. Some evenings there was another lecture to give, on most there were more home visits. Provincial surgeons often travelled more than ten thousand miles a year in the course of their work. London's concentration brought many of Astley's patients closer together, but he still spent so long sitting in the back of his carriage that he employed a secretary to travel with him and take dictation.

There were other opportunities for ambitious students to come into Cooper's presence. He threw frequent parties at his home, inviting his dressers and his favourite hospital pupils. At the start of each academic session the parties came in a hectic barrage, and students frequently arrived clutching some letter of introduction. As the years passed and the number of surgeons whom Astley had helped to train steadily grew, so the number of such introductions rocketed. At the end of each year's session the same concentration of socialising repeated itself. Ann had no appetite for these gatherings and avoided them whenever possible, driving out into the countryside to stay with her brother, who lived in Tottenham, or seeking refuge with City friends whose houses promised to be quieter.

The first textbook of paediatrics written in English recommended that infants under the age of four be allowed no alcohol stronger than beer – after that, anything went. A young blade – an up-and-coming man of the town – could be classed on the basis of how many bottles of wine he could take at a sitting. In 1751 Hogarth, whose drawings Hazlitt called 'works of science' and 'plates of natural history', had produced *Gin Lane* as a comment on the drink's contemporary influence on the poor, although he regarded beer and wine (the drinks of higher classes of society) in a different and more approving light. Astley, despite his occasional rides in London parks – ever rarer now with the success of his private practice – and a diet that many friends viewed as positively Spartan, began to put on weight. By 1814 John Flint South had grown from a boy with his face against a window into an apprentice with his backside on a bench at Guy's lecture theatre; he commented that although Astley turned up promptly for his afternoon lectures, he 'was generally not so punctual to time' at his evening ones. The comment has been taken as evidence that Astley was overly fond of a drink, but if it is a reference to alcohol it seems only to place him within a world where alcohol was consumed far more freely than today, especially in a working life in which playing a social part was as important as professional skill. Astley's efforts at improving himself had been undiminished either by marrying into money or becoming surgeon to Guy's Hospital. Neither politics, riches nor the death of his daughter had dulled his hunger for work. But an ever increasing amount of that work was now that of a successful society surgeon.

When a London merchant named Brown was discovered to have an aneurysm of his aorta, Astley was summoned. He knew that despite his limited success with operating on the carotid, no approach to the aorta was possible. A surgeon might attempt to patch up a deep wound to the chest or the abdomen, or to operate deliberately near their surface, but to open up either body cavity by choice was murder. Astley advised Brown to take early retirement and to adopt as quiet a life as possible, all in the hope that the aneurysm's growth might be restricted. Brown accordingly quit his work and moved to a comfortable house in rural Richmond to the west of London. There Astley visited him weekly for almost two years. By the end of that time the swelling had grown so pronounced that the front of Brown's abdomen began to bulge forwards. A few months later, with Astley in attendance, the increasingly thin walls of the aneurismal aorta finally tore. The blood poured out and Brown died.

John Saunders would have wished to have been involved in such a case, not least for the income it generated. The care of the chronically sick and constitutionally wealthy was financially rewarding. But Saunders, despite being a friend and protégé of Astley, was at a disadvantage. He had undertaken his training before coming to London, and when he moved into St Mary Axe he had felt too old to enter into another formal apprenticeship. That left him without the kind of official attachment to a hospital that was virtually the only way into the closed hierarchies of the day. Disappointed and discouraged, Saunders made an effort to leave London, only to be drawn back by the attractions of research and Astley's appeals. Prompted both by his own career difficulties and by an epidemic of eye disease in returning Napoleonic war veterans, Saunders had opened his own hospital in 1805. The London Dispensary for diseases of the eyes and ears was the first institution of its kind. The following year

Saunders, heavily influenced by Astley, published a book on diseases of the ear.

A few years later, Saunders's health was obviously failing. People believed that his decline was due to his laborious efforts in the dissecting room. From the start of his work in the dead-house he had appeared to suffer. Several times he turned frighteningly yellow, and his medical friends ascribed his jaundice to the hunched posture of an anatomist always at work on a body. On one occasion he collapsed, falling forwards over the corpse he was dissecting. On another occasion he punctured his finger, accidentally inoculating himself with some of the flesh of his corpse. The wound did not prove fatal, as similar ones did for many others, but his arm grew swollen and stubbornly inflamed, subsiding only after the application of almost two hundred leeches.

Late in 1809, with his vitality failing, Saunders resigned from his post as Astley's Demonstrator and from his work at the hospital he had helped to create. In February the following year, sitting with a physician friend after a meal and a bottle of wine, he complained of some numbness in his right foot. A moment later he seized his forehead in sudden pain, turned pale and sweaty, and began to lose control of the right side of his body. 'He looked at me,' reported his physician friend, 'and said, with a failing articulation, "Paralytic fit."'

Saunders managed to pronounce the name of his wife before becoming unconscious. His friend rushed to bleed him, taking ten ounces (about 300 millilitres) of blood from his arm and then opening up an artery over his temple and taking another sixteen (almost half a litre). Saunders became quieter. With the cohesiveness that marked a small profession, friends rapidly arrived. Saunders's house in Holborn was soon attended by a neighbouring surgeon, a second physician and then Cooper and Cline shortly after. Astley opened up Saunders's temporal artery once more but the blood, rather than pulsing out, oozed as though the vessel were a vein. Every so often Saunders's breathing stopped completely and then, with a retching gasp, spasmodically restarted. The gaps between breaths increased, the breaths themselves became more irregular and less lifelike, and within three hours of his fit Saunders died.

The crowd of medical men had failed to save him, but they had at least been there to bear final witness to the bonds of friendship that held them all together. And even with Saunders dead they found that there were still services that they could provide for him. Astley opened up the body, finding a fresh clot of blood inside his skull, the mark of the burst blood vessel that had killed him. Then he helped to organise the funeral, acted as a pall-bearer, and filled in at Saunders's eye hospital until a replacement could be found.

Family life continued to fill the gaps between work, but with Astley's time outside the hospital and dissecting room increasingly packed with private patients, Ann's discomfort with her city life continued. In the summers she retreated as much as she could to a series of rented homes in Tottenham and other villages. In 1810 the younger Astley, thirteen years old, began as a day boy at Charterhouse School. Schooling consisted chiefly of Latin and Greek, with Charterhouse's new master Dr Russell favouring a system whereby the older boys were put in charge of passing their lessons on to the younger. The choice of the school was convenient. At that time it lay on the north edge of London, but it was only a short distance south along the Islington Road from the village of Pentonville where Ann had taken a house. And at the south side of Charterhouse Square, across from the school, was Saunders's eye hospital.

Another child came to join the family. Henry Charles Cooper was the Reverend Samuel Cooper's third son, and at fifteen he was two years older than his younger brother Astley. It is unclear precisely when he came down from Norfolk, but since he too was entered at Charterhouse in 1810 he had certainly made the move by then.

In 1811, Ann persuaded her husband to buy a country estate. It was a lavish purchase, but Astley's income was now running into many thousands of pounds a year and continuing to rise rapidly. Ann's brother John found a manor and park called Gadebridge (spelt Gadesbridge in many older texts), out at the market town of Hemel Hempstead in Hertfordshire to the north-west of London. On the recommendation of his brother-in-law and the urging of his wife, Astley bought it without even visiting.

Gadebridge was a four-hour carriage ride from the City, an easy enough journey for weekend visits and to be still within reach of a dash back to London should a particularly pressing piece of private work come up. Ann spent much more time there, an escape from crowded city life and the bustle of patients and medical men who infested her London house. With her was Sarah, who turned nineteen in 1811. The two boys Astley and Henry probably boarded near Charterhouse, as did most of the school's paying students (residence within the school itself was reserved for those on scholarships). Their older brother Bransby, the Reverend Samuel's oldest son and the same age as Sarah, now also made an appearance. In 1805 at the age of thirteen he had tried for a career in the navy, gaining the patronage of Port Admiral Russell at Yarmouth and setting out as a midshipman on the 64-gun ship the *Stately*. Desperately missing home and overwhelmingly seasick he returned rapidly to shore and by 1811 had completed a surgical apprenticeship in Norwich. Astley helped organise a year's further study in London but, feeling that his adopted sons Henry and Astley might be disturbed by the residence of their older brother, did not invite Bransby into either of his homes. In the following year, 1812, Bransby's studies finished. Astley told him he still lacked knowledge and advised him to join the military. Early in 1812, with the Napoleonic wars offering rich experience for those who survived them, Bransby joined up. In September of the same year Henry Cooper left Charterhouse and went to live and study with Astley in London.

In May 1813 Cooper was appointed Professor of Comparative Anatomy to the Royal College of Surgeons. He launched feverishly into the preparation of his lectures and his specimens, employing an extra assistant to board in a room adjoining his own and limiting himself to only three or four hours' sleep a night. The new rush of work came at the same time as Sarah's marriage. Both bore rapid fruit, Sarah falling pregnant with her first child and Astley's fresh dissections once more making his well-attended lectures devastatingly perfumed. Lions, hyenas, elephants, cuttlefish, baboons, polar bears, walruses, lemurs, leopards, the lymphatics of a porpoise, kangaroos, tortoises, porcupines, panthers and seals and the stomach of a cormorant: every domestic or foreign animal Astley could get his hands on. Sarah's husband – a Mr Parmenter – was roped into family service in order to visit south coast fishing ports and see what he could bring back. Contemporary ideas of human evolution were also covered in the talks, and Astley 'dwelt for some time on the distinctive characters of the Caucasian, Mongolian, American, Ethiopian and Malay varieties of the human race'.*

---

* Down's syndrome – influentially described by John Langdon Haydon Down in his 1866 paper 'Observations on an Ethnic Classification of Idiots' – illustrates the ideas Astley had in mind. Caucasians were pictured at the top of a ladder that stretched back through shades of ever-darkening skin towards an affinity with chimpanzees and gorillas. Believing that each of us *in utero* passed through a similar chain of development, Dr Down felt that certain people were stuck at the level of the Mongol races. His ideas were widely accepted at the time.

That winter the Thames froze thickly, giving rise to the greatest frost fair that anyone could remember.* In spring, after the river had thawed and begun to flow again, both the lectures and the pregnancy came to a sudden end. On 12 April 1814, a sign was placed on the door of the lecture theatre, giving unexpected notice that the course had finished early that season. It had been brought to an early close by Sarah's death. The Coopers had lost another daughter, and their grandchild was stillborn.

Astley's grief at Sarah's death was sufficient to bring an early end to his lectures but they began afresh the following year. Ann's life – less securely anchored in the daily demands of work – was more permanently marked. She retreated to Gadebridge, finding what peace she could in the large gardens and the attractive countryside.

As before, when a child died, the Coopers assuaged their loss by another adoption. This time it was Parmenter, their son-in-law, whom they took in. He moved to Gadebridge to keep Ann company and to manage the estate.

While Astley and Ann were coping with domestic deaths, Bransby was engaged with the military. In 1814, during the Peninsular Wars, the 2nd assistant surgeon to the Ordnance Medical Department was bivouacking in the Spanish village of Sarre, soon to enter French territory. The evening had fallen when his servant came in and told him that there was someone to see him.

The muscular young surgeon stepped out of his tent to see a short and even more heavily built man who carried himself as roughly as he dressed. Mr Butler looked ill and tired, and he had good reason to, having walked and hitched several hundred arduous miles eastwards from Lisbon. He handed Bransby a letter:

> My dear Bransby,
>   Butler will tell you the purport of his visit. I hope you are well and happy.
>   Your affectionate uncle,
>   Astley Cooper

---

* It was also the last, partly because the replacement of London Bridge in 1831 meant the water flowed more swiftly and became less prone to freezing over.

Bransby asked the man what he wanted.

'Teeth,' he replied.

The unexpected messenger appeared to be on the verge of collapse, the journey having left him far too sick to continue his quest. Butler allowed Bransby to admit him to the military field hospital and to look after him until his strength had recovered. 'Oh, sir,' explained Butler as his health returned, 'only let there be a battle, and there'll be no want of teeth. I'll draw them as fast as the men are knocked down.'

For a while at least there was nothing for Butler to do but relax, recuperate, and dream of teeth. Bransby said later that once Butler had recovered he gave him some money and told him to forget the scheme. But given Bransby's devotion to his uncle that seems unlikely, and odd for a man whose training as a surgeon left him perfectly clear about where teeth and corpses came from and the extent to which Astley was involved in organising the trade. Butler may not have been sent specifically to fetch teeth, but Astley would not have dispatched him all that way without the hope that he would bring back some human trophy of war.

Whatever Butler's mission, he showed his gratitude for Bransby's medical care. Two years later, with both men back in Britain, he wrote to thank him, proudly mentioning that he had made £300 on his trip to the front line. He was not the only one of Cooper's London body-snatchers to make a fortune smashing in the mouths of the fallen. Many teeth from those foreign fields came back to mend the smiles of the English rich.

When Bransby returned from the war – having seen action in Spain, France and even on a secret military expedition to Quebec – he found his hopes destroyed. His younger brother Henry had become Astley's apprentice during his absence: and with that went the implicit promise of receiving, in turn, Astley's private practice and position at Guy's. Suddenly hopeless, Bransby decided to give up surgery entirely. He resolved on becoming a physician, and took himself off to Edinburgh to train. Most people would have preferred such a course, for it was still generally true that physicians gained far more by way of prestige and wealth than their surgical counterparts. But for Bransby it was the end of a dream. To be a surgeon like the uncle he worshipped had been all he had wanted since his failure in the navy. He did what he could in Edinburgh to console himself, and in the spirit of trying to build a new life for himself he found a wife.

After a rain-drenched day on the Continent, June 1815 saw Wellington defeat Napoleon. England celebrated, and Henry Cooper, now a maturing surgical student, rushed to the front line to offer his professional assistance. Astley, like many others, refused to take a fee from the hordes of injured men who returned from the war. His surgical practice was as large and as lucrative as he could ever have wished – his income for that year alone was the astonishing sum of £21,000, more than any other surgeon or physician in the country. Roughly translated it amounted to something around £1.26 million in modern terms. But in a society with a small middle class both property and labour were cheap, it was worth very much more. Feeling somewhat oppressed by the sheer quantity of private work being pressed upon him, Astley moved from the mercantile City of London towards the more rarefied region of the West End. He took a large house in Conduit Street, on the other side of Bond Street from Berkeley Square, oriented away from the teeming life of the City and towards the grander residences of the court and the nobility.

15

Surgeon to the Poet

The parties at Astley's house which marked the start of the winter season were attended by a wide spread of Borough Hospital doctors. Physicians, apothecaries and surgeons mixed with students whom Astley knew from the previous year or who had just arrived with their letters of introduction. Ann avoided the heat and the crowds of these entertainments, staying in Gadebridge and seeing her husband at the weekends.

By 1815 Astley had begun to grow slightly plump and red-cheeked. He was tall, muscular and partial to physical exercise when he could get it. His legs still had the sleek trim of which he was so proud. But he was forty-seven and age was beginning to tell, and the morning constitutionals on horseback around the London parks were not so frequent as they once had been.

In the time since his youthful tuberculosis had faded away, Astley had been generally healthy. There was the extended fever as a student, the fall on his head whilst with Cline and, later, a small bone broken in his leg on an icy London street. Otherwise he had stayed vigorous. Now, for the first time, a chronic illness began to emerge. It seemed nothing life-threatening – a series of giddy spells – but it was worrying. A surgeon could neither operate on nor offer consultation to a patient while the room was spinning around him so furiously that he needed to hold on to the furniture for support. And Astley was too familiar with man's mortality to have overlooked the link between his passing years and this new symptom.

Plenty of men lived into their seventies and eighties, but it was not the routine expectation that it would become almost two centuries later. Time was limited, even if the precise limits were often not clear. Astley attributed his attacks to the effects of overwork, and cut down on his private practice.

Among the new students in October 1815 was a short and physically striking young man. John Keats had finished five years' apprenticeship as a provincial apothecary and had signed on for a year at the Borough Hospitals. New legislation had come into force a few months earlier that meant all apothecaries now needed to attend a hospital for six months before they could practise. Keats chose to sign on for a full year. That signified his intention of qualifying as a surgeon.

The new hurdles for those wanting to train as apothecaries were a reflection of the growing strength of the public hospitals and the medical guilds. Together they were undermining the private surgical schools and apprenticeships, concentrating increasing power in the hands of those who held positions in the hospitals and the royal colleges. Mingled with the professional self-interest was an element of something admirable: the 1815 Apothecaries Act came about partly as a result of genuine concern over quality. Medicine was a massively expanding industry. Physicians were still the cream, even with Astley Cooper prominently out-earning all of them. But beneath both the physicians and the surgeons were the apothecaries who still filled the huge gap at the lower end of the market by prescribing as well as dispensing medicines. In 1815 such men were being spoken of by a new name: the term 'General Practitioner' was becoming common.

In St Thomas's Street, in the house of a tallow chandler only a few doors away from the hospital, lived two trainee surgeons. Frederick Tyrrell was one of Astley's apprentices; George Cooper, no relation, was effectively another, being his dresser. The two men were aristocrats of the world of student surgery, their positions with Astley promising them a bright future. Tyrrell's father had paid many hundreds of pounds for the privilege of his son's apprenticeship – fees could be in the order of £500. George Cooper seemed to have earned his by merit. Joining them was the young John Keats, placed with the two much more senior men by the personal intervention of Astley Cooper. The reason for Astley's involvement with this new arrival, a relatively poor apothecary from outside London, is a mystery. Keats had gone to school in Enfield and trained as an apothecary in Edmonton. Robert Gittings, the biographer of the poet, thought it probable that Astley had been struck with Keats's resemblance to a contemporary surgeon. But it seems more likely to have been the result of some direct recommendation. Thomas Hammond, the apothecary under whom Keats had been apprenticed, had himself trained at the Borough Hospitals, serving as a dresser to William Lucas, one of Astley's former colleagues. Keats, like many other young men, almost certainly arrived in the Borough with letters of recommendation. These would have been enough to admit him to Astley's company, but hardly to stir this active involvement. Unless there were something exceptional in the letters' texts – and there is no reason to suspect that there was – it must have been something in Keats's character that prompted Astley's further help.

Twenty years old and around five feet tall, there was nothing effete about this particular surgical student. He brawled, drank and studied with appetite and success. The Borough's narrow streets, at a time when at least one of the Borough's senior surgeons would not travel after dark without pistols and a sword, did nothing to intimidate him, although he found them crowded and oppressive. 'The Borough', he warned a friend, 'is a beastly place in dirt, turnings and windings.' Keats, like Shakespeare before him, attended the bear-baitings that, along with theatre, were traditionally on offer in the district. He seemed to enjoy them, mimicking for his friends not only the bear and the dogs but also the colourful audience. For someone with an interest in character and a tolerance for pain, the theatres of the Borough Hospitals were as enthralling as these other scenes of death. The sights and sounds of surgery, the smells and the fetid immediacy of dissection did nothing to dampen Keats's early enthusiasm for his training.

Each of the three senior surgeons had four dressers working for him. They took their duty in turns, each shift lasting seven days and coming around once every twelve weeks. While their period of duty lasted they slept in the hospital so as to be available for emergencies. In the daytime, if the work was quiet and their lodgings close enough for them to be easily summoned back, they might slip out home for a period. The dressers were the first ports of call for surgical emergencies. Trauma could come in at any hour. Patients came to have their wounds seen to, to have plasters or poultices changed, to have teeth pulled or blood let.

Within a month of his arrival Keats was offered the opportunity of a dressership when one should become available. It was an astonishing promotion for a young man without family or money to push favours into his lap. Given Astley's known involvement and Keats's lack of any other known supporters, it was most likely Astley who lay behind the appointment.

Since they were surgeons and not physicians or apothecaries, the dressers generally gave out no medicines. Lotions and leeches were permissible, as was cupping. Guy's had two rooms in which the dressers worked. The larger was fourteen feet square, and on benches around its walls sat the outpatients who made up the bulk of the dresser's work. The examination and treatment of those patients took place where they sat, amongst the crowd. If they needed a minor operation they could be led to a smaller room, about fourteen feet by five, and have it performed there. The rest of the time the smaller room was reserved for patients with enough money to pay something for their care.

While they worked, the dressers also had to study. If their ambition was to come to anything it needed to be stamped with membership of the Royal College of Surgeons. For that there were exams, and before the exams came lectures. Astley's remained the most popular ones available, and Keats was sitting in the audience as the senior surgeon strode in at the start of term. His accent swallowed a consonant here and there: customarily he greeted his audience with the exclamation 'Genelmen!'

'Take short notes of the Lectures,' Astley advised the class, '[then] having dissected generally go through the different parts particularly; and let me advise you to pay particular attention to Morbid Preparations for be assured there is no other true knowledge of Anatomy than that derived from observations of the Living, and on the Dead; and also by experiments made upon living animals.'

Keats followed Astley's directions, sketching his short notes on cream-coloured pages whose margins he crowded with doodles and drawings of flowers. He listened to Astley's mimicry of some of the capital's other doctors, in particular some of his Scottish colleagues. 'Weel, Mister Cooper,' ran one of Astley's favourite impressions, 'we ha' only twa things to keep in meend, and they'll searve us for here and herea'ter; one is always to have the fear of the Laird before our ees, that'll do for herea'ter; and the t'other is to keep your booels open, and that will do for here.'

Keats noted down with fascination Astley's account of an Italian vivisectionist who destroyed the eyes of a bat and watched it fly flawlessly around a room. He was struck by hearing about the wound received by a famous Polish revolutionary, who 'had his sciatic nerve injured by a pike'.

The story came only a few minutes before Astley switched to another famous patriot, this time Nelson. He explained to the class the ill-effects of a suture having been put through a nerve when Nelson's arm had been amputated. 'With all his heroism,' Astley told the class, 'he could not bear the least touch of the ligature, without uttering the most violent expressions.'

On the days when Astley walked the wards he continued to find a mob of students waiting for him, crowding the entrance of the hospital. Cline was well liked, but Astley was the favourite as John Flint South records: 'The pupils accompanied them in shoals . . . [they] pushed and jostled, and ran and crowded round the beds, quite regardless of the patients' feelings or condition.' And at the centre of it all, proudly carrying the plaster-boxes which were the symbols of their office, the equivalents of today's stethoscopes or bleeping pagers, were the dressers.

There were two scheduled ward rounds a week, but Astley often made more. A student, watching him walk the wards on Sunday mornings, compared him to a florist, visiting the beds where his flowers grew. Astley's wealth made a lot of people suspicious of him, but no one suggested that his enjoyment of worldly success had done anything to dim his genuine passion for surgery. 'His interest in his profession was genuine,' said his dresser, the man most likely to bear the brunt of any work that Astley shirked, 'independent of the additional incitement of the love of reputation or of gain. This was equally evinced in the dissecting-room, and in the wards of the Hospital: of the two, I should say, his passion was for minute anatomy.'

During the winter season of 1816–7 Henry Cooper, Astley's adopted son and planned successor, was struck down by fever while working away at his dissection. It was a common enough occurrence for a student in the atmosphere of the hospital or surgical school dead-house. The dangers were known, and Astley spoke about them in his lectures, telling the students of a young man a few years before them who had come over from the West Indies to study at Guy's. Pricking his finger while dissecting had brought on a fever and he died within days. Astley described the rotten and deliquescent state of his body at the post-mortem. Then he told of wounding himself in a similar fashion, suffering badly after cutting himself dissecting a man who had been hanged only a few hours before. The outcome of such wounds, he explained, depended partly on the nature of the material that was introduced, the portion of the dead that entered the flesh of the living, and partly on the constitution of the anatomist. Young men were weaker in spring after a long cold winter in London's dissecting rooms; in autumn, after a summer in the country, they were stronger. Astley recommended that they imitated him in 'temperance, early rising, and sponging [your] body every morning with cold water'. If all that failed, he said, a man's constitution was best preserved by a large bowl of hot tea each morning.

The points were seriously meant and seriously made, because the shadow of death hung over them. It was the heart of winter when Henry Cooper fell ill. Two weeks later, on 8 January 1817, he was dead. Neither connections nor youth nor the best medical advice in the country were any protection when it came to the hazards of dissecting.

Henry's death left a gap, and for Bransby, still up in Edinburgh training as a physician, there was no question of how to respond. His younger brother's death was sad but it was also an opportunity. Bransby abandoned his physician's career in an instant, rushing from Edinburgh to London to take up his scalpel, and called again at his uncle's house. This time the door opened for him.

Astley used Bransby's arrival to help with the changes to his life after his move westwards to Conduit Street. The pace of his life in the City had worn him out. He had more cash than he needed, less time than he wished and not as much worldly status as he fancied. To be paid £1,000 for a single operation on a rich merchant was one form of success: to be sought out by dukes, princes and ministers was quite another. As his nephew's experience and confidence grew, Astley was able to increasingly use Bransby as a deputy. That left more time for Astley to spend with the aristocrats. More time, jibed the *Quarterly Review*, 'to affect more silkiness of manner and finery of habits'.

Bransby replaced his brother Henry both as Astley's protégé and housemate, and when he moved in he brought his young wife with him. With Ann Cooper settled at Gadebridge, there was an immediate role for Bransby's wife in running the house. That made life more comfortable for Astley, and he added to its effects by changing his practice of almost a quarter of a century. He stopped seeing patients for free, directing Bransby to attend those who carried on seeking him out and asking his nephew to call him only if he found cases that were unusually interesting. Along with the reduction in his private practice, it was a change that made his life considerably more free.

The opposite was true for Keats, whose increasing seriousness about poetry coincided with a dresser's job finally becoming vacant in March 1816. Keats found himself carrying a box for William Lucas junior, the son of the man who had trained his old apothecary-tutor. Lucas was friendly and well liked, but neither his figure nor his accomplishments were impressive. Tall, stooped, shuffling and awkward, his occasional dexterity was undermined by a lack of both intelligence and knowledge. He had little skill when it came to either diagnosing a problem or dealing with it. As a young man, explained Astley, Lucas had never had the health and vigour necessary for spending hours in the dead-house. As a result he had never learnt the anatomy he needed. 'He was neat handed, but rash in the extreme, cutting amongst most important parts as if it was only skin, and making us always shudder from apprehension of his opening arteries, or committing some other errors.'

On one notorious occasion Lucas got into such a mess while amputating a leg that when he put down his saw and instruments he found that he had done everything back to front. There was a neatly fashioned flap of skin covering the part of the leg that had been removed, while naked bone stuck out unprotected from the patient's stump, glistening with blood and fluid. Exposed bone was deadly, and the patient had to suffer a second amputation immediately, this time higher up, in order to create enough spare flesh to cover up Lucas's mistake.

To his credit – for those willing to spend time on that side of the balance sheet – Lucas was partly aware of his defects. Astley noted that unless he or Cline were present in the hospital, ready to come to his rescue, Lucas was unwilling to operate. And it was also true that with operations needing to be carried out so swiftly, mistakes were easy to make. Astley himself once publicly fumbled an amputation, a bleeding femoral artery unsettling him so severely that he spent time senselessly clutching at its cut end with his fingers. His assistant rescued the situation by astutely pressing hard on the patient's groin, preventing blood spurting from the artery until Astley had recovered his senses. 'I was sometimes great,' said Astley of his operative ability, 'sometimes in difficulties from venturing too much.' He was confident in his own profound understanding of anatomy, nervous of the lack of physical delicacy that he knew he sometimes displayed. 'Quite unfitted by nature' was his verdict on himself when it came to such a tricky piece of manipulation as the removal of the lens within a person's eye after a cataract had formed.

Lucas was a bad surgeon, but there were plenty of those. His failures may have impacted forcefully on Keats, but it is not clear that this was what put the young man off a career in surgery. There was plenty of opportunity at Guy's and St Thomas's to see what could be achieved by good surgeons. To see the harm that could be done by men who were careless or unskilled was potentially even more of a motivation to do the job well. It is strange that Keats's many biographers so consistently conclude that horror and dismay hastened his exit from the profession. It was not Keats's character to slink away from what was difficult or painful, so it is odd to suggest that such a bad example as Lucas should have repelled Keats. In the face of other injustices Keats characteristically grew angry and forceful, determined to play a part in remedying them.

For Berlioz, who studied medicine in Paris in 1821 a few years later than Keats, the realities of hospital life were indeed destructive to the values and ideals of artistic composition:

Become a doctor! Study anatomy! Dissect! Witness horrible operations instead of throwing myself heart and soul into the glorious art of music! Forsake the empyrean for the dreary realities of earth! The immortal angels of poetry and love and their inspired songs for filthy hospitals, dreadful medical students, hideous corpses, the shrieks of patients, the groans and death-rattles of the dying. It seemed to be the utter reversal of the natural conditions of my life – horrible and impossible.

For Keats, there was no such opposition. After he decided to concentrate on poetry, the memories of medicine came frequently back to him. He wrote about his pleasure in discovering that he had not thrown his knowledge away, that both his mind and his library still contained the materials of his surgical studies. When his poetry went badly he thought of leaving it, of travelling to Edinburgh to train as a physician. Broken by tuberculosis and despair, he spoke of recuperating while working as a ship's surgeon. It was a serious thought with purposes beyond a warrant to sail under skies of sun-filled health. It was a way of making use of his life, and of earning a living, while his greater powers were absent, and it was also a way he imagined he might recharge them, poetically rejuvenating himself. Keats's continuing attraction to the symbolism of Apollo – god of poetry and medicine – also signifies something of the status of surgery in the minds of men like Astley Cooper. In 1802, in his preface to his and Coleridge's *Lyrical Ballads*, Wordsworth wrote:

Whenever we sympathize with pain, it will be found that the sympathy is produced and carried on by subtle combinations with pleasure . . . The Man of science, the Chemist and the Mathematician, whatever difficulties and disgusts they may have had to struggle with, know and feel this. However painful may be the objects with which the Anatomist's knowledge is connected, he feels that his knowledge is pleasure; and where he has no pleasure he has no knowledge.

As a young man Astley had decisively rejected the conservative values of his Enlightenment parents. After his first few London months of adolescent delinquency, he had responded to Henry Cline's radicalism by bursting through into a life animated by belief in revolutionary democracy and radical surgery. Now, middle-aged and a powerful member of the establishment, more concerned with opportunities at the royal court than with treating the poor, there was still some of his idealism left. The chill of the French Revolution and Pitt's repressive regime in Britain had killed off one part of Astley's belief in building a better world, in discovering a new way of living. His interest in radical politics was entirely gone. But what remained was the conviction that a surgeon was as much a worthy part of the world as a poet, that there was as much beauty in dissection as in sonnets.

William Hazlitt, the great critic of the age and the man to whose judgements Keats so often looked, understood this feeling. As part of an essay 'On Imitation' in Leigh Hunt's journal *The Examiner* of 18 February 1816, he wrote:

The anatomist is delighted with a coloured plate, conveying the exact appearance of the progress of certain diseases, or of the internal parts and dissections of the human body. We have known a Jennerian Professor as much enraptured with a delineation of the different stages of vaccination, as a florist with a bed of tulips . . . the objects themselves give as much pleasure to the professional inquirer, as they would pain to the uninitiated. The learned amateur is struck with the beauty of the coats of the stomach laid bare, or contemplates with eager curiosity the transverse section of the brain . . . the number of the parts, their distinctions, connections, structure, uses; in short, an entire new set of ideas, which occupies the mind of the student, and overcomes the sense of pain and repugnance, which is the only feeling that the sight of a dead and mangled body presents to ordinary men.

When Astley stood before his students in the hospital lecture theatre and spoke to them about surgery he wanted them to believe in its value as a human endeavour. It was essential that the world – or at least a small, thoughtful and educated part of it – was willing to see the beauty of surgical work, rather than just its necessity. Medical ignorance was everywhere, and it filled an imaginative life with excitement.

Astley's lectures also preached that tolerating pain was essential if men and women were to be helped. A surgeon, he said, needed 'an eagle's eye, a lady's hand, and a lion's heart'. It was a lesson that Keats, finding as much death and pain in the lives of his family as in the wards of his hospital, heard and understood. 'Do you not see how necessary a World of Pains and troubles is to school an Intelligence and make it a soul?' he wrote. There was no shying away from the touch of the dissecting room or the desperation of the operating theatre.

From the time of his appointment as surgeon to Guy's Hospital, Astley's imagination was almost entirely tied up with his profession. Even his family life, the only other area of existence to which he showed any devotion, moved in the same orbit, his adopted sons all being pulled into the field of surgery. He read poetry and was proud of the ease with which it stayed in his memory, but he felt no pull towards any other profession or avenue of life. Keats did not lack the stomach for surgery, nor, with his double-god Apollo, was he unable to perceive the aesthetic value of tending to a sick man or woman. There was nothing lacking for him in the world of early nineteenth-century surgery, nothing save the fact that it intruded on the single-minded immersion in poetry that he felt called to. When the short and vigorously animated dresser disappeared from the hospital wards, Astley showed no sign of noticing his passing. There were too many other keen young men whose careers he had an interest in fostering, and there were still his own more private ambitions.

Some biographical accounts of Keats suggest that from the time of his contact with Leigh Hunt his surgical duties slowly faded away. By February 1817, says Gittings, 'little trace remained of the dressership at Guy's, and [Keats] can only have carried out his duties there in the most perfunctory way'. In fact Keats completed his dressership successfully. It was arduous, but the busy times were intermittent. Each of the three Guy's senior surgeons took turns in charge of a week's intake, and for every week they had four dressers, one of whom would spend the time resident in the hospital dealing with emergencies. That meant Keats served roughly one week in twelve, with further study and clinic work fitted into the calmer times.

Keats finished his training, rather than let it fade away, although it is true that he neither took the examination to become a member of the Royal College of Surgeons nor collected an official certificate of completion from Guy's. Later in his life he was confident that he could get a job as a ship's surgeon – something that only such a certificate would have enabled him to do. Several of his contemporaries at Guy's requested these certificates only years later, supporting Keats's belief that it was something he could come back for. Guy's and St Thomas's also carefully recorded when dressers failed to complete their terms, and there are no such commentaries on Keats. So we know that Keats finished his year's training, squeezing his poetry in as he went, and that Gittings was wrong to imply that either the poet or the hospital was content to allow it to evaporate.

Keats's friend Charles Armitage Brown claimed that the poet quit surgery as a result of his terror of making a mistake:

He has assured me the muse had no influence over him in his determination, he being compelled, by conscientious motives alone, to quit the profession, upon discovering that he was unfit to perform a surgical operation. He ascribed his inability to an overwrought apprehension of every possible chance of doing evil in the wrong direction of the instrument. 'My last operation', he told me, 'was the opening of a man's temporal artery. I did it with the utmost nicety; but, reflecting on what passed through my mind at the time, my dexterity seemed a miracle, and I never took up the lancet again.'

In his biography, Gittings mistakenly elaborates on these concerns, suggesting that 'Brown's slip of memory or lack of understanding substituted what Keats was afraid of doing, "the opening of a man's temporal artery", for what he in fact performed successfully, the opening of a vein'. Gittings suggests that Brown's 'account, though confused, points to Keats's area of apprehension'.

In fact Brown was perfectly correct in suggesting that Keats had deliberately opened a temporal artery. It was the same treatment that Astley had carried out on his friend Saunders. But Brown was writing from memory many decades later, and did not know Keats during the period of his surgical training. A very different explanation for Keats's exit from medicine is given by the poet himself. In 1819 he wrote to Brown that 'in no period of my life have I acted with any self-will but in throwing up the apothecary profession'. To be forced out of a career by 'inability' is the opposite of exercising self-will. Keats made a deliberate choice to set medicine aside, although he kept his textbooks and notes and knew that it was something he could always come back to. At the end of his dressership in spring 1817, Keats handed on his plaster box and left the wards. He chose poetry.

16

The Lessons of Experience

For someone interested in tying off blood vessels, and seeing how well the body developed new ones, there was an obvious hierarchy of interest. The bigger the vessel, the greater nature's achievement in overcoming its obliteration and the greater the surgeon's credit for assisting. The popliteal artery behind the knee was commonly operated on and the collateral circulation developed well. The femoral vessels were even larger, being further upstream. If you put your hand in your groin, about halfway along the diagonal line from the top of your hips to the bony ridge above your genitals, you can feel the pulsing of the femoral artery. The sensation comes not from the movement of blood, since the blood in the artery is always on the move, but from the advancing pressure wave of each heartbeat.

If those big blood vessels were the Himalayas of the ambitious vascular surgeon, it was clear where Everest lay. The left side of the heart pumps out the same volume of blood as the right. But the right goes solely into the lungs, a relatively low pressure circuit, whilst the left drives blood through all the rest of the body. It is the left side of the heart that is larger, since it pumps against a much higher resistance. The name given to the main artery that emerges from the left side of the heart is the aorta. It arches upwards and backwards, slightly to the left of the sternum. Branches lead off into the head and neck and arms, but by the time the aorta curves over itself and heads down through the chest and abdomen it is still a couple of centimetres in diameter.

As a medical student I watched the blunt way in which a senior surgeon obtained what is called 'informed consent' for an operation in a man whose aorta had burst. She had asked to know the man's most recent blood pressure. I tried to measure it and failed, believing my lack of experience was to blame. She put it down to the man having too little pressure to be easily measured, and became brusque.

'If we don't operate now,' she told the man, 'you'll die. If we do operate, there's a good chance you'll die anyway.'

'What are my chances?' he asked, a little confused. 'Fifty-fifty?'

She shook her head – they were not nearly so good – and suggested to the man's wife that she kiss him and waste no time about it. Then she helped to push the trolley on which he lay towards the operating theatre.

I thought about her manner for a long term after. She was rude and brisk and I believe that she was also correct and admirable. It was a rude and brisk situation. The journalist John Diamond recalled that his own doctor had not been able to look him in the face when explaining that his cancer had become incurable. Diamond felt it was a mark of the man's humanity that he was too deeply upset by the news to be good-mannered about it. Haste may not be good-mannered, but it was vital enough to have been humane.

On a beautiful spring day in 1817, the porter Charles Hutson arrived at Guy's Hospital. He was thirty-eight years old and he had a swelling in his groin that extended upwards into his belly. The cause was an underlying aneurysm, its pulsing easily palpable over the broad mass of the swelling. Mostly the swollen flesh was tense and hard, but at one small point at the front of his abdomen it was soft and boggy. The disease in the aorta was not so sudden and catastrophic as that in the man I saw. This was a slow leak, the flesh surrounding it gradually eroding away.

The aneurysm was too high to be operable. It was above the femoral artery. There was no way of getting to it without tying off the aorta. It was an unthinkable operation to put someone through: horrifically painful in execution and pointlessly fatal in outcome. Astley explained this to Hutson and to the crowding students. For all his willingness to vivisect, he prided himself on avoiding pointless operations, on managing not to inflict needless pain on men, women and children who would not profit from it. Nature was always unpredictable, he said, and even in the most awful conditions there was a tiny chance of spontaneous recovery. Even if there wasn't, there was nothing to be done. Astley had watched many others, like the London merchant Brown, die of the same condition.

As the April days went by, the soft skin at the base of Hutson's belly began to ulcerate and rot. His admission at Guy's stretched itself out into months. Meanwhile Astley's brother Samuel had arrived in London for one of his regular visits. This time the normal routine of Samuel's dry humour convulsing Astley into unsightly snorts and eruptions of loud laughter was brought to a halt. Samuel's chest filled with water, most likely the result of some combination of heart failure, tuberculosis and pneumonia. He faded rapidly, dying at Astley's London house on 3 June in the arms of his eldest son, Bransby.

Just over a fortnight later, on 20 June, the day dawned bright and clear. By noon London was sweltering in the heat. Blood began to pour through the front of Hutson's abdomen. The junior surgeon on attendance was called and came quickly to the ward. He took a lint compress and pressed down on the broken flesh of Hutson's belly through which the blood was coming. The bleeding stopped.

They were hot days, the sun high and strong over the city. For Hutson, each one was gradually worse. He was slowly dying. Watching him, remembering Brown, Astley turned over the sensible decision that he had made not to operate. He knew that an operation was potentially possible. He had successfully tied the aorta in dogs. With Hutson so obviously slipping away, was not a vanishingly small chance better than none at all? In the evenings, when it had grown slightly cooler, Astley went to the dead-house and practised. But even on the co-operative dead the procedure was impossibly difficult. He tried different approaches and rejected them all. The operation could have no good outcome. It would be impractical and cruel.

The following day, as hot as the ones before, there was more bleeding. After a short period it spontaneously stopped but the next day, 25th June, it returned with more force. Although Charles Hutson was a remarkably brave man, when his blood was pouring out from the hole that had rotted open in his belly, he was scared enough to lose control of his bowels.

At nine o'clock that evening Astley saw Hutson was about to die. Desperate, he tried a smaller operation than tying his aorta. He sliced open the aneurysm itself and, pushing his finger upstream into the artery, tried to tie it from within. He failed. The bleeding continued, much worse now from the cut that Astley had made. There was no hope. Feeling beaten and discouraged, Astley got up to leave. He wrote:

As I was quitting the patient's bed, I felt a great regret, in which all the students by whom I was surrounded joined me, that the patient should be left to perish without giving him the only chance which remained of preventing his immediate dissolution from haemorrhage, by tying the aorta; and I therefore said: 'Gentlemen, this only hope of safety I am determined to give him.'

Hutson consented to an operation. He was placed flat on his back with pillows beneath his shoulders. Astley hoped that if he could keep the muscles of Hutson's belly relaxed then his guts might not spill out once he cut through them. 'I expected that a protrusion of the intestines would produce embarrassment in the operation', explained Astley. He anticipated having to push the bowels back in again, as he had once tried and failed to do as a student for the Borough woman who had sliced herself apart.

Astley ran his scalpel along the midline of Hutson's abdomen, with a small deviation to avoid cutting his navel in two. The muscles parted beneath the blade, exposing the membrane beneath shining wetly. It was the only thing now protecting the loops of Hutson's guts. Astley scratched through it with a fingernail, then reached into the abdomen with both hands. Only one small loop of bowel fell outwards as he did so. More would have done so, thought Astley, if Hutson's terror had not so successfully cleared his bowels out. As the operation progressed, with Astley's hands deep amongst his intestines, Hutson's fear made him open up his bowels once more.

There was no way for Astley to see what his own hands were doing. He proceeded by feel. The aorta lay underneath the guts, separated from them by another membrane and some surrounding fat. Astley opened it up twice with his fingers, once on either side of the spine. Then he reached through the intestines and attempted to get between the spine and the aorta that ran in front of it. At the moment of his success he paused. An admiring onlooker recorded that 'looking round, [he] said, "Gentlemen, I have the pleasure of informing you that the aorta is now hooked upon my finger"'.

There was an ease to Astley's performance that amplified much of his

success. He retained, said the *Quarterly Review*, 'the most perfect possession of himself in the theatre. He was, indeed, a great actor in more senses
than one. His admirable manual dexterity was not more obvious than the
love of display that he brought to the most critical of incisions.'

A student was more biting:

> *Not Drury Lane nor Covent Garden*
> *Are to my fancy worth a farden*
> *I hold them both small beer:*
> *Give me the wonderful exploits,*
> *And jolly jokes, between the sleights,*
> *Of Astley's Amphitheatre.*

The verse applies ambiguously to lectures as well as operations. A brave
patient might play a good supporting role within the theatre, but Astley's
audience were left in no doubt that the surgeon was the star. Charles
Hutson was in too much pain to notice.

In a modern hospital an emergency repair of the aorta is most likely to
fail. The situation is different if the operation is done electively, before
the aneurysm actually bursts. Then the vast majority of patients survive.
The aorta is opened and a graft, made of a material similar to Gore-Tex,
is sewn inside. A new blood vessel is formed inside the old. There is no
need to tie the vessel closed in the manner of Hunter or Cooper. Similar
fabric grafts exist for other arteries and, so long as the patient's heart and
lungs are strong, the operation is likely to succeed.

Charles Hutson stood his trial well, and the following day, almost miraculously, he was visibly better. His legs were warm. That meant blood was
successfully finding its way down to them. He himself was cheerful. But
he had also begun to vomit.

The following day, Friday, the weather finally broke. Showers came down
on the overheated city, and when the water had finished washing the walls
of Guy's Hospital the temperature dropped pleasantly. By then Hutson's
left leg had become cold, colder than it should have been. He was frightened and anxious, dribbling incontinently with urine and restless in his
ward bed. The first part of the night passed badly. He was sleepless and
the vomiting continued. His restlessness subsided into confusion and confu-

sion melted into unconsciousness. At eighteen minutes past one, in the darkness of the summer night, Hutson died. He had survived the operation by about forty hours.

In the medical school of Guy's and St Thomas's sits a small transparent case containing Charles Hutson's aorta. It has faded a little with time, but the preservatives have done their work and its structure is still intact. Around the lower part of it is a neat thread, tying it closed. Occasionally groups of American vascular surgeons come to visit, clustering around the aorta with their cameras and their professional amazement that anyone should have tried such an operation, and should have got so close to pulling it off.

Astley himself never had, or never took, the chance for another go at aortic ligation. Others did. Johns Hopkins Hospital in Baltimore reported the results of a series of seven attempts carried out up until 1922. Other hospitals made attempts in 1829, 1834 and in 1842. Every single one of the attempts at Johns Hopkins and elsewhere ended badly. Every single one of the patients died. But at least, from the second half of the nineteenth century, patients were spared much of the agony of operation. Anaesthetics had arrived.

The great constant in Astley's life was dissection. Before breakfast, in the gaps between morning patients, in the space that the afternoons and evenings allowed, he took up his probe and his scalpel and hunched himself over pieces of flesh. Publication gave a purpose to what he pursued for his own interest. In 1822 he published his second book, *A Treatise on Dislocations and Fractures*. It contained his lifelong manifesto:

> *I do not believe that, from the first dawn of medical science to the present moment, a single correct idea has ever emanated from conjecture alone. It is right, therefore, that those who are studying their profession, should be aware, that there is no short road to knowledge; that observations on the diseased living, examinations of the dead, and experiments upon living animals, are the only sources of true knowledge; and that deductions from these are the sole basis of legitimate theory.*

It was what he had learnt from Hunter and Cline, it was the essence of what he had to offer to his students. It was little more than an expansion of the conclusion that he had reached in his first published essays, and in the *Treatise on Hernias*:

> *It is my duty to state to you my opinion; you must think for yourselves, only do not rest contented with thinking; make observations and experiments, for without them your thinking will be of little use.*

To conceive that something was true because it seemed reasonable was unacceptable: it was gambling with the truth. In 1823, this point of view suddenly reached a larger audience than Astley had intended.

Thomas Wakley had qualified as a surgeon at Guy's in 1817. Four years later he met the journalist William Cobbett, whose radical newspaper *The Political Register* he greatly admired. With Cobbett's encouragement, Wakley founded a medical journal in 1823. The rising number of surgeons made a growing market, for those who supplied them with education as well as for those who brought them corpses. Wakley called his journal *The Lancet*. The name was a pun, referring both to a window and to a sharp surgical instrument. His new journal planned to let light in on the darkness of ignorance, as well as stabbing its sharp pen into the corruption, incompetence and rot of the medical profession. Wakley wanted to educate and he wanted to expose. He believed there were unpleasant elements in the medical profession, and wanted to cut them out just as much as he wanted to educate those who wished to learn.

To sell his journal, Wakley needed to make it live up to its name. His own aggression and well-developed sense of outrage provided plenty of material for his exposures. For his campaign of education, however, he needed help, and in his very first issue, he recruited Astley. He did it without permission and without discussion, announcing as a fait accompli in his opening editorial that:

> *As the Lectures of Astley Cooper, on the theory and practice of surgery, are probably the best of the kind delivered in Europe, we have commenced our undertaking with the introductory address of that distinguished professor given in the theatre at St Thomas's Hospital on Wednesday evening last. The course will be rendered complete in subsequent numbers.*

It was a terrific advertisement for both men, attracting readers to the journal and publicly announcing Astley's professional pre-eminence. But that, regardless of Wakley's potential breach of copyright, was part of the problem. Physicians and surgeons were fiercely competitive when it came to attracting patients, particularly rich ones, but they kept up a pretence of never advertising themselves. That was for vulgar merchants and shop-keepers, not for men who wished to appear above such mercenary inter-ests. By allowing his lectures to be published, Astley was accused of having crossed the line separating education from self-advertisement.

Astley dealt with the charge superbly, defusing the attacks upon himself by declaring that it seemed horribly true. The appearance of his first lecture in print, he told audiences, 'looked so much like quackery, so much like puffing, that I am unable to describe to you how much it annoyed me'. He pointed out that the publication of his lectures had been done without his assent and without his having had any warning of it. It was advertise-ment all right, but not of his making. He promised to take action.

The action he took, however, was not that of many of his colleagues, most of whom resorted to legal action when their lectures were printed without permission. The new journal was unsigned and its editorials anony-mous: it took Astley a few weeks to find out that Wakley was responsible. Having done so he called at his house, pretending to the servant who answered the door that he was a patient in need of Wakley's surgical atten-tion. Asked to wait until the master of the house was free, Astley did no such thing. The startled young editor was in the midst of correcting the proofs of one of Astley's own lectures when he looked up to find the surgeon striding across the room towards him. The coincidence, and Wakley's consequent embarrassment, were enough to bring out the warmer side of both men. Neither could resist bursting into laughter.

Astley agreed to his lectures being published but asked for his name to be removed. He has been applauded for such a selfless act, motivated as it was by caring more for the standard of general surgical knowledge than for his own glory or personal reward. In fact it was also an inspired piece of self-publicity. Everyone knew whom the lectures belonged to, so Cooper continued to gather all the prestige from the praise and attention heaped openly upon them. At the same time, he could declare himself free of any imputation of self-advertisement. It was a brilliant solution, and Astley benefited from it substantially. His lectures now became so well known that *The Times* quoted from them. ('This experiment, gentlemen, delighted me,' reported the paper in December 1823 when Astley announced the discovery of an effective stomach pump, an innovation with the power to save lives in a world where opium overdoses – deliberate and accidental – were common and there was no pharmacological antidote. 'I do not know if I have ever experienced greater pleasure in my life than I felt in going home from the hospital on that day.') Yet despite its appearance of wilful modesty, Astley's success was now too great – and his belief in himself altogether too robustly apparent – to divert all the criticism. Many of his operations had drawn accusations of self-publicity; people said that his motives in tying off Charles Hutson's aorta, for example, had been self-serving or at the least callously indifferent. And there were some, like Thomas Wakley himself, who found the nepotism that characterised London medicine to be revolting and offensive. Astley, the wrong side of fifty-five and widely seen as the crowned king of the nation's surgeons, was responsible for a good part of it.

17

Surgeon to the Parliament,
Surgeon to the King

To save money, William Cowles made the trip to London by travelling on the roof of the coach. A thirty-nine-year-old gardener from Beccles in Suffolk, he was travelling to the capital to seek help. No one recorded the reasons why he chose London and the Borough, but they did record the condition he arrived with: a swelling in his right groin. It was June 1808, a pleasantly balmy night, and despite lying on the top of the coach, Cowles managed to fall asleep. When he woke he discovered that the journey had made things worse. As he slept his weight had fallen onto his groin, and by the time he arrived at Guy's the following day the skin there was starting to blacken and die. Beneath the gangrenous flesh there was an easily felt pulsation. It was caused by a swelling of his femoral artery.

On the same warm day that Cowles arrived at Guy's, Cooper operated. His clothes and his hands were already stained with the blood of a man whose neck he had cut into a short time before. Cooper dissected the skin and fat and muscle of Cowles's leg, working his way downwards until he had identified and exposed the great blood vessels beneath. Using the tip of his finger and the end of a probe he separated out the vein, then passed a curved needle between it and the tight, pulsing muscular cord of the artery. On the end of the needle was thick thread which he then tied in a knot, shutting off the flow of blood through the artery. Cooper closed the wound with an adhesive plaster, taking care to keep the ends of the thread hanging loose so they could be pulled away when the inner portion rotted. By that time the artery should have scarred itself shut, and the body should have grown leashes of newer smaller vessels with which to supply the leg.

Everything went well, and Cowles survived the operation. It was a piece of good fortune for him, but it failed to set the pattern for the rest of his life. He lived a wandering existence, and came to rest almost two decades later in Heckingham workhouse about seven miles from Beccles, the Suffolk village from which he had first come. There he died, 'friendless and worn out'.

Although there was no one to mourn his death, the fact of it was noticed all the same. The local surgeon – a man with the wonderful name of Henchman Crowfoot – was aware that Cooper had operated on Cowles many years before. Cowles, said a young man called Arthur Dalrymple who lodged with Crowfoot, had 'wandered through many parts of the country but wherever he went he was (unconsciously) traced. The surgeon of the place he left corresponded with the medical practitioner of the place he went to.' When Cowles died, Crowfoot sent word to London. It was June 1826 and the days were long: at dusk the following evening, two men arrived at Crowfoot's house. They brought a box.

As soon as it had grown fully dark at about eleven o'clock, a party set out from the surgeon's to the workhouse graveyard. As well as the two London men, the group included Mr Crowfoot and his pupil, along with Arthur Dalrymple, whose only connection with surgery was that it had been his father's profession. The expedition was attractive to Dalrymple, with its exotic and macabre taste of adventure, risk, illegality and death. He went along for kicks.

The night was quiet, and as they dug down into the earth of the workhouse cemetery they could hear the chimes of the Beccles church a few miles distant. It proved a straightforward task to raise the body through the freshly turned and uncompacted soil. The two Londoners tidied the grave up with professional thoroughness. The body went into a sack and they carried it by gig back to Beccles. From there it went into its box and on back to London. The resurrection went undetected by the sleeping inhabitants of the Suffolk village.

The names of the two body-snatchers were John Bishop and Thomas Williams. One December morning five years later, they were hanged at the Old Bailey, having been convicted along with their accomplice May (the purveyor of the teeth with bits of gum attached) of murdering in order to obtain bodies. Bishop died quickly, his neck broken. Williams hung until his strength gave out, and the strangling noose suffocated him. May went to a prison hulk to await transportation to Australia. He died in its hold before he could set out.

Astley published his report of the operation in *Medico-Chirurgical Transactions* in 1813. The blood vessels of William Cowles's leg, prepared so as to highlight the delicate network of collateral vessels that grew to keep it healthy after his operation, are in a case at Guy's.

Before Astley's 1792 honeymoon in Paris, his father had told him that 'though you leave England a *Democrat*, you will be so far enlightened as to return an *Aristocrat*'. Samuel Cooper's confidence had been badly chosen, but he would have been gratified by his son's move across London to the more fashionable west. It was a deliberate step away from the limited merit-ocracy of merchant wealth, a step towards the pomp and ancestry of the nobility who clustered around Mayfair and St James's Park.

Astley's repositioning of himself was as successful as he could have hoped. His contact with nobility grew. He attended the king's brother, the Duke of York, and was called in repeatedly as consultant to the heroic Duke of Wellington and to Lord Liverpool, the Prime Minister. Ten years later Astley described him – with praise – as being High Tory. It was not the sort of judgement he would have made in 1792. (It was recorded amongst the notes that Astley later made of his post-mortem examination of Liverpool in December 1828, which covered liberally both the state of his corpse and the constitution of his late character.) Astley's politics had become those his parents had always encouraged him to hold. His eldest brother, one of the many Bransbys in the family, was in a position to feel particularly gratified by the change. He had qualified for the Bar but never practised, making a rich marriage instead and living the life of a country gentleman as a result. In 1818 he became Member of Parliament for Gloucester, winning a little over 800 of the 1,703 votes cast and entering the House as a staunch Tory.

After a few years of treating the upper ranks, the call came to the top. In 1820 Astley was summoned to serve the new king. George IV had taken up the throne that year, and he was fat, debauched and unpopular. Now a sweat gland on top of his head had become blocked. The gland continued secreting its sweat, but with no room for it to flow outwards the fluid accu-

217

mulated and formed a walled-off cyst. The more liquid contents were re-absorbed, leaving the cyst tense with a cheese-like accumulation of stagnant fat and prone to infections. The swelling was painful, inflamed and unsightly. The king wanted it removed, and he wanted Astley to do it, regardless of the existence of the sergeant-surgeon, the royal appointee who by protocol should have been responsible. The king summoned to Windsor the celebrity surgeon whose trim figure had been pointed out to him, riding about the parks and avenues of London. 'I have seen you in your little chariot,' he declared to Astley upon his arrival.

Astley refused the king's demand that he immediately cut away the tumour. The cyst was inflamed and angry, he explained, and it would be recklessly dangerous to perform the operation until it had settled down, even if this might take several months.

'By God,' the king remarked to Astley, after summoning him on another occasion and demanding that the surgeon work out why the royal person should have woken feeling a little unwell one morning, 'it is extraordinary that I should be thus heated, for I lived very abstemiously, and went to bed in good time.' In case the surgeon's clinical acumen was somewhat dull, a helpful servant took care to inform Astley that the king had actually stayed up until the early hours of the morning getting drunk. The prosaic explanation did nothing to dull Astley's growing feeling for the innate majesty of royalty. When the king announced proudly that he could cope with over a hundred drops of laudanum at a single go – the mark of a man addicted to opium – Astley spoke of it as though it were a mark of fortitude, of strength of character. He wrote:

The first time I ever saw George the Fourth was at the time he was Prince Regent. He was walking with the Duke of York and the Duke of Bedford, and he looked far superior to either. They were, however, the three finest men in England, but he was the Prince of grace and dignity.

It was a description so far from the truth that it might have been a joke, but nothing about Astley's newfound worship of royalty appeared to be anything other than earnest. To see the Prince Regent and the dukes of York and Bedford as 'the three finest men in England' was a breathtaking piece of self-delusion. Astley was able accurately to assess the nature of the bump on the top of the king's head, but his ability to make a judgement about the man beneath was clouded. A decade of unbroken success

had altered him. Money, prestige and power had achieved what intimi-
dation, pessimism and the sight of violence had never managed. Astley
had become a Tory. The radical William Hazlitt gave his biased but
contemporary definition of the term: 'A Tory accuses those who differ
with him on political subjects of being Jacobins, Revolutionists, and
enemies to their country. A Tory highly values a long pedigree and ancient
families, and despises low-born persons (the newly created nobility
excepted), adores coronets, stars, garters, ribbons, crosses and titles of
all sorts.'

In the spring of 1821, still troubled by the cyst that had flared up the
year before, the king summoned Astley down to his magnificent royal
pavilion at Brighton. In the early hours the habitually drunken king burst
into Astley's room: 'I am now ready to have it done. I wish you now to
remove this thing from my head.'

'Sire,' protested Astley, 'not for the world now – your life is too important to have so serious a thing done in a corner.' He named a noble lady
who had died of the infection – termed erysipelas – that had come on
after a similar operation. 'What would the world say if this were to be
fatal? No, too much depends upon your Majesty to suffer me, at one
o'clock in the morning, in a retired part of the Pavilion, to perform an
operation . . .'

'This is the second time I have been disappointed,' snapped the king.

'Yes, Sire, I am sorry for it,' apologised Astley. But he declared he was
unwilling to carry out the operation alone. He requested the presence of
Everard Home and Benjamin Brodie – the two surgeons whose formal
positions meant that by court protocol they ought to be present and responsible – and he asked for someone else also. He asked for Cline.

'Mr Cline, the world would say, would not advise anything without due
consideration, and from my long knowledge of him, too, I should like him
to assist me.'

'Well,' replied the king, 'I respect Cline, and I dare say he respects me,
although we do not set our horses together in politics.'

It was the sort of understatement that a royal would have found it
impossible to make a few decades earlier. But by 1821 George IV felt
comfortable enough with the thought of the persistently democratic Cline
to agree to Astley's demands. A government informer had once reported
Thelwall dramatically sweeping the head from his beer, declaring that he
would like to treat kings in the same manner. Now a king felt safe enough

to allow Thelwall's friends, Cooper and Cline, to stand above him with their scalpels sharpened.

There was more, however, to Astley's refusal than his unwillingness to operate in the early hours of the morning, or without professional support. He hoped to be able to avoid operating altogether. Behind the scenes he lobbied to avoid the task, calling on the Prime Minister and pointing out that it was really the job of the sergeant-surgeon to cut the king. Astley was not motivated in this by modesty. He was speaking out of fear. Should he be the one to operate, and an infection follow, his career would be over. Astley knew perfectly well that an infection was more than likely, and that it could easily kill. There was no predicting which wounds would go bad, and there seemed no surgical skill in the world that could eliminate the chance of its happening. Astley informed his friends that should the worst happen, he would make no attempt to carry on as a surgeon. It would be the end for him.

Instead, and to Astley's immense relief, his lobbying was successful. It was agreed that it would be the sergeant-surgeon, and not Astley, who should operate. But he and Cline were invited to attend the operation all the same, part of a large gathering of surgical and medical men. They were there partly to support one another and partly to try to improve their individual chances of grabbing any credit and avoiding blame.

When they approach the edge of an ice sheet, Adelie penguins will crowd together, peering over the edge and into the ocean. They know that predators lurk beneath the dark waters. They jostle, trying not to be first in, positioning themselves to have the best possible view should another penguin go first. Some penguins pretend to be about to jump, hoping to trick those around them into going first. If none is fooled and none volunteers, there is some surreptitious shoving. Everything stops as the first penguin falls. A row of beaked heads peers over the edge of the ice to watch what happens.

A few days before the cyst was due to be removed, Astley received a letter from Sir Everard Home, the sergeant-surgeon. He wrote to agree formally that as sergeant-surgeon he would undertake the operation himself. He also made sure that Astley and Cline received the invitation to attend.

On Thursday, the day of the event, the men gathered at London's Carlton House. The large and opulent house to the west of Trafalgar Square had been the king's lavish home during the years of his regency, and although he regarded it as unfit for a monarch he continued to spend time there while enlarging Buckingham House into a palace. Cline asked Cooper for final confirmation: 'Who is to do the operation?'

'Sir Everard,' replied Astley.

One of the men left the room and came back a moment later. He announced that he had been asked to communicate a change of plans. The operation, he declared, would now be done by Astley.

The Prime Minister Lord Liverpool was present, and seeing Cooper's sudden terror he made an effort to calm him.

'You ought to recollect, that this operation either makes you or ruins you,' he advised. 'Courage, Cooper!'

In the face of such a soothing piece of encouragement, and feeling suddenly giddy, Astley protested that he was physically unable to carry out the operation: he had not brought his surgical instruments, he explained.

Before anyone could reply the king entered the room. 'Where am I to sit?' he demanded.

Astley had been successfully out-manoeuvred. He took a chair and put it by the window, where the light was best. He ask Everard Home if he would be kind enough to lend his tools. The sergeant-surgeon graciously agreed to the request, then stood back. When the operation began to run into difficulties, it was Cline who stepped forwards to help. There were rumours afterwards that Astley had lost his nerve and needed his old master to rescue him. The cyst stuck tightly to the king's scalp and the two men struggled to remove it. After an effort they succeeded, and closed the wound with lint and plaster.

The following night, Friday, the king slept badly. The day after he declared that he felt unwell, and that his head seemed peculiarly sore. 'I immediately thought erysipelas was coming on, and that we should lose him,' noted Astley, who was attending the king several times a day to monitor his progress. As yet there was no outward sign of that dangerous infection, but the redness that characterised it was often preceded solely by pain. The next day, the Sunday, Astley spent the morning working away as usual. After a little time he took a break, and spoke miserably with a friend about the gloomy prospects for the king's life. 'It is now three days since the operation,' he said, 'which is about the time that erysipelas is most likely to occur, and if it should, it would not be a matter of surprise to me, considering the king's habit of body, if it terminated fatally.' As he finished speaking a messenger arrived from Carlton House, summoning him urgently to the king's presence. Agitated and alarmed, Astley rushed out.

In the complicated classifications of the day – based on the outward appearances of diseases – erysipelas was a skin infection, frequently affecting the face and head. It is caused by the same germ that brought about childbed fever and that had killed Mary Wollstonecraft. As they have become understood, diseases have been named after their causes rather than their appearances, and we would now regard both childbed fever and the king's erysipelas as being streptococcal wound infections. In the days before antibiotics, such infections were often fatal. Astley's fears for the king's life were not exaggerated.

Astley was massively relieved and also heavily crestfallen when he returned home a short time later. Disaster had slipped narrowly past. The king was in agony, but it was his toe and not his head that he was complaining of. The malaise of the previous day had been the forerunner of an attack of gout, not of erysipelas. Yet what should have been a moment for celebration had inexplicably become a time of disappointment. Despite the great success of the operation, the corpulent monarch had glared at Astley with disgust. In the moment of his great success and good fortune he had been greeted as though he were a monster. It was a harsh reward for a man whose concern for the life of George IV now matched that of any royalist in Britain.

Astley's friend pointed out that, in his haste and anxiety, he had rushed off to Carlton House without either washing or dressing especially for the king. In his haste to offer his aid he had gone exactly as he was. 'Why,' said the friend, 'I should have put on a white cravat and a clean shirt, or at least have washed my hands before I waited on his Majesty.'

Sunday morning, like any other, was a time for dissection and for private patients, and Astley was no more suspicious of a link between hand-washing and disease transmission than anyone else of his generation. In the hours before being summoned to Carlton House, he had performed some minor operations. As a result he had attended the fastidious king with his shirt and his hands still covered with the brick-red evidence of his profession: blood.

The king's displeasure did not last. The immediate value of the surgery to Cooper was twofold. He received a silver epergne of the king's own design: a large ornamental table piece for holding fruit and flowers that cost the artistic monarch 500 guineas to commission. And two weeks after the operation the king told Astley that he was to be made a baronet. The Prime Minister, George explained, had promised to award the honour 'but I will not suffer it, I shall do it myself'.

'Since your Majesty is so kind,' replied Cooper, 'let me say, if it be not entailed upon my nephew Astley, whom I have adopted and educated, it will lose much of its value.' The king agreed. Cline received neither honours nor silver. George asked Astley what the technical name of his tumour had been.

'A steatome,' replied Astley.

'Indeed!' said the king. 'I hope sincerely that it will stay-at-home for the future, and pay me no more visits.'

Astley remained fond of retelling the exchange. His over-estimation of its wit was partly due to his veneration of the king, partly to his own enthusiasm for lousy puns.

For some time Astley remained on friendly terms with the king, attending him both professionally and socially, until the relationship abruptly fell apart. The explanation was generally agreed upon, although the specifics were covered over. *Chambers's Edinburgh Journal* described Astley as 'hearty rather than elegant, [with] manners somewhat more disposed toward gaiety than to the gravity usually sought for in a "court physician"'. Such a sense of humour was too robust for a monarch who was not willing to be put into the shade by someone else's liveliness. Feeling high-spirited, Astley 'committed himself to some unlucky exuberance of jocularity'. It was enough to end his popularity with George IV.

Over the winter of 1824, Astley's episodes of sudden giddiness began to get increasingly frequent and more disabling. When they came he did his best to flee to Gadebridge, partly looking for shelter with his wife and his country estate but also in order to keep his illness as much of a secret as possible. By January of 1825, at the age of fifty-six, he felt that his health had become too poor to carry on any longer as a full-time surgeon. He resigned his position at Guy's, having held it for a quarter of a century. His understanding was that he had the right to nominate his successors. He chose two men to share the job that he had carried out alone, his old student South and his nephew Bransby. With his resignation accepted,

Astley learnt his wishes were to be ignored. Both posts were given to South and there was to be nothing for the less accomplished Bransby. Furious, Astley demanded that the governors of the hospital allow him to retract his resignation. They refused.

Angry and let down, Astley still retained sufficient personal sway in the Borough Hospitals to have the decision partly overturned. With the help of Benjamin Harrison, the treasurer who had encouraged him to abandon democracy for his surgeonship, Astley managed to persuade Guy's to split from St Thomas's and found an entirely separate medical school.* Prevented from handing his post over to his nephew, he created a completely new one for him instead. Astley felt that he was supporting someone whose value he knew, just as his uncle and Cline had once supported him. But Cline, who for decades had shown himself an accurate assessor of Cooper's behaviour, thought he was acting shabbily. For the first time relations between the two men grew cool.

One of the physicians at Guy's frankly accused Astley of behaving 'interestedly' in the affair. In response the far older Astley, already retiring due to ill-health, challenged the physician to a duel. It was not a vain threat. But like many challenges, the threat turned out to be enough: the physician apologised and wrote out a public retraction. Bransby, newly appointed to the post his uncle had created for him, read out the apology publicly in Guy's lecture theatre.

On 2 January 1827, at the age of seventy-six, Henry Cline died. His death was preceded by an intermittent fever over the preceding three or four months. Malaria, a chronic infection or a hidden cancer could all have been to blame.

Astley was upset at Cline's death, and wrote warmly about him afterwards. 'He was a man of great courage,' he declared. 'To me he was always kind, until he became prejudiced against me, during the last two years of his life.' He compared Cline to Washington. Both were men whose sense of patriotic duty outweighed any thought of personal gain. It was an admiring nod to their old days of democratic companionship and to the

* Guy's and St Thomas's reunited in 1982. St Thomas's had relocated in 1871, moving away from Guy's and to the south side of the Thames directly across Westminster Bridge from the Houses of Parliament.

youthful idealism that Astley had shared with the man who had helped to raise him.

Cooper praised Cline for his temper, his intelligence and his selflessness. He criticised him for not continuing with a programme of lifelong self-education in surgery. 'He never laboured in his profession as a learner after I knew him, which was when he was thirty-four years of age. Nor did he like to talk of his profession.' They were the words of a man who genuinely did constantly labour, and also liked to talk.

Astley had only ever seen Cline lose his temper twice. Once had been with a patient whose cowardice and indecision had led him to persistently agree to an operation only to back out repeatedly at the last moment. Cline had eventually ignored the man's last-minute change of heart and operated on him whilst he lay strapped on the table trying to equivocate. Astley approved of this exercise of paternal authority, and also of having once seen Cline rise into an instant fury on seeing a man hit a dog. In Astley's eyes cruelty to animals was revolting and infuriating; it just did not happen to include vivisection.

Cline's death enlarged a growing hole in Astley's life. He was showing an older man's difficulty in forming new friendships, and now he was without the advice of a man who had served many of the functions of a father. There was no one standing by now to reassure Astley of his unimportance in the great scheme of things, to puncture his vanity or to laugh him into taking himself less seriously.

To the end of his days, Cline had stuck both by his democratic principles and by his democratic friends. He had attended them in the Tower when they were awaiting their treason trials and he carried on attending them whenever requested. He looked after Horne Tooke during his final illness in 1812 and continued, for many years after Tooke's death, to hold an annual dinner in memory of his 1794 acquittal. He died in his home at Lincoln's Inn Fields, next door not only to the Royal College of Surgeons (which he had served as president) but also to the home of John Thelwall. While Astley had pursued surgical success when the waters of democratic change grew too cold, Thelwall had adopted a more restricted effort to help the downtrodden. He had taught elocution, managing with great success to help others overcome the stuttering that he had once battled his own way through. A visitor to Thelwall's home at Lincoln's Inn found the prospect of a cast of stutterers reciting Milton rather comic, but left both impressed and touched by the performance.

Late on in his life, preparing notes for Bransby to write his biography, Astley fell into the habit of writing about himself in the third person. 'In judgement,' one of those notes concluded about Sir Astley Cooper, 'he was very inferior to Mr Cline in all the affairs of life.' Even the ghost of Cline's memory was powerful enough to put his old protégé in touch with the kind of self-effacing modesty from which the glitter of his successful life distracted him. Writing pompously about himself in the third person allowed Astley the confidence to reveal his own sense of unworthiness compared to his memories of Cline.

Work went on. In February of 1827 Astley, as vice-president of the Royal College of Surgeons and along with the president and the leaders of the Royal College of Physicians, wrote to Peel (then Home Secretary) urging the importance of smallpox vaccinations. Mortality from the disease, they pointed out, had dropped from four thousand a year to around five hundred with the limited introduction of vaccines so far achieved. The letter was printed the following month in *The Times*. Later that year, Astley took over from Cline as president of the Royal College of Surgeons.

The following year, 1828, there was another catastrophe in Astley's life, this time in his attempt to hand over his practice to his nephew Bransby.

In a glass case at Guy's Hospital, near two large cabinets of Cooper's animal and human dissections, there is a small stone. It is rather pretty; oval in shape, perhaps three centimetres across at the most, and cut open to show the nested circles within. Internally the stone is solid. It is reminiscent of an eye-catching crystal on sale as an ornament. Concentric rings dwindle towards the centre, dancing with glittering reflections. The stone was removed by Bransby from a man's bladder. No one imagined such an operation was ever safe; Astley put his own mortality rate at one in eight, a good figure and one that he achieved only by avoiding surgery whenever possible.*

---

*Although he was very aware of the way in which an unfortunate case could blight a surgeon's reputation, his avoidance of needless surgery was also motivated by the desire not to inflict the experience on people pointlessly. In his lectures he gave an example: 'A patient came into Guy's Hospital to be cut for the stone . . . I saw that he was emaciated; he complained of pain in his loins, and his stomach was much disordered. I therefore said, "I will not operate upon this man, for he will die from the operation." In less than a month he died, and I was happy that I had not operated, as one kidney was found wasted, and the other at least twice its natural size, with its cavities full of a purulent secretion.'

A few days earlier Stephen Pollard had been boasting of how he was to be operated upon by the nephew of the great Sir Astley Cooper. Now he was strapped to the table, rope pulling his knees up to his neck and trussing his hands to his ankles, screaming in pain and dismay. The operation should have taken only a few minutes, but Bransby had difficulty locating the stone, repeatedly withdrawing from and returning to the ragged hole he created between his patient's genitals and his rectum. Pollard was unable to escape as that nephew probed and searched with forceps and gorgets and fingers inside his pelvis, loudly cursing the patient for having such abnormal anatomy that the stone could not be found. At one point Bransby even left the operating table to compare fingers with some of those in his two hundred-strong audience, seeking a man who possessed ones longer than his own. He thought the stone might simply be out of reach.

'Oh! Let it go!' Pollard cried, as Bransby persisted. 'Pray let it keep in!'

But Bransby ignored him and persevered, as his uncle had taught him to do, and eventually extracted the stone. He waved it about in triumph, turning his back on the patient who lay exhausted and bleeding on the table. The operation that should have lasted a few short minutes had taken closer to an hour. Stephen Pollard died a day later.

Despite its links with Astley, Wakley's *Lancet* published an article by a surgeon who had been in the audience. It accused Bransby of incompetence and a barbaric disregard for the suffering of his patient – and it suggested he had done nothing to merit his position other than being born a nephew of Astley Cooper. Bransby sued for libel and won, although *The Lancet* declared that the award of £100 in damages was so derisory that it represented a defeat. Accounts of the post-mortem differed but there seemed nothing in retrospect that was unusual about either the stone or Pollard's pelvic anatomy. Bransby had simply been making holes in the wrong places. Astley's original preference for Samuel Cooper's other sons may have had some basis in an accurate assessment of their talents. But to some extent Bransby's misadventure with the stone fits with Cooper's experimental ligations of the aorta or of the carotid arteries. There was no way to learn other than by practice. Cutting for the stone usually lasted a short time but its becoming drawn out was far from rare. Mistakes were simply not avoidable, however regrettable they might be, and it was unclear that a single botched procedure implied a man was unfit to be a surgeon.

'Give him time,' Astley said to the court when the case was heard. 'Let him work his way, and I have no doubt he will be a most excellent, a most thriving surgeon, a most brilliant operator.'

Wakley, defeated in court, raged in print. To every patient, regardless of the ability to pay, was due 'the best and most scientific practice of surgery as any nobleman in the land'. To modern ears – and in many ways Wakley was far more modern than the world he lived in – it sounds undeniably true. But there was no National Health Service at the time. Surgery was a commodity, to be bought and sold. How could anyone expect that the poor should be able to buy as good a service as the rich? And how, anyway, were surgeons supposed to learn if not by making mistakes? Non-anaesthetised operations had to be quick. There was limited scope to pause them for long periods to nurse a junior operator slowly through a proce-dure. Wakley, however, was certain that Bransby was to blame, writing:

> The unfortunate patient lost his life, not because his case was one of
> extraordinary difficulty, but because it was the turn of a surgeon to operate,
> who is indebted for his elevation to the influence of a corrupt system, and
> who, whatever may be his private virtues, would never have been placed
> in a situation of such deep responsibility as that which he now occupies,
> had he not been the nephew of Sir Astley Cooper.

*

In June 1827 Cooper spent an extended period at his estate in Hemel Hempstead. It was no longer enough for him to rely on fleeing there in the evenings in his carriage, a greatcoat thrown over his silk stockings and breeches. His giddiness had again become worse, crippling him while the attacks lasted and making him unable to work and frightened of having his illness discovered. At his worst he had to cling in panic onto anything solid, deserted of all sense of which way up the world was, devoid of any ability to orient himself.

Friends would drive out of London to join him. Ann still lived in Gadebridge year round, and the estate was managed by Parmenter, the man whose brief marriage to Ann and Astley's adopted daughter had ended in her death after labour. Coleman, with whom Astley had first heard John Hunter, was a frequent visitor. The two men often went out shooting, accompanied by the dogs they had not sacrificed, and Astley dissected the birds they killed, carrying out miniature post-mortems on each one.

Although Astley became more secluded as his intimate friends drifted away or died, his circle of colleagues and acquaintances remained wide. His pupils and dressers, his students and colleagues and his wealthy patients, many of them came regularly to enjoy his hospitality. Astley's interest in empire-building continued without serious abatement, and in 1826 he helped found an infirmary at Piccotts End near Gadebridge.* With his position, his personal charm and his sense of what work needed doing, he was forever finding jobs or projects for people. The network of those he knew, of those he was friends with, of colleagues he had once trained, of powerful people whom he had influence with, was now spread across the country. That was, after all, partly why he had been appointed president of the Royal College.

During Astley's June 1827 retreat to Gadebridge, Ann Cooper was struck down by erysipelas. It affected her head, just as her husband had been afraid that it would the king's. A redness began to spread over the skin of her face, and the hot flesh swelled painfully. Astley gave her calomel, hoping that the diarrhoea it caused would flush out from her body whatever was causing the disease. He followed that, for the same reasons, with a concoction of mercury to make her sweat. Then came quinine as a general tonic and treatment for fever.

After a short time the disease took a promising course and Ann began to recover. The infection faded away, the redness began to pale. Then Ann, just like the king, was seized with a pain in her foot. But for Ann the pain was not gout. Over a period of a few hours her right foot became discoloured, swelling up into a livid mass of purple and dark blue. The affected flesh turned gangrenous and Ann became delirious.

The infection in her head, the streptococcus, had spread. Bacteria make a flitting appearance in the bloodstream a few times a day, when you brush your teeth or scratch yourself. In the normal course of events they are rapidly cleared by the immune system. When that fails, the bacteria are able to breed within the blood and to seed themselves around the body. Nowadays that state is called septicaemia. Not so long ago, and in Astley's time, it was blood poisoning. The old term harks back to the confusion that only germ theory was able to clear away: something awful was clearly going on in such people, and it was apparent that it was being

---

* It has developed into today's 258-bed Hemel Hempstead Hospital, part of the West Hertfordshire NHS Trust.

spread by the blood. Without the notion of living bacteria it made sense to imagine that the causative agent was a blood-borne poison.

Astley knew that the mind had power over the body. When a man was struck down by grief, did it not cause a secretion to flow from his eyes? 'Some medical practitioners', he told his students, 'are so cold and cheerless as to damp every hope.' Such a state suited neither his personality nor his desire to keep his wife alive through her obviously serious illness. It was a medical man's duty to 'inspire confidence of recovery'. When all other measures failed, at least it was always possible 'to support hope, to preserve tranquillity, and to inspire cheerfulness, even when you are still doubtful'. Astley stuck to his optimism with such devotion that he seemed to those around him to be in no doubt whatsoever that the illness would end well.

Within a short time of her delirium beginning and eight days after the erysipelas first appeared, Ann died. Cheerfulness was no longer required of the doctor or expected of the husband. Astley collapsed into a state of moribund silence. He stayed at Gadebridge for some weeks, isolating himself. His giddiness immediately grew worse. There was no possibility now of carrying on with the life that he had known. In September he wrote a series of letters, letting it be known that he would no longer undertake any surgical work. His professional life was over, and he would remain at Gadebridge until his days came to an end. The prospect seemed very close, for he soon became feverish. A physician friend who attended him thought that he was on the verge of death. Livid blotches formed about his face and lips. They suggested the same process that had killed Ann, the same blood-borne spread of an agent capable of producing a rapid gangrene in widely spread bits of flesh.

The physician who attended Astley felt that it was quinine that saved him. As he began to recover he also began to speak again, filling his conversation with talk of Ann and her many qualities. Life, despite all of Astley's expectations, showed no sign of coming to an end. The world he knew had come to a close, and yet here it was again carrying on as normal. Soon the solitude of Gadebridge, the separation from the world of surgery that had filled his years, became a burden. He longed not for silence, not for peacefulness and death, but once more for company and for hard work. The habit of being alive reasserted itself.

He repented of his retirement, returned to London and took up private practice again that winter. The following year, in July 1828 at Trinity

Church in Marylebone, he even remarried. His new bride, Catherine Jones, was the daughter of a successful apothecary in Gracechurch Street, which lay close to the south side of Jeffries Square, on the direct route towards London Bridge. Catherine inherited from her father a large estate in Wales. Only one letter survives to her from Astley, from two years after their wedding. 'The Baronets are to have a Blue Ribbon and a Medal,' he tells her, and there is nothing in the short note save an enjoyment of the honours he has been awarded and a lively bit of local gossip.

From this point onwards honours came to occupy an increasing proportion of Astley's life. His passion for dissection and anatomy returned with the revival of his spirits; the remainder of his energies went into taking pleasure from his second marriage and from the professional and social success that he had spent so long acquiring. He returned with relish to attending the nobility, and was soon playing the part of the loyal servant of the monarchy. For a considerable period of time he attended the Duke of York, emerging from his Highness's sick room, when things looked bad, with tears in his eyes.

'Today,' he announced, as the royal end approached, 'the mortification has increased, and his Royal Highness has great flatulence.'

In the same month as his second marriage, Astley was given the official position that he had long filled in practice. July 1828 saw him made sergeant-surgeon to George IV, despite the end of friendliness between the two men. The position lasted for two years until the king's dissipation finally caught up with him. In 1830 George IV died. Even *The Times* was pleased: 'There never was an individual less regretted by his fellow-creatures than this deceased King.'

Three days after George's death, Astley cut him up. The king's body had already begun to rot. Despite the way in which it had swollen up with fluid in the days prior to his death, the most obvious finding was the 'very large quantity of Fat' to be found immediately on opening the body. Astley took notes as he went along, leaving *An Account of Appearances which were observed in inspecting the mortal remains of his Late Majesty* in hastily written pen. The paper is covered in a mess of stains, all long since dried out – the unavoidable splashes of dead monarch that accompanied the business of carrying out an autopsy while making notes at the same time.

William IV was installed in place of George and Astley became his sergeant-surgeon in turn. The reign was not a long one. In April of 1837 the king was having difficulty breathing. By May it was clear that he was dying. At Windsor Castle on 18 June, the anniversary of Waterloo, he received the sacrament for the last time. On the morning of the 20th he died. Astley was asked to attend one final time at five that evening 'for the purpose of Embalming The Body of His Late Majesty'.

Astley began by making deep cuts in William's muscles, gashing his calves, thighs, buttocks and shoulders in order to let the fluid seep out. He opened up the king's skull and removed his brain, then opened up his chest and abdomen and took out all the organs within. Heart, lungs, guts, brain and kidneys went into a basin of cold water for rinsing. In a cauldron he boiled up a mix of beeswax, resin, sheep fat and verdigris, into which he put a large roll of green cloth. While it soaked he stuffed the gashes in the king's limbs with a mixture of herbs, fruit and flowers – roses, marjoram, and lemon – then tied William's big toes together to keep his legs straight. The cauldron was so large that Astley needed to stand on a table to pull out the fourteen yards of green cloth. With it he started to wrap the king's body, starting at the head and working down. A warmed iron was on hand to seal down the edges of the cloth neatly. After the cloth came a wrapping of white silk, then one of purple. That was tied with four white ribbon bows and the body was ready. Astley helped lift it into the coffin, already lined with another mixture of 'sweets', this time lavender, marjoram, thyme, roses and wormwood all mixed with six bushels (over 36 litres) of bran. The viscera, bobbing up and down in their water bath, he drained and allowed to dry a little in the summer warmth. Once they were ready Astley put them into a cube-shaped urn, lead-lined and already filled with some of the herb and flower mix. The urn and the coffin were topped up with what remained of the aromatics, soldered shut, and William IV was ready for the grave. His niece Princess Victoria had just turned eighteen.

When Victoria was crowned queen, the sixty-eight-year-old Astley Cooper became her sergeant-surgeon. Other honours had also been accumulating. In September 1837 he travelled to Edinburgh and was fêted at the Royal Hotel by the College of Surgeons. 'When he looked back upon those days [his student days in 1787], and reflected on the fame and success which had attended him through life,' reported *The Times*, 'he was tempted almost to fall down on his knees and thank Providence.' Astley's reputation was international. There was his election to the National Institute of France (far more of a distinction in the early nineteenth century than being on the council of Britain's Royal Society) and his officer's rank in the French Légion d'honneur. (There is a letter from Baron Rothschild in late June 1832, to the French Minister of Commerce, suggesting the election was made at the baron's bidding.) The Scottish Royal College of Surgeons elected him an Honorary Fellow and the University of Oxford awarded him a doctorate. At the personal intervention of his friend the Duke of Wellington, William IV had given Astley the Grand Cross of the Order of Guelph. He became vice-president of the Royal Society and a Fellow of the Royal Society of Göttingen. The Russian Imperial University of Vilna awarded him a diploma. He was made a corresponding member of the first class of the Royal Institute of the Netherlands, a member of the Society of Natural Philosophy of Heidelberg, of the Physico-Medical Society of New Orleans, of the Academy of Medical Sciences of Palermo and of the Mexican Medical Society of Guadalajara.

The last years of a grandee's life are often happy ones.

18

Surgeon to Reform

In 1825 the second Charles Darwin had gone north to study medicine at Edinburgh. Along with his ill-fated uncle – whose death from a wound in the dissecting room had come in 1778 and before he could qualify – Charles's father and grandfather had both been physicians. He had prepared for his medical training by taking on the local poor of Shrewsbury as patients, discussing their care with his father as he went. But he found his Edinburgh lecturers dull and his anatomy tutor physically disgusting. He attended the operating theatre twice, and, as Francis Darwin quoted him saying, 'saw two very bad operations, one on a child, but I rushed away before they were completed . . . the two cases fairly haunted me for many a long year'. Above all, he was unable to get over his physical revulsion for the business of human dissection, a failing that he regretted throughout his professional life. He did not chiefly blame himself, he blamed his teachers. 'It has proved one of the greatest evils in my life', he wrote, 'that I was not urged to practise dissection, for I should soon have got over my disgust; and the practice would have been invaluable for all my future work.'

Abandoning his planned career as a physician, Darwin moved to Cambridge to study divinity. He grew friendly with the polymath Professor Henslow and the two of them fell into the habit of taking long walks together. During one of those walks they witnessed an illustration of what happened to men who were caught robbing graves to supply surgeons:

I once saw in his [Professor Henslow's] company in the streets of Cambridge almost as horrid a scene, as could have been witnessed during the French Revolution. Two body-snatchers had been arrested and whilst being taken to prison had been torn from the constable by a crowd of the roughest men, who dragged them by their legs along the muddy and stony road. They were covered from head to foot with mud and their faces were bleeding either from having been kicked or from the stones; they looked like corpses, but the crowd was so dense that I got only a few momentary glimpses of the wretched creatures. Never in my life have I seen such wrath painted on a man's face, as was shown by Henslow at this horrid scene. He tried repeatedly to penetrate the mob; but it was simply impossible. He then rushed away to the mayor, telling me not to follow him, to get more policemen. I forget the issue, except that the two men were got into prison before being killed.

Public disgust at the body-snatchers and grave-robbers had not abated. And as the 1820s passed and the number of those studying the human body grew, the supply of bodies could no longer keep up with demand. Change was needed. In 1828, the year of Astley's appointment as sergeant-surgeon to George IV, the Commons appointed a select committee 'to inquire into the manner of obtaining Subjects for Dissection in the Schools of Anatomy, and into the state of the Law affecting the Persons employed in obtaining or dissecting bodies'. Bodies were getting expensive, and the surgeons were suffering as a result. Students were starting to find it easier to travel to the Continent to learn their surgery.

For all the discomfort and inconvenience of the existing system, the surgeons had muddled through pretty effectively for a considerable period, and they had grown more powerful. Astley had many friends both in the palace and in the Cabinet. His older brother Bransby, a Member of Parliament, was even sitting on the select committee. There was a general desire amongst the surgeons not only to free themselves of the body-snatchers, thereby achieving a cheaper and more plentiful supply of corpses, but also to divorce themselves from the gibbet. To a profession that was growing in its humanitarian pretensions, it was increasingly unattractive to perform an office that had been designed as a disgrace. Astley led the profession's campaign for change, both on stage and behind the scenes. He was the select committee's first witness. 'There is no person, let his situation in life be what it may,' he told them, 'whom, if I were disposed to dissect, I could not obtain. The law only enhances the price, and does not prevent the exhumation.' Unless they changed the law to supply him with bodies, he would be forced to get them himself. The pointed boast that he could take Members of Parliament as easily as chimney sweeps was hard to ignore, but as well as the threat came an appeal. Astley told the committee:

> Without dissection there can be no anatomy, and that anatomy is our polar star, for, without anatomy, a surgeon can do nothing, certainly nothing well . . . I would not remain in a room with a man who attempted to perform an operation in surgery who was unacquainted with anatomy . . . he must mangle the living, if he has not operated on the dead . . . The cause which you gentlemen are not supporting, is not our cause, but yours; you must employ medical men, whether they be ignorant or informed; but if you have none but ignorant medical men, it is you who suffer from it; and the fact is, that the want of subjects will very soon lead to your becoming the unhappy victims of operations founded and performed in ignorance.

At the same time as he was making their choice clear to them, Astley also spoke to the select committee about the men who currently supplied him with bodies. They were filth, he said, implying they would murder in an instant if they thought that they could profit by it. 'They are as bad as any in society, and when I consider their characters I think it is a dangerous thing to society that they should be able to get ten guineas for a body.' It was a strange way to speak for a man whose record of standing faithfully by his body-snatchers had been so striking. In his relations with men whose poverty had driven them into such a dangerous and unpalatable criminal class he had been generous and supportive. Now he was in Parliament speaking about them as a lower species. Perhaps it was done as a show in order to get a certain effect, but it takes a certain effort of charity not to see it as breathtakingly ungrateful.

As a result of the select committee's report, in 1829 an Anatomy Bill was introduced into Parliament. Walter Scott, writing in his journal in that year, recorded his impression of it:

> For instance if it was now to be enacted, as seems reasonable, that persons dying in hospitals and almshouses who die without their friends claiming

*their remains should be given up to the men of science, this would be
subjecting poverty to the penalty of these atrocious criminals whom Law
distinguishes by the heaviest posthumous disgrace which it can inflict.*

Scott was correct, but those who supported the Bill pointed out that its
flaws had to be considered next to those of the present system. Already
it was generally the poor who were dissected, since their bodies were the
easiest to steal. By targeting those who had died without anyone to claim
them, was the new system not also selecting those without relatives whose
feelings would be hurt by the process? It was an argument that failed to
take into account the feelings of the poor themselves, who had no wish
to die with the knowledge of the lawful fate that awaited them. The popular
horror of being cut up remained. Even the wealthy who were comfortable
with the idea of a post-mortem grew anxious at the thought of dissection.
The former implied something modern and gentlemanly, the latter being
treated as a piece of meat.

The Duke of Wellington – now Prime Minister – had broader worries.
He opposed the Anatomy Bill, concerned that it came at too troublesome
a time to be permitted. Wellington's opposition to widening the political
franchise was absolute, and his Government was continuing to find it difficult to suppress popular agitation. Passing a law that victimised the poor
was not calculated to keep the peace. One victim of the political turmoil
was Bransby Cooper, MP, Astley's elder brother, who after speaking out
against the Emancipation Act of 1829 withdrew from the House of
Commons rather than face the pressure for democratic reform. A universal
franchise and the abolition of slavery were altogether out of keeping with
his traditional Tory values. In all of the furore about such wider issues the
Anatomy Bill was rejected, also in 1829. But public pressure for a reform
of the body-snatcher's trade was growing.

In November 1827, two years before the passage of the Emancipation
Act and the failure of the Anatomy Bill, an old man died in debt in a
lodging house in Edinburgh. Two of the lodgers sold his body to recoup
the money. They had no history of body-snatching, and even had to stop
in Surgeon's Square and ask a student for directions as to where to take
the corpse. But they received almost £8, an enormous sum for two men
who lived on the edge of destitution. When another lodger fell ill the
same two men were on hand. They quietened him with whisky and then
smothered him. This time they got £10. The lesson was clear, and they

learnt it well: they grew more active, luring the hopeless and the homeless to their deaths with promises of friendship and alcohol. Mary Paterson was a local prostitute. She was only four hours dead when she reached the surgeon. He was so struck by her naked beauty that he kept her preserved in whisky and on exposed display for three months before dissecting her.

The murderers were William Burke and William Hare, and the surgeon was Knox. Although Knox was never charged, he was widely held to be guilty for not having called attention to the freshness of the corpses. (There are grounds for doubt as to whether, and to what extent, Knox was complicit.) The killers were eventually caught in a piece of cartoon stupidity during a Halloween party in 1828. Burke made such a fuss of telling his guests not to go anywhere near his bed that they were provoked into doing precisely that. There they found Mary Docherty. Penniless and hungry, over from Ireland to search for her son, she had accepted Burke's offer of hospitality the previous night. She ended it stripped and dead, her corpse hidden in the straw of Burke's bed.

Popular imagination went berserk with what *The Scotsman* called 'Burking Mania'. The *York Chronicle* in 1831 said: 'The Burkophobia seems to be at its height in the metropolis at the present time, and scarcely a day passes but reports are circulated of the supposed sacrifice of fresh victims to the "interests of science".' As far as many people in Britain were concerned the murder of people in order to sell their corpses to surgeons was a nightly activity. Strong men were scared to walk home by themselves. Women and children lived in fear of the rough hand around their neck, throttling them into a posthumous existence as an anatomical subject. Burke and Hare had actually relied on alcohol and asphyxiation. Similar methods were used in 1831 in London, when John Bishop, James May and Thomas Williams dosed their victims with alcohol and opium before dangling them head first down a garden well to drown. Unlike Burke and Hare, all these men had worked as regular body-snatchers in the past, and all three had worked for Astley (including fetching specific corpses for him, like that of William Cowles). When their activities were discovered (they were arrested on 5 November 1831) it sealed the public perception that 'Burking' was going on all around them. Pressure to reform the body-snatching business became impossible to ignore.

Wellington, in the end, had things upside down and the right way up simultaneously. Reform in the trade of human bodies was certainly tied up with the weight of public feeling pushing for wider democratic representation. Both issues were bound together by the heavy freight of public interest they carried, but the shadow of the 1832 Reform Act was sufficient to cover the controversy of its little sibling. From 1832, one-fourteenth of the population was entitled to have a hand in choosing their Government. The right to vote was granted on the basis of a man's possessions. The composition of Parliament was altered to eliminate the worst of the rotten boroughs and to make way for the new constituencies of urbanising industrial Britain. In the same year as Parliament, the Lords and the king agreed to extend the right to vote, they passed legislation allowing the bodies of the poor to be seized by the state for the purposes of dissection. The Anatomy Act of 1832 made dissection the legal fate of many of England's poor. If you had no one to claim you – or simply no one who could afford the price of properly burying you – the state could send your body to the surgeons. It was a horrible end to offer to people whose fear of dissection still frequently outstripped their fear of death. The Act did make provision for anyone who wished to freely donate their body, but that was largely a piece of window dressing. When a woman called Charlotte Baume died on 16 December 1832, having expressed her wish that she be dissected, no one even knew what they were supposed to do next. The bequest was so unexpected that Charlotte's brother Peter was promptly arrested on suspicion of having murdered her. The charge was later dropped, having been inspired by little more than a general disbelief that anyone would have willingly offered themselves up for such an end, but it exposed the emptiness of the pretence that voluntary requests had ever really been expected.

Today the supply of bodies in Britain is entirely based upon voluntary donation, and more bodies are bequeathed than are actually needed. Medical students spend much less time on human dissection – there are many other facts to learn now, and detailed anatomy is reserved for those whose specialities require them to know it – but it is still a part of medical training. I remember the odd experience of trooping in with the rest of my class for a morning's dissection to find that the big toe of every single corpse had vanished overnight. Without warning or explanation, they were simply gone. Clean bits of bone and tendon stuck out where the toes had been.

It wasn't until the next day that the anatomy department belatedly

explained that an orthopaedic surgeon had been given permission to practise his technique. He had come in the night and removed all of the toes,
methodically working his way around the silent room until he had exhausted
his supply. Astley would have approved.

19

Surgeon to the Countryside

Whenever a man is too old to study, he is too old to be an examiner; and if I laid my head upon my pillow at night without having dissected something in the day, I should think I had lost that day. I do think a man must keep up his knowledge to the last.

Astley Cooper

Nostalgic and increasingly limited in what he could do, Astley kept up his studies as he grew older. His post as an examiner for the royal college, judging the knowledge of young surgeons, gave him a good excuse. An exchange of letters with Thelwall renewed their friendship in the closing days of the latter's life. 'John Thelwall had something very good about him,' said Coleridge in the summer of 1830. 'We were once sitting in a beautiful recess in the Quantocks, when I said to him, "Citizen John, this is a fine place to talk treason in!" – "Nay! Citizen Samuel," replied he, "it is rather a place to make a man forget that there is any necessity for treason!"' But although the letters that John and Astley exchanged were fond they were more in the manner of farewells than renewals. In February 1834, three weeks after complaining of an 'unpleasant symptom of the chest' and difficulty breathing, Thelwall died. In October that year Astley became a corresponding member of the National Institute of France – prestigious, but by now largely honorary. On an extended holiday to Norfolk in 1836 he devotedly made his way to the seashore each morning before breakfast, carrying his dissection tools along with him. On a September Sunday he dissected eels before church. The next day he rode along the beach and admired the industry of the fishermen. They were bringing in a full haul of herring and a few dogfish. Excitedly, Astley bought some. 'They are beautifully clean animals for dissection,' he wrote. The day after he cut up a gurnard, while the day after that was given over to dogfish and to herring brains. At the end of the month Astley noted in passing that there was rain coming down as he made his early morning journey. He dwelt with more feeling on how he had reluctantly turned down the offer of a porpoise. It was too big for him to handle, and instead he concentrated on dogfish again. There was still much to learn, even for a man whose horizon was drawing in.

There is something arresting about the thought of Cooper, in the last few years of his life, rising early to walk down to the beach and dissect. During the same trip away from London he began writing notes for his biography, scribbling down memories that he planned to hand over to his nephew. His dissection was always animated by a belief in being himself fundamentally similar to the creatures before him, the feeling that a surgeon's life uncovered the stuff of which everyone was built. It is impossible to imagine that the correspondence between autobiography and dissection did not occur to him.

Energy and enthusiasms, deeply felt convictions and vigorously acted beliefs all mark the early part of Astley Cooper's life. They are more than encouraging, they are electrifying; there is something galvanising about colliding with a life that has been richly lived. Something of its impulse of energy – the energy of eternal delight that Blake, eleven years older than Astley, spoke of – communicates itself across the gap.

Unfortunately there are also moments when another life communicates dullness. To read about the early deaths and the tragic disappointments, the lives crushed into mockery by accidents of fate and society, is to be infected with discouragement. Finding Wordsworth's poetry fading away from him, seeing Keats dying, in his description, not 'in warm blood like Romeo', but making his 'exit like a frog in a frost': those things are dispiriting. Is there much cause for encouragement, at the end of Cooper's life? What are we to make of all the honours and ornaments? What would the young Astley Cooper himself have made of them? In some respects he would have found them tasteless, even objectionable. There is no nobility, the young man said, save what is earned by a person's character. When Astley walked and rode along the Yarmouth beaches in 1836 at the age of sixty-eight, he was filling the office of president of the Royal College of Surgeons for a second time. It implied no particular vigour, no arresting energy or dynamic mental quality. It was a bureaucratic sinecure, a part of his semi-retirement, as much a medal on his chest as was the Order of Guelph. It was a token of past achievements and past efforts.

Yet certain of Astley's finer qualities remained throughout his life, surviving as glimmers and glints beneath the carapace of complacency and conservatism that hardened about him as he aged. The man who made his slow way along the beach, and wrote carefully afterwards about the construction of the dogfish, retained something of his youthful spirit.

In his retirement, Astley retreated more and more to the countryside, to the Gadebridge estate in Hemel Hempstead that his first wife had loved and tended and that he had bought and enlarged and now shared with Catherine. When the expanding railway threatened to come too close, he used his influence to make sure the line took a distant detour. He took pleasure in buying up sick horses from Smithfields, animals that were being sold cheaply for their meat, and letting them rest and recover in his pastures until they were fit and strong and could work again.* He was a poor farm manager, losing money and blaming others for it, critical of his staff and unreasonably bad-tempered with them. The same man who had so successfully built up an empire of worshippers in hospitals all around the country behaved with irritable inefficiency. It was the bluster of an old man, increasingly frail.

When I first began thinking of studying medicine, I went to the local public library to look at the medical journals. I thought they might give me some kind of a window into the life of a doctor.

I recall what I read. It was a copy of *The Lancet*, and it contained a long piece about Geoffrey Keynes, younger brother of the economist John Maynard Keynes. Geoffrey Keynes was a friend of the poet Rupert Brooke while the two studied at Cambridge, and afterwards he became involved with London's Bloomsbury Group. Keynes served in the First World War and survived. He became both a surgeon and a student of literature. He did some important literary work, and his efforts led to a re-evaluation of William Blake among others. He saved Virginia Woolf's life by pumping her stomach after an overdose, and he pioneered an operation that was a

---

* In this, as in many things, Astley was fashionable. His interest in rehabilitating horses reflected the growing popular concern for animal welfare, just as his beachside dissections mirrored a widespread contemporary study of Britain's fish.

triumph of good intentions and good science: lumpectomy rather than routine radical mastectomy. Keynes showed that it was often better to remove the cancerous portion of a breast, rather than needlessly performing the far more massive operation of cutting away the whole breast and much of the chest wall underneath it.

Geoffrey Keynes was born in March 1887. In 1910, having finished studying pre-clinical medicine at Cambridge, he became a student at St Bartholomew's Hospital in London, near Smithfields Market. During his studies he wrote a short monograph on Astley Cooper. He made no mention of what first attracted him to the man, and there is a chance that it may have been Keynes's own surgical ambitions, but given his devotion to literature, it is likely that he was drawn to Astley through the surgeon's relations with John Keats. Keynes was even a distant relation of one of the poet's great friends, the monumentally eccentric painter Benjamin Robert Haydon. (Haydon knew Astley; when he went to make a portrait of the Duke of Wellington in 1839, he found Astley and Wellington sitting comfortably together in the duke's drawing room.)

Keynes felt that Ann Cooper had no influence on her husband:

> The tenor of his life suggests he was more closely wedded to his profession than to his wife, since the one continued for the remainder of his life to engage his attention practically to the exclusion of all else; while the other had to content herself with occasional hurried visits from her husband when he could spare the time for a trip into the country.

There is no evidence that Keynes was correct in this assessment, and there is every suggestion that he was wrong. Astley was deeply moved, even in old age, by the memory of his first love as a teenager in Norfolk. His and Ann's only child followed so hard on the heels of their wedding that the marriage must certainly have started off with some ardour. The lack of any further children probably had something to do with the first pregnancy and the child's death, although it is by no means clear exactly what. It may be that Ann was left unable to bear more children, or that the couple practised some form of contraception, or that their sexual relationship never recovered. Intimate relations between Astley and his Ann are opaque from this distance. But when she died he was crippled with grief, and when he recovered he remarried rapidly. He had no need then either for money or to find some kind of housekeeper (Bransby's wife was there for that role). He tried to give up all surgical work after Ann's death and found that he couldn't, that he simply did not know how to carry on with life without it. Something similar seems to have happened with his remarriage – he tried to retire from an intimate relation with a woman and found that he couldn't. There is no evidence of whether Astley was faithful, which has the mild implication, since he led such a public life, that he may have been.

The youthful Keynes, who later replied to a question about how he achieved successful careers in both surgery and literature by explaining he had done it by neglecting his family, may have been projecting his own anxieties on to Astley. Or, since he seems to have used only Bransby's biography and Cooper's surgical writings as his sources, he might have simply been cutting corners when he made his guess.

Keynes was bitter about the older Astley Cooper, regarding his conservatism as a form of senility. He bemoaned the old man's complacency, his insularity and occasional violence of temper, his self-deception and his fatuous patriotism. By the time he wrote his study of Astley, he had already begun his far more serious work on William Blake. The poet and painter who had visions of angels and human souls rather than of anatomies and human societies had also decayed as his life progressed. Both Cooper and Blake had their lives damaged in some way by the devastating failure of the optimism that promised, for a few moments at the end of the eighteenth century, a radically fairer and more humane society. Astley fled into conservatism and Blake drowned himself in obscurities. For Keynes, to expose the vitality and genius that remained in Blake, hidden away in his convoluted philosophies and wrenchingly odd paintings, was part of his own life's work. What Keynes missed out on, in his revulsion at what Astley had become, was that in his life too a vital part of what was admirable stubbornly continued to thrive.

In the work that Astley was doing at the end of his life, both sides of his character are apparent. He wrote about the human breast, and he did it with the voice of the pragmatic Victorian, weighing up human lives as commodities, declaring that a 'woman who has children and suckles them is undoubtedly a better insurable life than a married woman who has no children, or one who has remained single'.* But the same work also contains

---

* An accurate observation with a long history, the health benefits of having children having first been noted some centuries before in the high rates of breast cancer noted amongst nuns.

the more attractive Astley Cooper, the man who thirsted after knowledge at first hand and who found beauty in it, and whose hard-won habits of scrutiny made him insist on the value of reality over ideals:

The breasts are slung upon the chest . . . and they are projected at the nipple forwards and outwards. I have, in my work on the Testis, pointed out the errors of those who paint or chisel from imagination, and not from observation of nature, in placing those bodies of equal height, although the left is usually much lower than the other; and the same remark may apply to the breasts. Modellers, sculptors, and painters sometimes represent the nipples as being pointed forwards and place them as their imagination leads them to conceive them to be, and not as they really are. It is modern artists who fall into this error, for the ancients modelled from the living subject, and gave accurate representations of nature.

To this clear-eyed respect for nature Astley added the sensibilities of British natural history, in which meticulous description and a belief in purposeful design went hand in hand with prose that was often highly emotional.

This natural obliquity of the mamilla, or nipple, forwards and outwards, with a slight turn of the nipple upwards, is one of the most beautiful provisions of nature, both for the mother and the child. To the mother, because the child rests upon her arm and lap in the most convenient position for suckling . . . it is wisely provided by nature, that when the child reposes upon its mother's arm, it has its mouth directly applied to the nipple, which is turned outwards to receive it; whilst the lower part of the breast forms a cushion upon which the cheek of the infant tranquilly reposes. Thus it is we have always to admire the simplicity, the beauty and the utility, of those deviations of form in the construction of the body which the imagination of man would lead him, a priori, to believe most symmetrical, natural and convenient.

Astley had never intended to cover the anatomy of the breast, only to deal with the treatment of breast cancers. But he was so appalled by the general state of anatomical knowledge that he changed his plan. For years he had worried over the contemporary inability to differentiate between malignant tumours of the breast that required an operation, and such condi-

tions as chronic abscesses that might only need the most minor of procedures to open up and drain. His lectures contained a warning against the
'ignorance of this circumstance, [from which] you might subject your patient
to a cruel operation, where a small incision would have done'. Now he
submerged himself in trying to sort out the muddled understanding that he
found most people possessed of the breast's basic anatomy. His descriptions
were youthfully innovative, managing carefully and clearly to describe what
was half known about and often ignored, and describing for the very first
time aspects of structures that no one had ever managed before to trace
and accurately observe. He was the first to detail the lymph drainage of the
breast, a piece of painstaking work involving meticulous dissection as well
as carefully locating the minute lymphatic ducts and injecting them with
mercury until they appeared as a filigree of quicksilver.* The ligaments that
support the breast are still named after Cooper to this day, and when a study
used ultrasound to explore the anatomy of the lactating breast in 2006, it
cited Cooper's work as its direct predecessor. ('The previous major study on
the anatomy of the lactating breast was published in 1840. And there haven't
been any definitive studies since that time,' said Peter Hartmann, one of
the authors.) Beyond the technical achievement of Astley's work, there is
something impressive about the man who was able to do all of this, to spend
so much time cutting up the breasts of the dead, and not have his sense of
beauty destroyed. He dealt at length with inflammatory and benign diseases
of the breast, including their operative treatment. He described a case of
echinococcus hydatid cyst, in which he had cut into a swollen breast and
found it full of pus and what appeared to be animal parasites. He jotted
notes to his assistants requesting 'breasts of any age (old women or young)'
and yet was still able to write, beneath an illustration:

> *This sketch was made in great haste, and by candle-light . . . There was
> very little difference in colour between the areola and the surrounding
> integuments. There were no hairs. Four or five prominences were apparent
> beyond the areola and superiorly. Two rows of tubercles were slightly visible
> . . . The parts, generally, much resembled those of the Venus de Medici
> according to my recollection of that Statue.*

---

* Lymphatic ducts drain lymph, eventually returning it to the blood. Lymph consists of the extra-
cellular fluid that is not part of the blood, and the cells of the immune system that have migrated
out of the bloodstream to penetrate and protect the tissues of the body.

There is one other record from his preparations for the book that, at the end of his life, shows a bright thread of continuity with the young man he had once been. In dark blue and black ink the picture appears to be that of a Romantic forest. Intricate and elegant leaves branch out delicately from sinuous trunks, all against a background of impenetrable darkness. But although the scene is of nature, it is not of dark clustered trees that murmur in the wind. The trunks are ducts, and the leaves are glands where milk is made. The picture is an image of the human breast, dark and wild and mysterious. Astley's attachment to Romantic politics dissolved in the complacent sweetness of success, but his passion for exploring the world within, for feeling the burden of its mystery, never faded.

20

Heart Failure

By 1835 Astley had reached the age of sixty-seven. Today that would be enough for doctors like myself, whose wards are packed with those in their eighties, to prefix the word 'young' to any mention of him. In the nineteenth century it was different. When a rumour reached Bransby of his uncle's death from an epileptic fit, it seemed frighteningly possible. Unable to travel and find out for himself, Bransby wrote a letter to discover the truth. The reply was enlightening:

> My dear Bransby,
>
> It is with much self-gratification that I assure you that I am not dead and that the only fit I have had is a fit of hunger, to which disease I have been extremely liable ever since I was born. Indeed, it is my full intention to practise my profession for the next thirteen years: after that time to retire for twenty, and then to be at God's disposal for as many more as he pleases.

Those who met Astley for the first time were struck by how much energy he retained. In 1839 a visiting professor from Philadelphia remarked on his appearance, calling him 'tall, elegantly formed ... with a remarkably pleasing and striking countenance, red, and fresh as a rose ... very agile and graceful in all his movements'. The only obvious sign of age was his hair. It had become completely white.

Yet despite this late appearance of health, by the end of 1840 Astley began to find himself becoming short of breath whenever he took a few steps or tried to dress himself. The cause was apparent to him. His chest was starting to fill with fluid. He began to cough at night. The fluid gradually increased. He became unable to lie flat in his bed. If he did so, the fluid spread too extensively through his lungs, filling the space where air needed to be. As his chest worsened Astley found he needed to spend the nights sitting sharply upright. It was the only way to keep enough of his lungs above the water to carry on breathing. His working life drew to an end, and a short time before Christmas he performed his last operation. He sent an assistant on ahead to check the number of stairs that led up to his patient's bedroom, where the operation was due to be held.

'If there are more than lead up to my own bedroom,' he told his aide, 'I leave it to you to manage that the lady shall be moved to an apartment in a lower storey, otherwise I shall not attempt to operate.'

There were not so many steps, and Astley managed to struggle up them. He completed the operation successfully.

At the end of January 1841 Bransby called at Gadebridge. He had last seen his uncle only a month before, and was shocked at the change. As he came into the room he saw Astley sitting with his head slumped forwards onto his chest. 'Instead of greeting me in his wonted lively and affectionate manner, he scarcely moved; but, with a half-extended hand, and melancholy expression, watched narrowly what impression his altered appearance excited in my mind.' Astley's legs had begun to swell, the flesh pale and stretched and studded with indentations where shoes, stockings and probing fingers had made lingering dents in its soft surface. Gout bit into his left hand, making it exquisitely painful. The fluid within his chest crackled wetly with each laborious breath.

Astley's own doctors, all friends, began meeting by his bedside. As he grew worse they began to meet daily. News of his illness was reported in the press. His doctors prescribed remedies '*of a most active character*'. That meant drugs to make Astley vomit, urinate, sweat and defecate, along with minor surgical interventions to draw off extra fluid: puncturing the legs with thick needles to allow the fluid to trickle out, tapping it off from the abdomen through a tube pushed directly through the muscles of the belly. But Astley's condition only grew worse. The meetings to examine him and to plan changes to his treatment began being held twice daily. *The Lancet* reported to its readers that Sir Astley was declining, that his chest was filling with water, and that only faint hopes were entertained of his recovery. The mechanism of death in heart failure is no different today – an accumulation of fluid around the body and in the lungs as the pumping of the heart weakens. It is one of the few conditions for which bleeding offers some benefit (modern drugs perform the job better, making people urinate out their extra fluid, but opening up the vein of someone dying of heart failure is still occasionally practised as a treatment of desperation). When there is nothing more that can be done to prolong life, there are drugs that can prevent the worst of the physical sensations of dying. The most effective of these agents are opiates, good at taking away the panicked pressure of breathlessness that comes when a patient's lungs fill up with water. Opium was available in Astley's day, but was under-used, as it continues to be to a lesser extent today.

On the morning of 10 February, after a consultation between Astley's two physicians and his nephew Bransby, he responded to the news of their new plans for him with a polite refusal:

> My dear sirs, I am fully convinced of your excellent judgement, and of your devotion to me, but your wishes are not to be fulfilled. God's will be done! God bless you both! – Bransby, my dear, kiss me. You must excuse me, but I shall take no more medicine.

The following day *The Times* announced that though the 'eminent surgeon is still living . . . no hopes of his eventual recovery are entertained'. Over the next forty-eight hours, attended by a suitably large array of friends and family, Astley drowned while sitting in his chair. The lack of oxygen made him confused and distressed. The suffocation increased slowly, punctuated by paroxysms of coughing and gasping. On the afternoon of Saturday 12 February, at six minutes past one o'clock, at the end of a violent struggle for breath, he died. His fortune, suggested *The Times*, was in the order of half a million pounds.

Astley left instructions for the preparation of a final publication to add to those that he had authored while still living. He wished his autopsy report to be published in the Guy's Hospital medical journal, and he wanted certain things paid particular attention to. Just as Hunter had directed his friends to inspect the parts of his body that had troubled or interested him in life, so Astley did the same. There was the cured hernia he had suffered as an adolescent, and another smaller one that had appeared in his navel towards the end of his life, and there was also the tuberculosis that he recalled suffering from as a child. He wanted them all examined.

His friends opened him up on the day he died. They found evidence of all the three conditions he had predicted. They also found that his liver had taken on the appearance of nutmeg, not from alcohol but from the stagnation of his blood that preceded his death. And there were collections of fluid sitting in both lungs and in a constrictive band around his heart. The most likely cause for it all was heart failure, the gradual collapse of his heart's ability. That may have been caused by a heart attack, but the re-emergence of his childhood tuberculosis could also have been to blame.

Astley was entombed in a stone sarcophagus locked in a crypt beneath the chapel at Guy's. It was partly in case any of his former employees should take it into their heads to try to resurrect him. Unless they secretly managed it, his bones are still there, in the darkness of a National Health Service hospital, close to the south bank of the Thames and sealed in a dark hush from the noise of London overhead.

Astley's life was built upon the desire to look into things and see them clearly. 'He took no pleasure in lopping off a limb, or excising a tumour,' said *The Times*, 'but he appeared to delight in being able to dispense with the performance of operations.' It is not clear whether he knew, when he assigned his nephew to write his biography, that Bransby would spend two long volumes doing the opposite and covering up much of the truth of his life.

Bransby Cooper suffered a number of crushing disappointments. After his brother Henry's death he was able to take his place at Astley's side, but in 1828, when his cack-handed lithotomy killed a man and *The Lancet* damned him for it, his reputation was publicly blighted. 'It left a lasting mark upon him', judged Bransby's biographer from the Royal College of Surgeons, 'and throughout the remainder of his life he was unduly emotional.' When Astley appointed Bransby as his successor, having split the Borough Hospitals to do so, Bransby was left bitterly aware of how widespread and profound had been the opposition to his taking up the job. 'As a man,' says his biographer, *he was well made, muscular, a good oarsman and pugilist, and a good shot. It is told of him that, when Demonstrator of Anatomy, he came to the rescue of his pupils during a fight between St Bartholomew's and Guy's . . . He was beloved of his pupils and was never referred to otherwise than as Bransby.*

In his life Bransby was penalised for the way in which he idolised Astley. 'He would perhaps have done better, and he would certainly have been happier, had he remained an army surgeon.' Bransby could be 'warm-hearted, sympathetic, and jocular' but he had little faith or confidence in himself. His private practice was never large and towards the end of his life it fell away. He concentrated instead upon biochemistry, and spent his hours analysing body fluids and poring over bladder stones. His lovingly written biography of Astley received poor reviews.

There was something well-meaning about Bransby's attempt to immortalise his uncle. He tried to preserve, to praise and to protect the memory of the man he had loved and looked up to throughout his adult life. But he did so by destroying Astley's papers and diaries and betraying the principles that represented the best part of his life. After the terrific energy of Astley's life comes the shuffling figure of his nephew. Bransby was a flawed human being, but his flaws were those of his period, they were not unique to him, and in his life he received a great deal of cruel treatment as a result. He may have deserved much of it, but it remained cruel.

For a time towards the end of Bransby's life, the base of his tongue ulcerated, either from infection or cancer. On 18 August 1853, when he was aged sixty-two, a blood vessel suddenly eroded through. In London's Athenaeum Club, blood flooding out of his mouth and down into his lungs and stomach, he died. His body was buried at St Martin's in the Fields, across from Trafalgar Square.

In 1887 the *Dictionary of National Biography* (edited at that stage by Leslie Stephen) called Cooper's first biography 'a most tedious performance but [one that] includes much interesting matter'. In reviewing the book in April 1843, *The Times* commented that:

Sir Astley Cooper, moving, as he did, in a circle composed of such motley variety, within whose verge we may descry the monarch and the meanest of his subjects – the beaux and beauties of May-Fair grouped in juxtapo-

sition almost with dog-stealers and body-snatchers – the hall of science and the desecrated grave-yard – these furnish materials for scenes of more startling contrasts and thrilling interest than the imagination of a novelist ever bodied forth in his terrific or pathetic pages.

But they damned the account that Bransby had managed to produce. During the Second World War Sir Russell Brock, Cooper's successor both as surgeon at Guy's Hospital in London and as president of the Royal College of Surgeons, wrote a second biography. Slimmer than Bransby's two-volume production, it focused on an analysis of the anatomical, surgical and pathological studies that Cooper had published. Bransby had commented repeatedly on the amount of documentation that his uncle acquired as he went through life, that he was invariably scribbling in notebooks, journals and diaries, despite being a somewhat poor letter writer. Yet Brock used no new original sources. A few libraries (Southampton, Yale, Lincolnshire) hold a small number of letters from Sir Astley on professional matters, but only the Royal College of Surgeons holds a significant amount of material. There, in a few cardboard boxes, are a handful of letters about patients, two sides of notes written by Sir Astley about his childhood and the account book from his honeymoon in Paris. A portrait by Sir Thomas Lawrence hangs in the main hall of the Royal College of Surgeons, and a statue looms in the shadows of St Paul's Cathedral. But the bulk of the evidence of Astley Cooper's life, his papers, is gone. I believe Bransby burnt them, worried that they did not show his beloved uncle in the proper light, and convinced that destroying them was the most honourable way to preserve Astley's memory. He could not have been more wrong.

Astley's world was strange and gripping. The emergence of modern science took place against a wider revolution – started by the printing press, inflamed by the English Civil War, and set incandescently on fire by the American, French, commercial and industrial revolutions. Astley and his colleagues sought out lives touched by death, disease and decay. There were profits to be made, but their aim was not solely financial. The image of Astley that one of his students bequeathed, of him visiting his patients as a florist visited his flowerbeds, is a rich one. Surgery was a commercial undertaking, but those who did it well could see past its revolting exterior to the meaning and the beauty within. The willingness to accept and inflict pain and the desire to find meaning in the struggle, to do the world some great and lasting good, characterised the period that Astley lived in and the profession that he followed. The hours in the stinking rooms of the rotting dead, the appalling operations on the screaming patients, the horrific roll of animal experiments: we would hardly expect any humanity to be left in the surgeons that lived through it all. Yet their humanity was often what drove them.

After Astley's death a friend wrote down some anecdotes as a contribution towards the obituary being prepared by the *Gentleman's Magazine*. Thomas Streatfeild wrote approvingly that 'latterly he was a firm Conservative'. Streatfeild also told of a poor neighbour of his, dying in distress and poverty, who heard a rumour that Astley occasionally saw patients for free and asked Streatfeild if it were true. In an offhand way Streatfeild wrote to Astley on Christmas Eve, asking if perhaps he would visit the man the next time he happened to be in the area and with a bit of idle time. 'The next day was Christmas day, a cold wet blanket of [a] day, but no matter, Sir Astley mounted his horse, and rode over on purpose *to do a kindness.*'

Afterword

As I write, the spring is finally arriving. Normally the daffodils are in bloom here by the start of March, but this year they have hardly got started and we are well into April. But the tulips by the garden gate have buds that are beginning to blush red at their tips and birdsong is everywhere. Most of all the light, now that the clocks have changed, is suddenly endless. June might have days that are longer, but they never seem such blessings as those immediately after Greenwich Mean gives way to British Summer.

For the past fortnight a small bird has tried persistently to make its way through my bay window. It has ignored the large envelope I've taped there – an effort to explain to it the difference between solid objects and clear bright air – and it desists only for a minute whenever I try to chase it away. I cannot decide what the bird most advertises. Futility, perhaps, but the bird shows such spirit that I have found myself drawn into admiring it. It is better, far better, said Cyrano de Bergerac, that the fight is hopelessly, irreparably and incorrigibly in vain. He would have admired the long-tailed tit that seems so determined its will-power should prove stronger than glass.

I have dreamt of Astley Cooper while writing this book, and in my dreams he has often worn a collar made of the same scarlet cloth that frames him in his portrait at the Royal College of Surgeons in London. It is the colour of fresh blood, the colour of his profession and the colour that my garden-gate tulips are beginning to turn. I started this book while working as a doctor in an Accident & Emergency department, frequently covering myself with freshly spilt blood in the course of a shift's work. The start of Astley's own rather bloody story is tied up in my mind with a hot English summer, and the endless complaints of people bitten by wasps or burnt by the sun. Seas of twisted ankles and broken bones, of cuts and heart attacks and strokes, alternated for me with the even darker world of eighteenth-century hospitals and the dead-houses and dissecting rooms that supported them. Rewrites took place during what Americans would call a residency or fellowship in internal medicine; what in Britain doctors call a registrar training as a general physician. Attending to the geriatric sick, many of them dying and demented, oscillated with sitting quietly in my 1820s living room, rich with the atmosphere of a former world. The conjunction of these experiences has kept me aware of how medicine and surgery have changed, of how much more powerful they have become. Our surgical and pharmacological tools have improved, and so have our mental ones. Astley Cooper was part of the first generation of medical practitioners for whom statistics were starting to seem a useful way of finding out the truth of the world. Since then the techniques associated with clinical trials have opened up ever more effective ways of exploring the worlds of our bodies. Well-designed, large-scale trials are the only way we have of eliminating our biases, of keeping our hopes and prejudices from contaminating our understanding. Intelligently collected statistics have helped evidence displace expert opinion in virtually every medical speciality, including those of surgery. Increasingly, we know very precisely what works and when and under what circumstances. Guesswork, so often presented under the appealing guise of clinical intuition, has departed from huge swathes of medicine and a large dose of mystery has vanished with it. The flair of an individual doctor has become less important. More and more treatments can be applied by a set of rules that a practitioner needs to follow far more than they need to understand. At the same time doctors, I think, have in general become more humane than ever before. I suspect it is partly due to the increasing numbers of women doctors, but I believe it is also true that the world we live and work in has softened and become more merciful. Anaesthetics and analgesics, and our ability to banish physical agony, make it easier for us to maintain our sympathies for the emotional agonies of illness and age and death.

The training of surgeons and physicians has become more routine, more organised: very occasionally it is even well organised. We are better at helping doctors learn how to make decisions and carry out procedures, at reducing to a minimum the human costs of the mistakes that they unavoidably make as they learn their profession. There is no longer so much of a role for the celebrity surgeon when operations are driven by protocol, when we know the conditions in which a procedure should be carried out and the methods by which it should be performed. The space for personality to conjure up a healing spell of its own is still there, but it is much reduced. A surgeon today can become excellent, or they can become an idiosyncratic innovator. It is very difficult now ever to be both.

A biography cannot avoid reflecting the writer, any more than biographical stories can avoid being twisted by the prejudices and beliefs of those that record them. One of the great constants between Astley's world and our own is the worship of learning, the belief that there is something valuable about understanding the world. It is part of what makes it such a pleasure to sit with a book, reading and imagining. The other constant is that great drive to *do something*, to be stirred into action. The robins are dancing away their rivalries in the forsythia a few yards from my desk, the sun is warm on the lawn that has been mown for the first time in months, the hammering of the long-tailed tit against my window continues unabated. On the days when my alternating life of books and patients has worked, when the demands of each have married in some creative manner, writing this book has been a fertile experience.

Much of what made Astley Cooper a great man was his charisma. The effect he had on the people around him, encouraging them and vitalising them, came palpably across the centuries. He taught generations of surgeons, influenced physicians and scientists, kings and hospitals and provincial railway routes, and made a number of innovative discoveries in anatomy and surgery. In a world where drugs still tended to do far more harm than good, the limited operations available to surgeons were genuinely of benefit – most of the time, and so long as they were appropriately timed and chosen. But for Astley, as for most men of science, his world was crowded with the talents of those who would probably have made similar discoveries had he died of his childhood tuberculosis or slipped into adolescent delinquency. He is remarkable not so much for what he did that could have been done by no one else, but for his vigour and his élan, and above all for the way so many of the themes of his world expressed themselves with full-throated ease in his life.

'Of what shall a man be proud,' wrote Robert Louis Stevenson, 'if he is not proud of his friends?' A man, I think, can be proud of the people he has taken the trouble to know, even if they have never met him, even if they were dead long before he ever walked out into the sunshine for the first time. Parts of Astley Cooper's character were objectionable, but much of what drove him, much of what brought him to life, had something admirable about it. His love of learning and his belief in the benefits it might bring never left him. It was the comfort of his old age, the source of the optimism that sustained him as he began to decay, walking along the seashore while his days drew to a close. Astley's conviction of the value of books and study, debate and education, was strong. It still raps persistently away at the window, and it leaves me lingeringly fond of this vain, egotistical, nepotistic and rather wonderful old man.

Sources and Bibliography

Unattributed quotations relating to Astley Cooper's life, letters and opinions are taken from Bransby Cooper's *Life*, 1843.

Archives

Guy's Hospital Physical Society, Minutes

Correspondence and papers of Sir Joseph Banks, Series 1, Subseries 15, Item 15(1a) – 15(20). Notes for an address to the Royal Society, National Library of Australia.

Library of the Royal College of Surgeons, in particular the collections relating to Astley Cooper and Henry Cline

Lord Chamberlain's Office, letter to Astley Cooper, 20 June 1837, in the Wills Museum at Guy's Hospital

Old Bailey Proceedings Online (www.oldbaileyonline.org, 26 July 2006), February 1794, trial of Daniel Isaac Eaton (t17940219-71).

Society of Antiquaries of London, letters of Thomas Streatfeild, containing memories of Astley Cooper apparently submitted as a contribution towards the *Gentleman's Magazine* obituary, reference SAL/MS/987/1,1841

Suffolk Record Office, Bury St Edmunds branch, letter concerning Astley Cooper, reference HD588/7/6, c.1810

Journals

Annals of the Royal College of Surgeons of England
British and Foreign Medical Review
Gentleman's Magazine
Guy's Hospital Reports
London Medical Gazette
Medical Adviser
Medico-Chirurgical Transactions
Morning Chronicle
Provincial Medical and Surgical Journal
Quarterly Review
The Lancet
The Times

Bibliography

Ackroyd, Peter, *Blake*, Quality Paperbacks Direct, 1995

Ackroyd, Peter, *London*, Vintage, 2001

Allard, James, 'John Thelwall & the Politics of Medicine', *European Romantic Review*, vol. 15, no. 1, pp. 73–87, March 2004

Almeida, Hermione de, *Romantic Medicine and John Keats*, Oxford University Press, 1991

Arrowsmith, R. L., *A Charterhouse Miscellany*, Gentry Books, 1982

Bailey, Brian, *The Resurrection Men*, Macdonald, 1991

Bamforth, Iain, *The Body in the Library*, Verso, 2003

Barnard, John, '"The Busy Time": Keats's Duties at Guy's Hospital from Autumn 1816 to March 1817', *Romanticism*, in press

Barrell, John, *Imagining the King's Death*, Oxford University Press, 2000

Bate, W. Jackson, *John Keats*, Chatto & Windus, 1979

Beales, Derek, *From Castlereagh to Gladstone*, Nelson, 1969

Belloc, Hilaire, *On Something*, Kessinger, 2004

Berlin, Isaiah, *The Age of Enlightenment*, Oxford University Press, 1979

Berlin, Isaiah, *The Roots of Romanticism*, Chatto & Windus, 1999

Bettany, G. T., *Eminent Doctors*, John Hogg of London, 1885

Blandy, John and Lumley, John (eds), *The Royal College of Surgeons of England, 200 Years of History at the Millennium*, Royal College of Surgeons of England and Blackwell Science, 2000

Bowlby, John, *Charles Darwin*, W. W. Norton, 1990

Briggs, Asa, *A Social History of England*, Book Club Associates, 1983

Brock, Russell, *The Life and Work of Astley Cooper*, Livingstone, 1952

Bynum, W. F. and Porter, Roy, *William Hunter and the Eighteenth-Century Medical World*, Cambridge University Press, 2002

Cameron, H. C., *Mr Guy's Hospital*, Longmans, Green, 1954

Christison, Robert, *The Life of Sir Robert Christison*, Blackwood, 1885

Coleridge, Samuel Taylor, *Specimens of the Table Talk of the late Samuel Taylor Coleridge*, John Murray, 1835

Colquhoun, Patrick, *A Treatise on the Commerce and Police of the River Thames*, Joseph Mawman, London, 1800

Colquhoun, Patrick, *A Treatise on the Police of the Metropolis*, Joseph Mawman, London, 1800

Cooper, Astley, *The Anatomy and Surgical Treatment of Hernia*, Cox, London, 1804

Cooper, Astley, *A Treatise on Dislocations and on Fractures of the Joints*, Longman, Hurst, Rees, Orme & Brown, Paternoster Row, London and E. Cox & Son, Southwark, 1822

Cooper, Astley, *Illustrations of the Diseases of the Breast*, London, 1829

Cooper, Astley, *The Anatomy of the Thymus Gland*, London, 1832

Cooper, Astley, *On the Anatomy of the Breast*, Longman, Orme, Green, Brown & Longman, London, 1840

Cooper, Astley, *Lectures on the Principles and Practice of Surgery*, Philadelphia, 1836

Cooper, Astley, *Practical Surgery*, London, 1841

Cooper, Astley and Travers, Benjamin, *Surgical Essays*, London 1818–19

Cooper, Bransby Blake, *Life of Sir Astley Cooper*, London, 1843

Cooper, Maria Susanna, *The Exemplary Mother*, Becket, 1769

Darwin, Francis, *Charles Darwin*, London, 1892

Dobson, Jessie, *John Hunter*, E. & S. Livingstone, Edinburgh and London, 1969

Ellis, Harold, *A History of Bladder Stone*, Blackwell, 1969

Fido, Martin, *Bodysnatchers*, Weidenfeld & Nicolson, 1988

Forman, Maurice Buxton, *The Letters of John Keats*, 3rd edn, OUP, 1948

Gatrell, V. A. C., *The Hanging Tree*, Oxford University Press, 1994

Gentleman's Magazine, obituary of Astley Cooper, pp. 538–41, 1841

Gittings, Robert, *John Keats*, Heinemann, 1968

Handler, Clive (ed.), *Guy's Hospital*, Guy's Hospital Gazette Committee, 1976

Hazlitt, William, *The Round Table & Characters of Shakespear's Plays*, Everyman's Library, J. M. Dent, London, 1936

Hill, Christopher, *Reformation to Industrial Revolution*, Pelican, 1969

Holland, Henry, *Recollections of Past Life*, Longmans, Green, 1873

Home, Everard, *A Short Account of the Author's Life*, George Nicol, 1794

Hunter, John, 'Observations of the Structure and Oeconomy of Whales', *Philosophical Transactions*, vol. 77, pp. 371–450, Royal Society, 1787

Hunter, John, *Observations on Certain Parts of the Animal Oeconomy*, 2nd edn, J. Johnson, St Paul's Churchyard, 1792

Hunter, John, *A Treatise on the Blood*, George Nicol, 1794

Joliffe, John (ed.), *The Diaries of Benjamin Haydon*, Hutchinson, 1990

Keynes, Geoffrey, *The Life and Works of Sir Astley Cooper*, John Murray, 1922

Lobban, R. D., *Edinburgh and the Medical Revolution*, Cambridge University Press, 1980

London Topographical Society, *The A to Z of Regency London*, London Topographical Society, 1985

Lonsdale, Henry, *Life of Robert Knox*, London, 1870

Low, Donald, *Thieves' Kitchen*, Alan Sutton, 1987

Macalpine, Ida and Hunter, Richard, *George III and the Mad-Business*, Pimlico, 1991

Marshall, Tim, *Murdering to Dissect*, Manchester University Press, 1995

Moore, Wendy, *The Knife Man*, Bantam, 2005

Motion, Andrew, *John Keats*, Faber & Faber, 1997

Murray, Venetia, *High Society in the Regency Period*, Penguin, 1998

Palmer, Alan, *George IV*, Cardinal, 1975

Pearce, Edward, *Reform!*, Pimlico, 2004

Picard, Lisa, *Dr Johnson's London*, Phoenix, 2003

Plarr, Victor, *Lives of the Fellows of the Royal College of Surgeons*, Royal College of Surgons of England, 1930

Porter, Roy, *The Greatest Benefit to Mankind*, HarperCollins, 1997

Porter, Roy, *Flesh in the Age of Reason*, Allen Lane, 2003

Ottley, Drewery, *Life of John Hunter*, London, 1835

Oxford Dictionary of National Biography, ed. Matthew Collin, Brian Harrison and Lawrence Goldman, Oxford University Press, 2006

Qvist, George, *John Hunter*, Heinemann, 1981

Rae, Isobel, *Knox: the Anatomist*, Oliver & Boyd, 1964

Ramsay D. *et al.* 'Anatomy of the Lactating Human Breast redefined with Ultrasound Imaging', *Journal of Anatomy*, vol. 206, no. 6, pp. 525–34, June 2005

Richardson, Ruth, *Death, Dissection and the Destitute*, Penguin, 1988

Ripman, Hujohn (ed.), *Guy's Hospital*, Guy's Hospital Gazette Committee, 1951

Ritvo, Harriet, *The Animal Estate*, Penguin, 1990

Ritvo, Harriet, *The Platypus and the Mermaid*, Harvard University Press, 1997

Robinson, Andrew, *The Last Man Who Knew Everything*, New York, Pi Press, 2006

Roe, Nicholas, *John Keats and the Culture of Dissent*, Oxford University Press, 1997

Roe, Nicholas, *Fiery Heart: The First Life of Leigh Hunt*, Pimlico, 2005

Rollins, Hyder Edward, *The Keats Circle, Letters & Papers*, Howard University Press, 1948

Rupke, Nicolaas, *Vivisection in Historical Perspective*, Routledge, 1990

Rutledge, Robb H., 'Cooper Ligament Repair of Groin Hernias', in Robert Baker and Josef Fischer (eds), *Mastery of Surgery*, vol. 2, Lippincott, Williams & Wilkins, London 1997

Sanger, 'Lord' George, *Seventy Years a Showman*, J. M. Dent, 1927

Schama, Simon, *The Fate of Empire*, BBC Books, 2003

Schama, Simon, *Citizens*, Penguin, 2004

Schonberg, Harold, *The Lives of the Great Composers*, Abacus, 1970

Shapin, Steven, *A Social History of Truth*, University of Chicago Press, 1995

Shapin, Steven, *The Scientific Revolution*, University of Chicago Press, 1996

Shapin, Steven and Schaffer, Simon, *Leviathan and the Air-Pump*, Princeton University Press, 1989

South, John Flint, *Memorials*, Centaur Press, 1970

Sprigge, S. S., *Life of Thomas Wakley*, London, 1897

St Clair, William, *The Godwins and the Shelleys*, Faber & Faber, 1989

Stevenson, Robert Louis, *Travels with a Donkey in the Cevennes*, Könemann, 1997

Sykes, A. H., *Doctors on the Streets of Paris*, Cerebrus 2004

Thelwall, John, *The Peripatetic*, 1793

Thelwall, John, *An Essay Towards a Definition of Animal Vitality*, Rickaby, 1793

Thelwall, John, *Poems written in Close Confinement*, Ridgway, Symonds & Eaton, 1795

Thelwall, Susan, *The Life of John Thelwall*, London, 1838

Thomas, Keith, *Man and the Natural World*, Penguin, 1984

Todd, Janet, *Mary Wollstonecraft*, Weidenfeld & Nicolson, 2000

Tomalin, Claire, *The Life and Death of Mary Wollstonecraft*, Penguin, 1992

Twiss, Richard, *A Trip to Paris in July and August 1792*, Minerva Press, 1793

Uglow, Jenny, *The Lunar Men*, Faber & Faber, 2002

Ward, Aileen, *John Keats*, Secker & Warburg, 1963

Warren, Edward, *Life of John Collins Warren*, Boston, 1860

Wells, Walter, *A Doctor's Life of John Keats*, Vintage Press, 1959

Wilks, S. and Bettany, G. T., *A Biographical History of Guy's Hospital*, London, 1892

Winston, George, 'John Keats and Joshua Waddington', *Guy's Hospital Reports*, vol. 92, no. 4, 1943

Wise, Sarah, *The Italian Boy*, Pimlico, 2005

Wootton, David, *Bad Medicine*, Oxford University Press, 2006

Wright, William 'The Fellowship of the Royal College of Surgeons of England', *Canadian Medical Journal*, vol. 26, no. 5, pp. 600–1, May 1932

Index

Lancet, The 80, 212–13, 227, 243, 250, 252
Lavoisier, Antoine 123
Lawrence, Sir Thomas: Sir Astley Cooper 254, 256
Leonardo da Vinci 54
lithotomies see bladder stones, operation for
Liverpool, Robert Jenkinson, 2nd Earl of, Prime Minister 217, 221, 223
London (1784) 32; see also Borough, the; Thames, River
London Bridge 33, 59, 191n
London Corresponding Society 122, 134, 135, 137, 143, 167
London Dispensary (eye hospital) 187, 189
London Hospital, Whitechapel 144, 167
Louis XI, of France 77
Louis XVI, of France 108, 112, 122
Love, Mrs (wetnurse) 13
Love, John 19, 20, 79
Lucas, William 196
Lucas, William (son) 200–1
Lunar Society, Birmingham 89–90, 98
lymphatic ducts 247 and n

Mackenzie, Henry 91
Maconochie, Alexander (later Lord Meadowbank) 91
Marie Antoinette 112
May, James 150–51, 216, 217, 238
Mead, Richard 38
Medico-Chirurgical Transactions 182, 217
Money, General 112 and n
Monro, Alexander (father) 88
Monro, Alexander (son) 93–4
Morning Chronicle 139, 141
Morning Post 139–40
Munchhausen's syndrome 133

Napoleon Bonaparte 168, 175, 192
National Institute of France 232, 241
Nelson, Lord Horatio 15, 177, 198
Newby, Eric 53
Newgate Prison: hangings 57–8; AC contracts fever 85; Thelwall imprisoned for treason 139, 140
Newton, Sir Isaac 15, 23, 30

nitrogen, discovery of 92
Norfolk and Norwich Hospital 26–7, 28–9
North, Lord (Frederick North) 34

opium 29, 71, 77n, 138, 158, 214, 251
Osbaldeston, Charles 171–2, 183
Oxford University 12, 36, 37, 58, 69, 89
oxygen, isolation of 98

pain, infliction of 5, 82–4, 133, 202; AC's attitude to 79, 82, 84, 147, 173–4, 183–4, 203
Paris: storming of the Bastille 100 and n; the Coopers' 'pilgrimage' to 106, 107–15; see also French Revolution
Parkinson, James 167
Parkinson's disease 167 and n
Parmenter, Mr 190, 191, 228
Parmenter, Sarah (AC's adopted daughter) 141–2, 144, 148, 162, 168, 189, 190, 191, 228
Paterson, Mary 238
Peel, Robert 226
penguins, Adelie 220
Pepys, Samuel 29
Percival, Thomas 24
Physical Society, the 40–41, 71; weekly meetings 41–2; AC's early attendances 42–3; and his first dissertation 43; fines AC 43, 46; elects AC to committee 64; Haighton as member 96, 97; AC's lectures 99, 101, 103; AC as rotating president 118, 121; Thelwall on management committee 118, 121–2; reprimands AC for awarding prize for late dissertation 119; and Thelwall's paper on 'Animal Vitality' 122–4, 125; and Hunter's heart failure 130, 131; and lectures on medical cases 132–3; and Thelwall's lecture on physiology of the brain 134–5; and his radical politics 135; discussion of Thelwall's lecture blocked 135–6; turns against Thelwall 136, 142; resumes with less contentious subjects 136–7